Coming Alive from Nine to Five

Coming Alive from Nine to Five

THE CAREER SEARCH HANDBOOK

Sixth Edition

Betty Neville Michelozzi
Corralitos, California

MAYFIELD PUBLISHING COMPANY
Mountain View, California
London • Toronto

Library of Congress Cataloging-in-Publication Data

Michelozzi, Betty Neville.
    Coming alive from nine to five: the career search handbook/
Betty Neville Michelozzi. — 6th ed.
        p.   cm.
    Includes index.
    ISBN 0-7674-0216-2
    1. Vocational guidance.   2. Job hunting.   I. Title.
HF5381.M46   1999
650.14—dc21   98-53450
                                                              CIP

Manufactured in the United States of America
10 9 8 7 6 5 4 3 2 1

Mayfield Publishing Company
1280 Villa Street
Mountain View, California 94041

Sponsoring editor, Franklin C. Graham; *production,* Publishing Support
Services; *copyeditor,* Patterson Lamb; *design manager and text/cover
designer,* Susan Breitbard; *cover image,* Paul Schulenburg; *manufacturing
manager,* Randy Hurst. The text was set in 10.5/12.5 Sabon by TBH Typecast,
Inc., and printed on 45# Highland Plus by Malloy Lithographing, Inc.

 This book was printed on recycled, acid-free paper.

Contents

Chapter 5

WORKPLACES/WORKSTYLES: Companies That Work   142

Chapter 6

TIMESTYLES/WORKSTYLES: Alternatives That Work   176

Chapter 7

THE JOB HUNT: Tools for Breaking and Entering   214

Chapter 8

DECISIONS, DECISIONS: What's Your Next Move?   258

Chapter 9

Preface

Coming Alive from Nine to Five is a unique handbook that develops, demystifies, and integrates the various facets of career/lifestyle search and choice. A handy reference book, it draws together into one comprehensive, practical, easily usable and reusable source the essentials of career/life decision making. Flexible enough to be adopted in whole or in part by individuals or groups, previous editions have been used in semester-long courses, workshops, individual counseling sessions, colleges and high schools, and industry and business. In short, *Coming Alive from Nine to Five* is intended for anyone searching for meaningful life activities—from students to retirees, from managers of households to managers of corporations, from job trainees to career-changing professionals.

This updated version of *Coming Alive from Nine to Five* focuses on career preparation not only for the last shred of the twentieth century, but for the twenty-first century as well. Using the same personal approach as earlier texts, the sixth edition expands still further awareness of the career search process as it relates to a person's whole life.

Writing yet another edition has provided me an opportunity to develop new material, integrate overlapping exercises, eliminate what seemed less helpful, and update innumerable bits of data.

The book begins with an upbeat discussion of success and moves quickly into self-assessment activities. It then considers a variety of societal factors that influence work and workplaces. Because vast social changes are happening very rapidly and the next hundred years will no doubt be very different from the present, Chapter 4 enables us to look at the future in terms of challenges, options, and opportunities.

Chapters on workplaces and various styles of work follow. While reading about workplaces of interest is helpful, the book offers a guide for obtaining firsthand information from people in the field.

The leader/instructor's manual includes a discussion of study skills especially useful in a career course as well as other materials to facilitate the task of assisting students with this most important activity: reflection on life goals, including, specifically, career choice.

B. N. M.

Acknowledgments

Acknowledgments are a very personal thing. They point out the impossibility of accomplishing anything of importance alone. I am grateful to all of these people:

Peter, my husband, for his caring support, "thought-full" suggestions, and assistance with many tasks. He helps me keep perspective on life's deeper meaning when a sea of paper and words threatens to engulf me.

Supportive colleagues at West Valley and Mission Colleges who read, reviewed, and gave helpful feedback and/or materials: Bill Allman, Joanne Anderson, Veronese Anderson, Chloe Atkins, Don Cordero, Ken Gogstad, Tom Heffner, Carolyn Hennings, Michael Herauf, Jo Hernandez, Sharon Laurenza, Joyce McClellan, Susan Monahan, Gladys Penner, Richard Przybylski, Jack Seiquist, Sylvia Selleck, Pat Space, Jill Trefz, Pat Weber, and Jan Winton; Patti Yukawa, Dave Fishbaugh, and the Mission library staff.

All the caring, careful typists who contributed way back, especially my neighbor Ruby Garcia, who goes beyond neighborliness to heroism, and Kay Koyano at West Valley College, whose patience with the first manuscript was unmatched. Aptos, Santa Cruz, and Watsonville library staff, who at the drop of a phone call searched out many details and even called back—in minutes!

Academic reviewers who use the text and made valuable suggestions and comments: Lynn Hall of Bakersfield College, Carey E. Harbin of San Jose, California, Dolores McCord of Valencia Community College of Florida, Sydney E. Perry, Jr., of Old Dominion University in Virginia, Sharon L. Speich of Inver Hills Community College in Minnesota, Charles Ward of Pasadena City College, Susan Wood of Indiana University Southeast. The following people also provided helpful reviews before preparation of the sixth edition began: Susan Coady, Ohio State University; Jennifer Jones, New Jersey City University; Beth Kaiama, Pasadena City College; Joe Livingston, West Valley Community College; Sarah Moore Schoffner, University of North Carolina at Greensboro; and Charles Washington, Midlands Technical College.

West Valley and Mission College students who taught me to teach Careers and Lifestyles and shared the beauty of their life journeys. Staff and students in many places who attended workshops and lectures and gave generous feedback. Career people who share their stories and give support and resources to career searchers.

Colleagues and resource people in many places who have been supportive and given assistance and information: Judy Shernock, for her work on the Personality Mosaic, and Cora Alameda, Sally Brew, Dorothy Coffey, John

French, Mel Fuller, H. B. Gelatt, Lynn Hall, Phyllis Hullett, Jean Jones, Barbara Lea, Ritchie Lowry, John Maginley, Gene Malone, Lillian Mattimore, Stephen Moody, Art Naftaly, Chuc Nowark, Ruth Olsen, Alex Reyes, Kay Ringel, Mary Kay Simpson, Pat Thompson, Ed Watkins.

Instructors who shared class time to test materials—too numerous to mention by name but remembered with gratitude.

People (past and present) at Mayfield who have been so great to work with: Naomi Angoff, Liz Currie, Bob Erhart, Laraine Etchemendy-Bennett, Frank Graham, Pat Herbst, Yaeko Kashima, Carol Norton, Don Pond, Nancy Sears, Laurel R. Sterrett, Pam Trainer, April Wells-Hayes. Manuscript editors Susan Geraghty, Carol King, Victoria Nelson, and Patterson Lamb contributed above and beyond the call of duty, as did Vicki Moran of Publishing Support Services.

And thanks to those dear relatives and friends who, besides professional help, have given more than generous encouragement: Fr. Gary Byrne, Thérése Gagnon, Carolyn Grassi, Julie Martin-Pitts, Jo-Ann Seiquist, Judy Barry-Walsh. Thanks too, to Dan Anderson, a recent graduate who gave invaluable suggestions and more invaluable support.

Family and friends, who gave me "living love," you have all enriched me.

Betty

Introduction

A Letter to You

Career search can be a special, very precious time to orient and organize your life. It can be a time when you look deeply at yourself and what you have been doing. It can lead you to question how you intend to spend your life for a time, or your time for the rest of your life: to keep or not to keep certain goals, to change or not to change certain behaviors, to aspire or not to aspire to certain positions—all with a view toward life enrichment.

Career search involves more than simply figuring out what job might suit you best. (That is the short-range view.) Your perspective expands when you ask yourself what you want that job to do for you. Once you ask this question, you may very quickly find yourself face to face with some of your deepest values. Do you want power, prestige, profit? Peace, harmony, love? Are some values incompatible with others? Can you have it all?

Can you work sixty hours a week moving up the corporate ladder, nurture loving relationships with family and friends, grow your own vegetables, recycle your cans on Saturday, jog daily, be a Scout leader, meditate, and play golf at the country club? How fully can all your interests and values be actualized in the real world? What is the purpose of work? What is the purpose of life? These questions lead to that all-important question, What do *you* want out of *your* life?

This text is written for those who are in transition and would like the opportunity to learn a "thought-full" career/life decision process: beginning college students, graduating seniors, parents whose children are grown, the newly divorced or widowed, job changers, the disabled, the unemployed,

PEANUTS reprinted by permission of United Feature Syndicate, Inc.

grandmothers and grandfathers kicking up their heels, corporate tycoons stopping to smell the flowers, people in mid-life crises, veterans, ex-clerics, people becoming parents and providers, people retiring, and all others willing to let go of behaviors that are no longer appropriate and risk new ones. A book about career choice is inevitably a book about life and all its stages for people from nineteen to ninety-nine.

Because a career decision is so important, some people approach it with fear and trembling lest they make a mistake. Others avoid the process altogether, certain it will nail them down to a lifelong commitment they can never change. Still others feel that any job will do just to get them started on something! And then there are those who feel that even if they did a thorough career search, it would turn up absolutely nothing. In reality, a careful career search can help everyone. It can help *you* to see many possibilities, develop flexibility, and gain a great deal of confidence. It can even help people who have already made a career decision better understand themselves and their connection to the work world. The result can be greater career/life satisfaction.

The Process

What process should you use in making a thoughtful career decision? Many people choose their first career using the "muddle-around method." They consider subjects they've liked in school: if it's math, then they'll be mathematicians; if it's history, they'll be historians. They consider the careers of people they know and ask the advice of friends—a good beginning, but not always a broad-enough perspective. If Uncle Jim the firefighter is a family hero, a new crop of firefighters is launched. If the career seekers fry hamburgers for a time, they're tempted to judge the whole world of business through the sizzle of french fries. If models and airline pilots capture their attention, they long for the glamorous life those people seem to have. They may try one job, move from here to there, get married, have a family, and move again, trying differ-

ent positions, grabbing different opportunities. Then one day, they aren't sure just how it all happened, but there they are: spouse, children, house, job— "the whole catastrophe," as Zorba the Greek said. And they may wonder, "Is this all there is?"

Some folks make very early decisions: "I knew when I was two that I wanted to be a chimney sweep." Although deciding early may work out well and satisfy the need some people have to firm up choices, in other cases it means the person has closed off options that might have been more satisfying. Career choice is sometimes treated as trivial. Adults ask six-year-olds what they want to be when they grow up. Are they going to sell shoes at Penney's or invade the corporate complex of Microsoft? Will plumbing be their outlet or travel tours their bag? Even while quizzing the children, many adults aren't always sure what their next career would be if they had to choose.

At least occasionally, however, the image of life's wholeness will flash before you and you will catch a glimpse of the time and energy that you will invest in work. You see that work will affect your life in many ways. But unless you keep a tight lid on it, the ultimate question will eventually present itself: "What's it all about?" If you deal in depth with career choice, you are bound to slip into philosophic questioning of life's meaning. To do otherwise is to trivialize a profound experience.

Stages and Steps

Because you are reading this book, you're indicating that "muddling around" is not the way you want to approach your career decision. There are stages and steps in the career search process. For many people, the journey begins at ground zero with not an idea in sight. As you gather career information, you may reach a point where you seem to be engulfed by too many ideas; things seem to get worse before they get better. Eventually you must begin to lighten

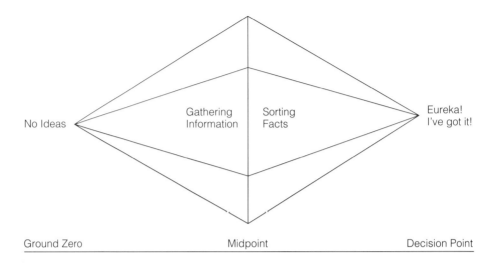

Where are you on the Career Search Continuum?

_____ Ground zero: You have no idea what career to choose.

_____ You are gathering information about yourself, the work world, and the issues that affect work.

_____ You have gathered as much information as you can. Now you need to sort it out.

_____ You are sorting out the facts by talking to people and visiting workplaces in your areas of interest. You are reviewing the information and weighing the pluses and minuses.

_____ Eureka! You have decided exactly what you would like to do and where! You know it is possible.

The Career Search Continuum

the burden by choosing. You simply can't follow every career in one lifetime. The calmer you stay, the more easily you will arrive at your decision point.

The steps you need to take to reach a career/life decision must be part of a clear, understandable, and reusable *system,* one that

1. helps you articulate who you are and what you do well.
2. describes the work world as simply and completely as possible.
3. helps you see where your personal characteristics fit into the work world.
4. empowers you to secure the job you have chosen by improving your job-hunting skills.
5. sharpens your decision-making skills, for you probably will make many decisions, and each choice leads to others.

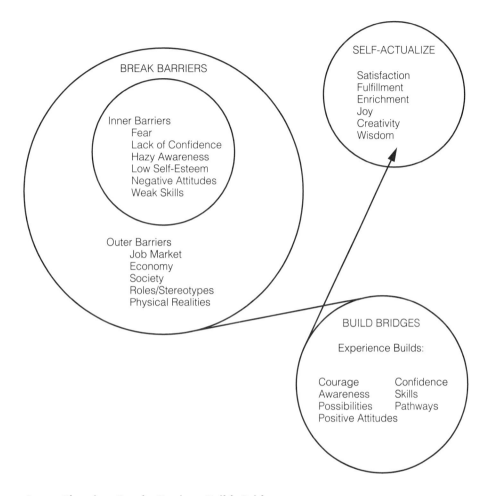

Career Planning: Breaks Barriers, Builds Bridges

6. raises your consciousness about work as only one part of your personal journey, one aspect of your total lifestyle.
7. addresses issues of global concern, showing how work is part of the world picture with its many challenges and how the solutions are provided by your work. Career planning breaks barriers and builds bridges.

In *Coming Alive from Nine to Five,* you will find such a system. It is based on identifying clear values that lead to good decisions. At first glance, this book may look like a conventional careers manual. Read the book, fill in the blanks, and (even if you're already over forty) you'll know what you want to be when you grow up.

You *will* find blanks to fill in as part of the step-by-step process of getting to know yourself and the job world. You *will* find exercises to explore your needs, wants, and values, to discover your personality orientation. You will be guided to examine your past and select the activities you've enjoyed as well as the skills you've developed over the years. A job group chart will help you to put *you* and *work* together in a meaningful way. A final inventory will collect all this "you" data and help you to see it as a unified whole.

Each of these steps represents small decisions designed to fall into a general career pattern that is compatible with your personality. This in turn leads you to choose an appropriate educational pathway such as a college major; a career that will lead you into a field of your choice; and a lifestyle that both results from and supports your career choice.

No two people will do the process in exactly the same way. Some people find that doing every exercise will lead them to a career. Others may want to use this book for ideas but not follow it exactly. Some may wish to skip around, looking for what is most helpful as long as they are not doing so to avoid the issues involved in making a career/life decision. For example, those who find decision making difficult may want to read Chapter 8 for more structured decision-making exercises.

But this book also touches on some of the heavier issues of life. How can you fulfill your potential? Be happy? Be content? It deals with such issues lightly—sometimes whimsically—because life is meant to be joyful. After a good chuckle, you will get serious and *think* again because your life is also serious and sometimes even sad. Career search, then, is really a time to *stop out* to see who you are and where you're *growing*.

This handbook works best when the searcher approaches it in a relaxed, lighthearted manner. But a serious career search also calls for commitment and motivation. Those who get thoroughly involved will experience new confidence in themselves and greater clarity about their lives. Their goals will be easier to recognize and reach. Besides providing a living, a career can satisfy some of your deepest longings. The career search, then, will become a profound journey of personal growth on the path toward self-actualization.

 The Career Search Guide

Most people base career decisions on incomplete information. As you begin your career search, it may help to focus on some important questions.

1. Gather Information about Yourself

a. Needs, wants, and shoulds

What do you *need* to survive? What do you *want* to enrich your life? Do your *shoulds* help you or hold you back?

b. Interests and values

The choices you've made over your lifetime have developed into a strong pattern of interests. These reflect what you value most in life. Are your values clear?

c. Skills

Analyze your most enjoyable activities. Through repeated choices in your areas of interest, you have developed many skills. Of all the skills you have, which do you enjoy using the most?

2. Become Informed about Societal Issues That Affect Your Career

a. What are the major challenges that face the world today?

b. What are the many positive and viable options already being taken to meet these challenges?

c. How do your values affect your work and your work affect your values?

3. Job Market Exploration: Where to Start

a. Explore the job market

Interest and skill inventories lead you to an overview of the entire job market. What jobs fit your self-image?

b. Research workplaces

What are the important characteristics of various workplaces? How do you find out which will work for you?

c. Research job market opportunities

Check the job market outlook and relate it to needs and wants in society. Will there be a need for people to do the job you'd like? What workplaces will you choose? Do you have alternatives?

d. Information interview

Have you talked to people in careers that interest you? Have you surveyed and evaluated possible workplaces? Does the survey show that you need to reevaluate your choices?

e. Tools for the job hunt

Do you know how to network, to portray yourself effectively through résumés, applications, interviews, letters? Can you talk fluently about yourself?

4. The Final Analysis: Wrap-Up

a. Decisions: Finalize your decision.

b. Goals: Set realistic goals with time lines

c. Strategy: Develop a strategy for action
d. Values/Philosophy: Review the whole picture to make sure it fits your value system, your philosophy of life and work

 *Self-Assessment*

Before you begin your career exploration, discuss either in writing or with a group where you are on the Career Search Continuum (p. 4) and how you feel about doing a career search process at this time.

1 /

Needs, Wants, and Values

Spotlighting YOU

FOCUS

- Define success in terms of your needs, wants, and goals.

- Examine important values in your personal and work life.

- Identify steps to help you decide on desired changes in your life.

Success Is Everybody's Dream

Everyone who begins a career search dreams of what he or she would like the process to achieve. Some simply want a job of any sort, the sooner the better. Others may be able to take the time not only to choose a career but also to get any education it requires. In any case, when a change is in the air, success is the goal.

Hold up the word *success* and almost everyone will want to follow it. It's so upbeat, so cheerful, so, well . . . successful! We certainly favor it over failure. Success, though an elusive concept, is compelling in its power. We chase it, we work for it, we long not only to be successful but to be considered successful by everyone we know. But many career searchers forget to define this coveted creature in terms that are uniquely theirs.

What is success? Is it attained by high-speed movement? Go places, hit the floor running, travel in the fast lane. Is it beating the competition? Get ahead, be number one, swim with the sharks. Is it battle? Set your sights, maneuver, get to the top. Is it labels and logos? The right outfit, the right house in the right place with the right car? Media images of success bombard our consciousness; the successes that family and friends imagine for us confuse but compel us; our own half-formed dreams lure us up one pathway and down another.

The pragmatic often wins over the Puritan. Many of us are no longer grateful cogs in the industrial wheel working to the rhythm of the mechanized clock. Today we can hotly pursue the American success dream rushing to the exacting beat of the finely split digital second, no longer set only by our masters but also by our inner desire to excel, look good, and make it. The values match: work hard, set high goals, and reach them. They still sound like the old Puritan work ethic. But their true values have gotten lost in the race for a sort of success our pious forebears might find hard to recognize.

These images can make the thoughtful person's head swim. Furthermore, society seems to demand one success after another without end. Yet achieving success is a basic human need. From getting a meal to making a deal, both the street person and the billionaire work each day to succeed.

Success Defined

Success has many layers and many definitions. We generally think of it in broad terms: a person *is* successful. We seldom ask what that means, what it consists of, how a person gets there, how that compares with our idea of success, and whether that is the kind of success we would enjoy. The fact is, success is "all in your head"; it is what matters most to *you*.

DILBERT reprinted by permission of United Feature Syndicate, Inc.

Some people see success as a secure niche they'll occupy when they have finished the hard work of achieving and changing. But we are all in transition and usually required to meet new challenges and draw on new abilities throughout life. No one stands still forever. Growth, marriage, family, divorce, deaths of significant people, degrees, promotion, transfers, new technology, layoffs, cutbacks, mergers, reorganization, management changes, company bankruptcy, illness, disability, and retirement represent some of the changes that affect life and careers and make us face new choices.

Goals that were appropriate for us at an earlier age fall by the wayside as we acquire and uncover new skills, as our values become more certain, as our experience opens up new horizons. What we view as a great and exciting success today may fall into a more modest perspective later in life as we move toward greater maturity and fulfillment. Our definition of success changes as we grow.

Sometimes people really are successful right now, but they aren't giving themselves credit. The powerful image of the dynamic, hardworking businessperson reaping tons of profits, prestige, and power can make other types of achievement seem trivial. Someone noted that today's maxim is "Nothing succeeds like excess." Artist Thomas Hart Benton lamented that the ideals and practices of the go-getter were ranked "above all other human interest."[1] We often honor the workaholic, who in fact may be quite self-destructive. We revere the ideal of individual success—being number one; but some might ask, at what price? We continually "up the ante" in the amount of material goods that make us look successful. We have to question such prevailing madness and ask "Must success cost so much?" And further, "Must my success be the success defined by others?" Some people measure success in terms of their ability to simplify their lives, to live with less.

People often accept life roles based on stereotypes that may prove a stumbling block to success. You are born male or female, of a certain race and ethnic background. You may grow up in a certain religion. You are student, engineer, or cook. You become spouse, parent; you are divorced, widowed; you become a sage. Each person plays these roles differently. Some let stereotypes limit their actions and narrow their views. They may think that women should not . . . , only men can . . . , blacks are . . . , Muslims believe . . . . Stereotypes can be helpful in a general way—a doctor can fix your sagging back; a carpenter can fix your sagging door. But stereotypes often fail to show that people can exhibit a full spectrum of behaviors from timid to tough, from outgoing to introspective, from flamboyant to cautious, whether they are male or female, black or white.

In the latter part of the twentieth century, stereotypes have been under scrutiny, bringing about a sea change in awareness. Women, minorities, disabled people, and older individuals have shown that they are capable of much more than people give them credit for. But we cannot assume that change based on this awareness is in any way universal. For example, *no* country in the world treats women as equals of men. In the United States, women can expect to earn on average 74 percent of the wages of a man. Most countries fall far below that mark.

These realities can inhibit *you* when it comes to making career or life decisions. You may feel that because you are female or belong to a certain minority or are "too old" that you can't fulfill your dreams. Examining the attitudes that hold you back can give you the courage to move ahead toward success in achieving your goals.

At the very least, success is finding happiness, which may be defined as being reasonably content with the choices you have made in life. Unless you see more broadly, with a more penetrating look, you may simply continue searching for success—and hence, happiness—where they are not to be found. Through self-exploration you will begin to see how capable you are, how much more is possible for you, and how wonderful you are and could become on the road to success.

If you have grown accustomed to feeling "unsuccessful," find success by setting one small, short-term, realistic goal each day and achieving it: exercise for five or ten minutes; learn five dates in history; straighten out one drawer. And then congratulate yourself on your achievements. Expand your goals little by little each day.

Luck is preparation meeting opportunity![2]

Success also relates closely to failure. We achieve, and then we find ourselves looking at the next step. Some steps work and some don't. What we learn becomes a part of our life experience. The steps that don't work might be considered failure, but they are temporary and they are also learning experiences. Thomas Edison tried hundreds of different filaments before he found one that worked in the electric lightbulb. When asked about all those failures, he said, "What failures? With every test, I discovered another material that didn't work."[3] We also need to recognize that no one has the time, energy, and interest to "do it all," to become good at everything.

Failure often causes us to reassess our goals, strive harder, and hence attain greater success. Most successful people admit they have had some "good luck" that helped them along the way. Chances are they have had "bad luck," too. They have made some mistakes, but they were not defeated. Success comes most often to those who set realistic and reasonable goals and who work hard persistently and with enthusiasm, without giving up when things go wrong.

Townes Duncan, chair and CEO of Comptronix, in Gunersville, Alabama, once said:

> Seymour Cray was a friend of my dad's. I asked him once what it was like to know the genius who had built the world's first supercomputer company. My dad said, "Well, actually, son, he wasn't so much smarter than me. He just made mistakes a hundred times faster."[4]

Sometimes people "fail" when actually they are resisting following the goals others have set for them. Failing becomes a way to exert independence. As surprising as it may seem, some people are afraid to succeed. Success brings more responsibility, higher visibility, and the expectation that the good performance will continue. Success requires continued effort to get there, to stay there, and to continue growing. The person who accepts failure, however, no longer has to keep trying.

Surprisingly, the setbacks we experience in life are often those that precipitate deeper, more valuable, and often painful insights into ourselves that cause us to make changes. Author Bill Cane asks, "Is it possible to accurately plot out a lifetime without budgeting in the possibility of change, darkness, and personal pain?"[5] When they look back, people are often grateful that a failure led them away from some serious pitfalls. People who never risk will never fail—or will they? Avoiding failure at all costs may be the greatest failure of all.

Failure is a greater teacher than success.
—*Clarissa Pinkola Estés*[6]

Clarifying Needs, Wants, and Values Leads to Successful Goals

All our activities are motivated by human needs and wants, and based on our value system. Work is one of the chief ways to fulfill those needs and wants, express our values, and find success. To start the career process at its roots, ask yourself what you *really* need. A genuine need is something you *must* have to survive, something you literally cannot live without. After these basic needs are identified, begin to look at your *wants*. Wants can enrich life beyond the level of needs. Then look at *shoulds* because sometimes they create confusion about what we really want. What we want reflects our *values* and gives meaning to our lives. Looking at needs, wants, shoulds, and values is the root of a career search and can open a new phase of personal growth as well as clarify goals.

Basic Needs Relate to Our Survival

We can divide all human motivation or needs into four areas: physical, emotional, intellectual, and altruistic or spiritual. These needs can be thought of as a hierarchy, with physical needs first on the agenda, then emotional, then intellectual, and then altruistic/spiritual, according to psychologist Abraham Maslow. All human beings have basically the same needs. Minimal survival needs in each of these areas are the foundation for becoming a fulfilled and self-actualized person. If a person's most basic needs are unfulfilled, it is difficult for that individual to be motivated by higher needs.

> Even God cannot talk to a hungry man
> except in terms of bread.
> —*Gandhi*

Air, water, food, clothing, shelter, energy, health maintenance, exercise, and the transportation required for these necessities are the vital elements of our physical need system. We also must feel physically safe and secure, and we must have the time and usually the money to satisfy our physical needs in a dependable and orderly world.

Yet we've heard stories about orphaned infants whose physical/safety needs were met but who nevertheless died mysteriously. We've heard of old people "dying of loneliness" or of a person dying after learning of the death of a loved one.[7] Human beings need love, some kind of faith and assurance that they are lovable, and someone to give them courage in order to develop self-esteem and a sense of self and belonging. University of California historian Page Smith asks, "Can't we state this as the most basic natural or moral law of the universe? That we can't live without love, that none of us can deserve

POT-SHOTS NO. 179

I DON'T NEED A GREAT DEAL OF LOVE BUT I DO NEED A STEADY SUPPLY.

love as much as we need it and that we cannot have it without sacrifice of self? Is there anything plainer underneath the sun?"[8]

We fool ourselves when we say we have no need for others, that we can do it or have done it ourselves. Without the support of others, we would not have survived. Without their caring, we would have little or no sense of self-worth. The how-to-get-rich-quick, look out for number one, and win-through-intimidation books override the basic need that people have for caring and cooperative emotional support that "swimming with the sharks," "winning with weapons," and using "guerrilla marketing attacks" don't quite fulfill. A certain level of emotional nurturing is important for survival and growth.

We may tend to view intellectual needs as nonessential, but every culture has a system to teach its young how to satisfy needs. Education begins when we are born and does not stop until we die. In this complex, fast-paced, high-tech world, it is ever more important for survival. Ideally, education leads to deeper knowledge and understanding of ourselves, others, and the world around us and to the wisdom needed to make good life choices. School is only one avenue to education because people learn in different ways. Those who relate best to the physical world seem to learn through their hands. Some learn best through their ears, some through their eyes. Some learn best from the emotion-laden words of people they love. Media-lovers learn easily from books, pictures, diagrams, and other symbols. But however we learn, our intellect lights the way.

Altruistic needs—setting aside our desires to meet the needs of others—sound as if they are only the frosting on the need cake and not a real need at all. But actually, a certain degree of altruism—looking out for others, winning by cooperation—is necessary for our individual survival. As we begin life and often as we age, we are dependent on the altruism of others. In a recent magazine article, authors Growald and Luks say that "scientists are now finding that doing good may be good for the immune system as well as the nervous system" and "may dramatically increase life expectancy."[9] There is no doubt that our individual decisions affect other people and the planet. Most societal problems are the visible product of many individual choices made without regard for the wealth and well-being of all. In an interview on "Bill Moyers' World of Ideas" on U.S. public television, the Rev. F. Forrester Church reminded us that our very survival depends ultimately on our seeing that our self-interest is the same as the self-interest of others and acting accordingly.[10] If you have survived modern life thus far, a good share of your basic needs have already been fulfilled. Many people have contributed to your well-being on all levels along the way.

> In this age we can no longer
> afford to be self-aggrandizing.
> —*Joanne McKohn*
> *California business owner*

When people reflect on their own needs and those of others, they often feel drawn to find answers to the riddle of life, to understand the problems that face them, to live a more meaningful life. They also sense that simply having knowledge does not imply that they will have the wisdom and will to act for their own good and that of others. A desire to develop morally and spiritually often results. As they search for answers to the whys of their existence, they may find motivation to live nobly and to accept with a graceful and adventurous spirit all that life brings them.

> I have the audacity to believe that people everywhere
> can have three meals a day for their bodies,
> education and culture for their minds, and
> dignity, equality, and freedom for their spirits.
> —*Dr. Martin Luther King*

Needs Relate to Wants

Satisfaction of needs is absolutely necessary for life. A cup of water, a bowl of rice, and a few sprouts a day, one set of clothes, and cardboard box for shelter will do. Twenty percent of the world's people exist at this level on less than $1 a day.[11] Because most people choose not to live at a survival level if they can help it, they begin to search for the means to satisfy their wants. It's important to know what is clearly necessary for survival and what can wait—a great difference. Risks such as changing jobs are less frightening if you know that you can survive on very little. Once your basic needs are satisfied, you can work more calmly toward achieving your wants.

If all our needs and wants were completely satisfied, all the action in our lives would stop. Need/want satisfaction is not a straight line where at some point we have "finished." Some people find the struggle for survival needs so all consuming that they have only minimal time or energy left for the pursuit of emotional, intellectual, or spiritual needs. Others get so caught up with amassing great quantities of material goods that they neglect more enriching pursuits on other levels. The tiny, exquisite, and rewarding moments in life—a smile from a special person, a kind gesture, a word of concern, a work of insight and beauty—can be lost when we are constantly rushing for more. We have little time to savor and to taste the beauty that life brings us.

Think of basic needs and those wants that are truly enriching: clean air and water; nourishing food; simple, attractive clothing and warm, decent shelter; adequate health care; simple, practical transportation; reasonable protection from risk; close relationships with caring people; the opportunity for satisfying work; a job that provides money, time, and leisure to enjoy these things and to be creative; and personal, intellectual, and spiritual growth not only for ourselves but also for others.

What makes up survival needs is lost amid the surfeit of goods and services in which the postmodern person lives. The glitter of technological wonders, the bounty of markets and malls, the ease of movement from place to place, the ever-present ability to be entertained at any hour of the day and night all take enormous amounts of time and energy away from friends, family, work, and personal enrichment and growth. To gain perspective about abundance in the developed countries, consider that a person who earns $25,000 or more is in the top 1 percent of income in the world.[12]

In altruism, all the needs and wants come together: we share, we feel, we see, we do. We share what material things we can—our time, our security; we feel love, friendship, and compassion for and with others; we see with wisdom the common bonds, the connection of all people with each other and the earth; we do what we can so that we all can be liberated into a more joyful life.

> A person is rich
> in proportion to the number of things
> he can do without.
> —*Henry David Thoreau*[13]

Needs and Wants Relate to Feelings and Shoulds

How does each person's unique set of wants evolve? Most wants come from the culture in which a person lives. Ideally people are taught by parents and teachers to find the balance called *common sense* that exists between going for everything that feels good, and reasoned judgment telling us that not everything that feels good is good for us. Life experience teaches us over and over that some things work and some do not.

Everyone has a range of emotional responses to life's events. Growing means learning to understand and manage these responses, not letting them manage you. Anger, for example, can be a natural response to adversity. Staying angry, "grinding" about bad luck, and plotting revenge keep a person from using "anger energy" in a productive and positive way to grow through the problem. It's obvious that impulsive people may act on feelings to such excess that they bring harm to themselves and others.

But it's less obvious that overly cautious people may become so dependent on rules that they are slaves to shoulds. When you say, "I should," you are implying that you neither need nor want to do this thing, but some force or some person outside you is saying you ought to. Shoulds are energy drains because they create a feeling of resistance and apathy. They cause people to shift responsibility for their choices somewhere else. When you make life changes, it's important to know whether your shoulds are value inspired. Shoulds will either evaporate as unimportant or, if value related, will be owned as a want.

Needs and Wants Relate to Values

Needs are absolute survival minimums on the physical, emotional, intellectual, and altruistic levels. *Wants* go beyond survival to a place of enriched choices. When you make such choices based on reasoned judgment, good feelings, and common sense with no pressure from shoulds, you are clearly indicating that this choice is something that *you* value. You will generally feel confident and enthusiastic about your decision. Making an important value decision may also bring some feelings of regret or guilt. Other good choices may have to be left behind; shoulds may still linger. But in time, a true value will become a comfortable part of your life pattern. Values are what you *do*, not what you *say*. Becoming aware of what you really value and cherish is a lifelong process.

Surprisingly, struggles, disappointments, worries, hopes, and dreams indicate a value area as well, for if something is not a value, it will not be of concern. There are bad values as well as good ones. Sometimes people sense that they are choosing values that are not good for them or others, that do not nurture them; they may struggle against a "good value" decision. Murky values can result in many conflicts. People who seem turned off, confused, inde-

cisive, complaining, hostile, alienated, or "lazy," and who overconform or over-rebel probably have conflicts over values.[14]

Values are unique to each person. For King Midas, gold was everything. For some people, it is the love of a pet as we have seen when a person astounds the public by leaving a million dollars to a pet cat. Sometimes your choices can lead you far from the kind of success you originally had in mind. Hoping for attention and love, people who acquire all sorts of status symbols may instead alienate those they are trying to impress. Endless acquisition of satisfiers on one level can cause neglect of needs and wants on other levels. A wise person once said that everything you own owns you. Clarifying your values helps you avoid pitfalls on your journey. You don't want to find yourself halfway down the block before you realize you've turned the wrong corner.

You are not alone when you are trying to clarify values. In 1997, a group of the world's most eminent doers and thinkers met in Prague to find a set of minimum and common moral principles. These thinkers feel that the world is in a crisis of values and must change. Some people think it is simple-minded to search for common values and then hope that the world will agree to them. But Jose Ramos-Horta, 1996 co-winner of the Nobel Peace Prize for his work on East Timor, said, "A lot of changes for the better have come about through the so-called naive people, not by bureaucrats and state leaders."[15]

Values Act As Motivators for Decisions

Your values lead you to make decisions about your whole life, not just your career. All the components of your lifestyle, including family, love and friendship, home and work environments, religious preference, education, work, and recreation—in short, all the elements of life choices you make—will reflect your personal values.

Your choices will in turn clarify and perhaps change some of your values and will thus influence your lifestyle in many ways. In your career, for example, you will learn new skills, change some behaviors to fit your new role, make new friends, and learn a new vocabulary. Recent college graduate Dan Anderson chose to teach English for a year as a volunteer in the African country Namibia. He found the people impoverished in a material sense but rich in joy and relationships. His discovery led him to rethink the values he had acquired as a typical American college student. Your work can lead to new involvements and even new ways of seeing yourself.[16] In fact, work roles are given such importance that some people find it hard to relate to a new acquaintance without knowing what that person does for a living.

Most important, the work you choose will fulfill many of your needs and wants and will directly reflect your values. Without needs and wants to motivate them, people would not work. Most people work for money to fulfill their basic needs. Some people work because the work is intellectually satisfying. Others go to work to be with people, to be noticed, to be approved of, and for a whole host of individual enticements. Those with enough resources to fulfill their basic needs and wants then work for enrichment and for the good of others.

For some, consumerism, people-collecting, and degree-collecting become goals to make them look more successful. But these activities drain resources from the planet as well as from the lives of others.

It may seem difficult or impossible at times to align your lifestyle with your values. Life is not always obliging. To write the Great American Novel may be on your dream agenda, yet you find yourself typing engineering specs. Your choice says that you value feeding yourself and your family over feeding your love for writing.

Sometimes you can feel very alone when you struggle with a values-related decision. A recent survey, however, found that Americans have a high level of agreement on basic values. The author of *The Seven Habits of Highly Effective People* noted that an overwhelming number of those surveyed agreed on these points: personal freedom must be tempered with responsibility; people have a responsibility to help others; families are more important than ever; a spiritual or religious belief is essential to a fulfilling life.[17]

Clarifying your values and their order of importance can eliminate a great deal of conflict as well as help you set goals. When you have realistic goals, both immediate and long term, you have a far greater possibility of actualizing your dreams. With this book you will be clarifying many values as you learn about yourself and your own characteristics. You will be making decisions based on those values. And achieving your needs and wants in harmony with your values spells success. This process is bound to enhance your personal growth.

> The unexamined life
> is not worth living.
> —*Socrates*

Personal Growth

Getting acquainted with yourself—your feelings, needs, wants, and most cherished values, changing shoulds to wants or dropping them—is a continuous process of growth. Growing as a person means adjusting but not losing our dreams and desires as we explore the realities of the world. The need for growth on all levels is a powerful force within us. It means expansion into new and exciting areas of life. Never before in the history of humankind have people of all ages had such opportunity for growth. Many people now live longer, are more affluent, have access to vast amounts of technology, and are more aware of possibilities. There are new dimensions to life that were not present even twenty years ago. People are going back to school at ages seventy and eighty and even ninety, getting degrees, starting businesses, publishing their first books, painting, initiating nationwide political action groups, or teaching swimming! One very energetic eighty-year-old took a careers and lifestyle class to help plan the rest of her life. People are discovering that often their powers are about as strong as their attitudes: physical (including sexual) ability, the ability to learn, the capacity to develop new ideas.

The alternative to growth is a diminished life that closes out self by putdowns and lack of confidence; many shoulds that close out others by bitter, angry thoughts and blaming/projecting, or by viewing them in a narrow way; and many demands that close out life by tension, guilt, and anxiety.

Growth is not always easy. Sometimes exploring these ideas and feelings with a trusted guide can help you learn to channel your energy in positive ways and to accomplish your goals more effectively.

Reviewing past experiences can uncover important clues to your skills and interests as well as promote growth. Your "free spirit" years, those beginning at about age five or six when you became independent enough to make some choices, are especially important. You weren't as worried about what people thought as you might have been when you were ten or twelve. What gave you satisfaction then and what proved disappointing? Some people find great motivation in striving for success in what was once a so-called area of failure. Timid speech students become noted speakers; inept Little Leaguers become strong athletes.

Times of transition can be fearful periods in which life seems so empty that we'd give anything not to face reality. But when we do face it, we are amazed at how much more there is of all good and joyful things. We begin to like ourselves better and are able to care more for others. We gradually begin to see life differently. In a sense, we create our own world. Ken Keys, Jr., believes that "a loving person lives in a loving world."[18] Self-awareness leads to self-acceptance, which leads to self-confidence. Then we are on the way to self-actualization.

When minimal needs are fulfilled on every level, when our wants are becoming reality, when our shoulds have dissolved or turned to wants, when our feelings are helping rather than hindering the process, endless vistas of growth seem to open up for us. Psychologist Abraham Maslow said, "We may still often (if not always) expect that a new discontent and restlessness will soon develop, unless the individual is doing what he's fitted for. A musician must make music, an artist must paint, a poet must write, if he is to be ultimately at peace. What a person can be, he must be. This need we call self-actualization."[19]

A self-actualizing or growing person might be described as follows:

- is authentic, open, doesn't hide behind roles or masks
- is ruled neither by ego nor emotion
- is simple, natural, with little need for status symbols
- is autonomous, centered, not pulled along by every fad
- can make decisions, take responsibility
- takes life seriously, with a generous touch of whimsy
- can see through the pretenses of others with a benign view and maybe even a chuckle
- is emotionally balanced, enjoying peak experiences, delighting in people, art, nature, yet able to "get the job done"
- feels secure, worthy, cared about, respected, connected with others
- is not burdened with the anxiety, guilt, or shame that go with shoulds
- is spontaneous, passionate, creative, an enjoyer of life—yet is moral, ethical, concerned
- sees all useful work as dignified and treats all workers with respect
- takes time for self-renewal and relaxation
- can be alone or in a group with equal ease
- values self as well as others
- is able to find common ground in opposing views and to help reconcile people's differences
- values privacy, yet feels one with humankind
- tends to form deep personal relationships, based on love and caring, with other self-actualizing people
- has a basic set of beliefs, a philosophy of life
- acts not out of greed, fear, or anger, but out of love and caring for the whole world

The flowering of our growth brings aliveness, effortlessness, individuality, playfulness, completion, richness.

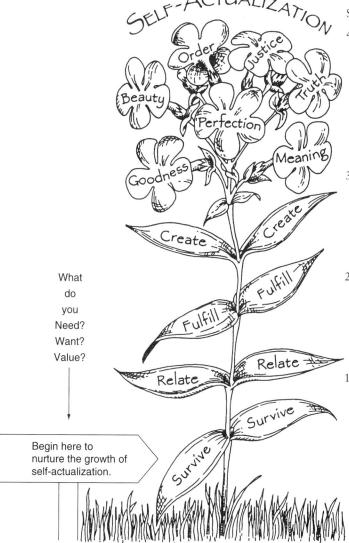

SELF-ACTUALIZATION

4. ALTRUISTIC NEEDS: We all must interact with others to survive, but to live life fully is to have that generous, loving spirit that promotes truth, goodness, beauty, justice, perfection, order, meaning, and all that is noble and good in the world.

3. INTELLECTUAL NEEDS: A degree of knowledge and understanding is necessary for survival, but a truly developed mind is one in which wisdom and creativity flourish.

2. EMOTIONAL NEEDS: Basic caring from others is necessary for our growth. Rich relationships bring us joy and the courage that comes from emotional support, love, and respect.

1. PHYSICAL NEEDS: We all have needs for food, clothing, shelter, safety—the things that keep us alive. Our carefully chosen wants enrich us and enable us to simplify our lives and feel self-sufficient.

Four NEED/WANT/VALUE areas lead to Personal Growth and Development.

The Flowering of Personal Growth

The possibilities for an enriching life are endless. Maslow intimates that when people have good homes, clothing, and food, many will take time for intellectual, artistic, and altruistic/spiritual interests. But in affluent, consumer societies, people may miss the enrichment that comes from growth in these areas.

As they find balance and sufficiency in their needs and wants, however, their lives become greatly enriched: fulfillment of physical needs and wants is ample yet not excessive; relationships bring respect, support, love, and joy; honesty, courage, faithfulness, fariness, generosity, wisdom, and creativity flourish; and the human spirit becomes noble, compassionate, and good.

A study by the Stanford Research Institute found that many affluent people feel they have enough and have chosen to live lives of voluntary simplicity. A poll conducted by Louis Harris and Associates Inc. agreed and reported that a large majority of the American public place importance on the following activities: "teaching people how to live more with basic essentials than [to reach] higher standards of living (79 percent vs. 17 percent); learning to get our pleasure out of non-material experiences, rather than on satisfying our needs for more goods and services (76 percent vs. 17 percent); spending more time getting to know each other better as human beings . . . instead of improving and speeding up our ability to communicate with each other through better technology (77 percent vs. 15 percent); and improving those modes of travel we already have rather than developing ways to get more places faster (82 percent vs. 11 percent." Harris sums it up: "Taken together, the majority views expressed . . . that a quiet revolution may be taking place in our national values and aspirations." He says this reflects our realization that our resources are limited.[20]

Beyond Needs and Wants

When people have it all, where do they go next? The answer is that they often astound and inspire us by their incredible courage in setting aside their own wants and by their tender care for others. Heroic deeds make up the fabric of their lives as they achieve the highest form of self-actualization. At this level, a person is motivated by natural altruism or spirituality. These are the people who delight and inspire us and give us new energy and courage. Service to others becomes the primary value, and the person strives for what Jakob von Uexkull, founder of Right Livelihood Awards, called "the ability to empower, uplift, and heal the human spirit."[21]

For example, Millard and Linda Fuller wondered why so many people in rural Georgia were living in run-down shacks. Instead of getting angry, they got busy, organizing volunteers and raising money. They began to build low-cost housing in partnership with needy people who pay the cost back so that more homes can be built. The organization they founded, Habitat for Humanity, has built over 70,000 homes worldwide since 1976.

Anita Roddick, founder of the successful company The Body Shop, leads workshops on new ways of doing business that take into account the rights of people and the planet. The word *activist* hardly begins to define Naomi Gray. At sixty-seven, she still puts herself on the line as she challenges communities to give deserving young black people and their families the tools they need to improve their lives.[22]

Pat Cane brings school supplies and teaches art and relaxation techniques to war-torn, poverty-stricken countries of Latin America, but above all, she brings love. Gradually, others are joining her in her ministry of healing for an afflicted world. She writes, "All of these communities are very poor, some in the countryside are without running water and electricity. Most of the families earn less than $10 a month. Their lives are, for the most part, simple and very humble, but very rich in love and faith and truth and many of the deep human values that matter most of all. What they have to share with us is a very different view of reality not found in the media nor in the rhetoric of the powerful and wealthy of our world. And this can lead to many awakenings within ourselves of the deeper meaning of love and justice in the world."[23]

Ruth Hunter at age eighty-two travels to poor, war-torn countries to work for human rights. She met with and tells Americans about Guatemalan Flor de Maria Salguero who represents women working in the garment industry under terrible conditions. Flor was kidnapped and brutally raped and beaten but refuses to give up the struggle for others.[24] Flor is presently living in a cardboard box shack while helping a thousand families petition the Guatemalan government for land on which to live.

Encouragement for helping others appears in many guises. Former U.S. labor secretary Robert Reich tells graduates not to retreat from the demands of the common good as many affluent people are doing. "Doing better together creates the right [best] conditions."[25] Attorney Bob Gnaizda represents the Greenlining Institute that fights institutional economic discrimination.[26] Frances Moore Lappé, founder of the Food Institute in Oakland, California, now heads a group called Center for Living Democracy, which provides hopeful news stories to the national media. Their motto is, "Democracy is not what we have. It's what we do."[27]

David Suzuki talked to destitute homeless children on the streets of Brazil and found amazing altruism. One child said, "I wish I was rich. And if I were I would give all of the street children food, clothes, medicines, shelter, and love, and affection!"[28]

In every field, people are working to make a positive difference in the world. The more talents you develop and the greater your contribution to improving the world you live in, the more self-actualized you are on all levels—from physical through emotional, intellectual, and altruistic/spiritual. This world is filled with challenges. It is our work that provides many of the options and solutions.

Hope . . . is not the same as joy that things are going well,
or willingness to invest in enterprises that are obviously heading
for . . . success, but rather, an ability to work for something because
it is good, not just because it stands a chance to succeed.
—*Vaclav Havel, former president of Czechoslovakia*[29]

The Work Ethic: A Personal Philosophic View

An integral part of our value system and a reflection of our personal growth is our attitude toward work, our *work ethic*. Is work really necessary? Is it valuable? Demeaning? Enhancing? Often we are ambivalent. While necessary, work is viewed differently by various cultures. In the modern technical world, people are expected to work hard and achieve much, leaving enjoyment and fun for ever-shrinking leisure hours.

The American work ethic has its roots in early colonial days when the maxim "Idleness is the devil's workshop" was a basic belief, along with Ben Franklin's dictum, "Time is money." Americans value those who have "made it" and often look down on people who haven't. People should work hard for their just rewards. Thus, by and large, we are work addicts—striving, struggling, sometimes becoming ruthless and immoral to succeed. (Work itself sometimes becomes the devil's workshop!)

The backlash from our national policies and attitudes was vividly described in 1973 in *Work in America,* a special task force report to the secretary of Health, Education, and Welfare that is still relevant today.

> Because work is central to the lives of most Americans, either the absence of work or employment in meaningless work is creating an increasingly intolerable situation. The human costs of this state of affairs are manifested in worker alienation, alcoholism, drug addiction, and other symptoms of poor mental health. Moreover, much of our tax money is expended in an effort to compensate for problems with at least a part of their genesis in the world of work. A great part of the staggering national bill in the areas of crime and delinquency, mental and physical health, manpower and welfare are generated in our national policies and attitudes toward work. . . . Most important, there are the high costs of lost opportunities to encourage citizen participation: the discontent of women, minorities, blue-collar workers, youth, and older adults would be considerably less were these Americans to have had an active voice in the decisions in the workplace that most directly affect their lives.[30]

Not everyone subscribes to the American work ethic. Senator Edward Kennedy recounts how, during his first campaign for the U.S. Senate, his opponent said scornfully in a debate, "This man has never worked a day in his life!" Kennedy says that the next morning as he was shaking hands at a factory gate, one worker leaned toward him and confided, "You ain't missed a goddamned thing."[31]

Somewhere between these two extremes of workaholism and alienation you will develop your personal work ethic, your personal perspective on the meaning of work for you.

Just a Job, or a Career?

Your career choice will more completely match your values when you clarify your work ethic and decide on the degree of commitment you are willing to make to your work. Do you want a career or just a job? A job might be defined as something one does to earn money, requiring little involvement beyond one's physical and mental presence. Many people of all levels of intelligence and creativity approach work this way: some, because their job is the only work they want or can get; others, to support hobbies and creative activities for which there seem to be no work opportunities.

In contrast to a job, a career can be seen as a series of work experiences that represent progression in a field. This kind of work usually absorbs much of a person's energy. A career is often planned for and trained for, and it often involves dedication of time and talent beyond the minimum required.

Two people may do identical work, yet one may view the work as "just a job" whereas the other sees it as "my career." Sometimes a person trains and sacrifices to achieve a career only to face disillusionment and ends up just putting in time. Conversely, some people have been known to perform what society calls "menial" work with a level of dedication worthy of a career professional.

A demanding career may cause a loss of family, health, friendship, and leisure. How much are you willing to sacrifice? Some people can pursue a career with great dedication and yet manage to keep a balance. How much involvement is enough for you? Keep the question of commitment in mind, as well as your other values, as you consider your career choice. When you find work that matches your needs, wants, values, interests, and abilities and see that it brings you many rewards, your respect for your workplace and colleagues will grow. You will be eager to put forth your best effort, and you will enjoy the challenges that each day brings. What began as a job may become your career.

We seem to be in a period of rising expectations about ourselves and about work, even in a frequently shaky job market. As T. George Harris, former editor of *Psychology Today* once said, "We were doing all right until some idiot raised the ante on what it takes to be a person and the rest of us accepted it without noticing."[32] Well, why not? Why not expand our vision? To paraphrase nineteenth-century feminist Elizabeth Cady Stanton, the true person is as yet a dream of the future.[33] Why keep that idea forever in the future? Why not begin to make it a present reality? The premise of this manual is that people can find joy in work and life and be more than they thought possible! For the first time in history we can allow ourselves the luxury of thinking of work as both fulfilling and a responsible way to provide good things for ourselves and others. And each person will find that fulfillment in a unique way. A carpenter will fit each piece of wood more tightly; a secretary will prepare reports with extra-special care. We can all contribute in some way to the well-being of others as well as to ourselves as responsible, productive, and contented workers.

If we can find a place where we feel some measure of success, some value, we will find new energy to put into our work. Dr. Hans Selye, a world-renowned biologist, describes the relationship among aging, work, and stress: "Work wears you out mainly through the frustrations of failure. Most of the eminent among hard workers in almost any field lived a long life. Since work is a basic need of man, the question is not whether to work but what kind of work is play."[34] And Yehudi Menuhin expressed it well when he said, "All my life I have reveled in the sound of the violin."

We have many resources of mind and spirit. Can we move to a place of greater joy in work and in life? Harvard researchers, Bartolomé and Evans tell us, "You will fit your job/life activity, and we can say, be more successful if you feel confident, enjoy the work and if your moral values coincide with your work."[35] Reflecting on what success means to you, what your values are, is essential and may be quite surprising and different from what you have expected.

As you go about the process of choosing a career, your image of success will sharpen. May your career choice contribute to *your* dream of a successful future.

 ## *Self-Assessment Exercises*

Self-assessment exercises throughout the text are designed to help you with your career search. Each set will prove helpful for the chapters ahead. Use *only the ones that are useful to you. You may not need to do them all.* In Chapter 9, "Work Affects the Soul: The Final Analysis," you will find a place to summarize all the exercises.

1. Needs and Wants: Dream Your Goals

a. Survival needs plus: Your enriched wants reflect your values

What lifestyle is important to you? Dream—let your imagination soar; describe your ideals in the following areas and what you expect from each, or write a paragraph or two about those most important to you:

Your home _____

Your clothing _____

Your food _____

Your family _____

Your friends _____

Your associates _____

Your transportation _____

Your pets/plants _____

Your gadgets and playthings_____

Your activities_____

Other _____

b. Fulfillment needs/wants

Dream again! If you could instantly be in your ideal career/lifestyle, already skilled and trained, what would it be?

■ To delight yourself and amaze your family and friends?

_____

_____

■ To improve the world?

_____

_____

c. Check the balance in your life.

What do you do, over and above absolute need, to contribute to your well-being on each of the following four levels?

Physical _____

Emotional _____

Intellectual_____

Altruistic/Spiritual _____

2. Tapping into Feelings and Shoulds

What seems to block your effectiveness? It's easier to make career/life decisions if problems are not getting in the way.

a. Life problems checklist

Identify the factors that you feel are a problem for you. Rate the items listed by checking the appropriate columns: I am happy with; I am managing with; I am having trouble with. Year + = this problem has been going on for a year or more; Chronic = this problem has been present for a great deal of my life. Then go back and circle the items you would like to change.

	Happy	Managing	Trouble	Year+	Chronic
Parents/brothers/sisters					
Spouse/children					
Family closeness					
Friends/relationships/love					
Privacy/freedom					
Dwelling					
Work					
Finances					
Personal achievements/success					
Confidence					
Health					
Diet/drugs/drinking/smoking					
Exercise					
Physical appearance					
Physical well-being					
Time/leisure					
Recreation/hobbies					
Emotional/mental well-being					
Status					
Intellectual ability					
Artistic ability					
Education					
Social concern					
Political concern					
Spiritual/religious well-being					

b. Feelings checkpoints

Check (✓) any of the following feeling responses that often create problems for you. Mark with a plus (+) those areas you'd like to improve.

_____ Anger	_____ Fear	_____ Pessimism
_____ Apathy	_____ Frenzy	_____ Resentment
_____ Boredom	_____ Frustration	_____ Skepticism
_____ Confusion	_____ Hostility	_____ Violence
_____ Depression	_____ Hurt	_____ Worry
_____ Discouragement		

c. Shoulds

List and examine the shoulds that hold you back. Can you drop them or change them to wants? Answer below.

_____

_____

_____

_____

3. Rating Values

Here are five incomplete sentences that encourage you to think about values. In the lists that follow each one, check (✓) every word that finishes the statement correctly for you as you or your life are *now*. Put a plus sign (+) in front of every word that describes things you would like to *develop more*. Feel free to add, delete, or change words on each list.

a. Career values

In my career, I do (✓); I would like to (+):

_____ Create beauty	_____ Improve society
_____ Create ideas	_____ Make things
_____ Design systems	_____ Manage/organize people
_____ Experience variety	_____ Organize things
_____ Explore ideas	_____ Perform physical tasks
_____ Follow directions	_____ Take responsibility
_____ Help people	

b. Result values

I have (✔); I'd like to have more (+):

_____ Adventure	_____ Money
_____ Beautiful surroundings	_____ Pleasure
_____ Comfort	_____ Possessions
_____ Fun	_____ Power
_____ Happiness	_____ Prestige
_____ Independence	_____ Security
_____ Leisure time	_____ Structure

c. Personal qualities

I am (✔); I'd like to be more (+):

__✔__ Accepting	_____ Famous
__+__ Affectionate	__+__ Friendly
__+__ Ambitious	__✔__ Good-looking
__✔__ Balanced	__✔__ Healthy
__✔__ Brave	__✔__ Honest/Fair
__✔__ Calm	__✔__ Intelligent
__✔__ Caring	__+__ Joyful
__✔__ Compassionate	__✔__ Kind
__✔__ Competitive	__✔__ Loving
__+__ Confident	__✔__ Loyal
__✔__ Conscientious	__✔__ Mature
__✔__ Cooperative	__✔__ Neat
__✔__ Courteous	__✔__ Needed
__✔__ Creative	__✔__ Optimistic
__✔__ Decisive	__+__ Peaceful
__+__ Disciplined	__✔__ Poised
__+__ Efficient	__+__ Prompt
__✔__ Enthusiastic	__✔__ Self-accepting

__+__ Sensitive	_____ Understanding
__+__ Strong	_____ Verbal
__+__ Successful	_____ Warm
__✓__ Trusting	_____ Wise

d. People satisfiers

I have (✓) good relationships with; I'd like good (or better) relationships with (+):

_____ Spouse/lover	_____ Children
_____ Relatives	_____ Friends
_____ Parents	_____ Neighbors
_____ Siblings	_____ Colleagues
_____ In-laws	_____ Supervisors

e. Personal growth satisfiers

I am satisfied with my development in the following need/want areas (✓); I'd like to develop more in (+):

_____ Physical	_____ Intellectual
_____ Emotional	_____ Altruistic/spiritual

f. Global values

I am working toward (✓); I would like to work more toward (+):

_____ Economic development	_____ Industrial/technical development
_____ Environmental protection	_____ Weapons control
_____ Ethical/spiritual development	_____ World food or housing supply
_____ Human rights	_____ World peace and prosperity

g. Values checkpoint

Star (*) your top three values in each section a–f. Write a brief paper, describing who you are, using these value words. Explain any contradictions.

4. Goal Setting

Set goals! Go back over the above exercises and pick one area for improvement. Write down a key word and post it someplace where you can see it, perhaps on the bathroom mirror. What specific steps, little or big, can you take to improve your life? Perhaps see a counselor to talk over such issues as problem areas, strong feelings, or values conflicts.

I'd like to improve: _____

Steps to take: _____

_____

_____

5. Your Expectations

At this point, do you feel that you want a career or "just a job"? Explain.

_____

_____

_____

6. Candid Camera—3-D

Each activity you've chosen to do contains important clues about you, your skills, and your interests. This exercise will be one of the first steps on the road to career decision making. It is also the first step toward preparing a résumé and getting ready for an interview. Your life in 3-D will help you discover who you are, decide your goals, design your strategies. Spend an intense hour doing this exercise as outlined here. Use scratch paper. Then save it and add to it, refine it, and organize it according to the exercises that follow.

- **Loves:** Make a list of ten to twenty activities you love to do, not *like* or *should* but *love*. Don't *think* too much; just list whatever comes to mind first.
- **Jobs:** List five to ten or more of the jobs most important to you that you've done for pay, way back to baby-sitting or lawn mowing.
- **Other:** List five to ten of your most important extracurricular activities, community volunteer jobs, hobbies done at home or on vacation, sports, anything that gave you confidence and good energy.
- Then take a separate sheet of scratch paper for two or three of the most important items above and begin to list in detail what you did to accomplish each activity. For example, if skiing is on your list, you might write buying/organizing equipment, doing fitness exercises, choosing a slope, making reservations, trying new techniques, teaching friends, what else?

- **Data, People, Things:** Using your lists, note when you deal with people or things. Notice when you are dealing with ideas and information alone as, for example, when reading, analyzing, and organizing material—just what this exercise requires. You will see that in dealing with people and things, you always need ideas and information (data). Then code each activity D, P, or T. We will use this code later to help you sort out various types of job qualities.

> P = activities when you deal directly with people (some use of data always implied).
>
> T = activities when you deal directly with things (some use of data always implied).
>
> D = activities when you deal just with ideas and information, called data (there is little or no interaction with people or things).

7. Data File

Here is an example of file cards done by students to organize and summarize information from Candid Camera about their past jobs and important activities. Notice that any activity can be expanded with more detail. Making a file card for each of the jobs and activities that is important to you will help you in creating a résumé and preparing for a job interview.

X-Mart, Inc.   Supervisor: Buster Brown

347 Snow Valley Lane   Salary: $5.20/hr

New Castle, DE   Dates: June 1998–present

Title: Cashier

- Process customer merchandise through check stand

- Collect cash and make change

- Verify check or credit card information

- Bag items and present sales slip

- Help unpack merchandise in storeroom and stock shelves

Happy Lake Summer Camp   Supervisor: Jane Golden

Route 555   Salary: $50/week plus

Happy Lake, Wisconsin 53950   room and board

Title: Camp Counselor   Dates: Summers 1998, 1999

- Supervise group of 8 children ages 8 to 10
- Organize swimming activities
- Teach leather crafts
- Do conflict resolution, listen to problems
- Oversee bunk room

8. Drawing a Self-Portrait: Your Autobiography

You may wish to choose one of the following to use as a basis for writing the story of your life. Some people may find doing more than one useful as background for their history.

a. Briefly write the story of your life.

b. Use the value words in Exercise 3 to describe your values and how they have evolved over the years.

c. Examine your free-spirit years and summarize what you discover.

Between the ages of five and ten, what activities did you enjoy most? Remember various seasons, indoors, outdoors; remember friends you played with. List and then check (✓) those you enjoyed most.

_____	_____
_____	_____
_____	_____
_____	_____
_____	_____
_____	_____

d. Fill in your lifeline on the following chart and summarize the data asked for.

Even very young people have had significant experiences that changed them. Beginning with your young childhood period, draw a lifeline representing the ups and downs of your experiences at various times of your life. Draw your first impressions without concern about detail. Imagine yourself gliding over the surface of your life, noting the high and low points, times of joy, and times of unhappiness. Look for people who had profound and positive effects on you.

	Young Childhood Teddy Bears/Goblins 3–5 years	Elementary School Free-Spirit Years 6–13 Years	High School Teenage Traumas/Triumphs 14–17 Years	New Beginnings College/Work 18–22 Years	Developing an Adult Lifestyle 23–28 Years	Family/Commitment Career Involvement 29–39 Years	Midlife Crises Is There Life after 40? 40–45 Years	Settling In Facing Up 45–55 Years	Putting It All Together Once More/Preretirement 56–70 Years	Reflecting/Integrating A Time for Wisdom 70+
High Points										
Low Points										

- List your low points/hardest times.

_____

_____

_____

_____

_____

- List your high points/happiest times.

_____

_____

_____

_____

_____

_____

■ List your most important life decisions.

_____

_____

_____

_____

■ List three to five people who influenced you the most either positively or negatively (include teachers, authors, etc.). Tell what they did. Indicate the current
importance of their influence by rating them: 1 = Very important; 2 = Important; 3 = So so; 4 = No longer important.

_____

_____

_____

_____

e. Use the following three circles diagram as a basis for an autobiography.
   Discuss each item in the past, present, and future circles as it applies to your
   life.

f. Make a poster or collage using magazines or old photos that illustrates you.

g. Create a personal "I Wheel" like the one on page 40.

Group Discussion Questions

In addition to the group discussion questions below, you might like to share
with others your answers to the previous exercises in this and all the chapters.

   1. Do the basic human needs change over time? Discuss with a group what
      basic needs you could supply for each other and how much money that
      would save you. What wants are important for you? Have you covered all
      the need/want areas: physical, emotional, intellectual, altruistic/spiritual?

   2. What is the connection between our needs and wants and the work we and
      others do?

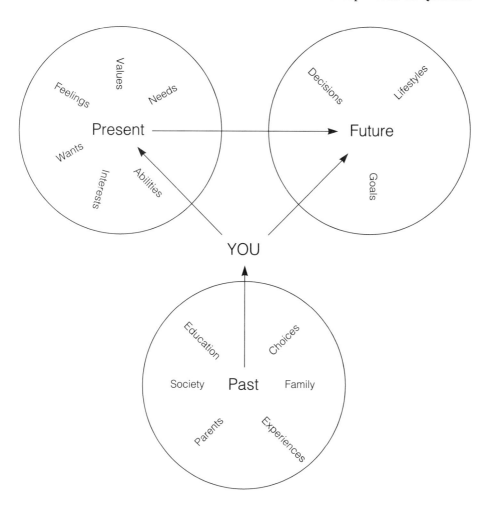

3. What limits and demands do your personal wants place on your career choice?

4. Name the last five items you've purchased. What basic needs did they fulfill? What wants? Could you survive without them for a year?

5. List all the devices in your home that use electricity. On a scale of 1 to 10, rate how necessary each appliance is to you. If you could use only five, which ones would you choose? Is electricity a basic human need?

6. Discuss success and failure.

   a. Define success and failure for yourself.

   b. Try substituting the word *happiness* for *success*. Is there a difference?

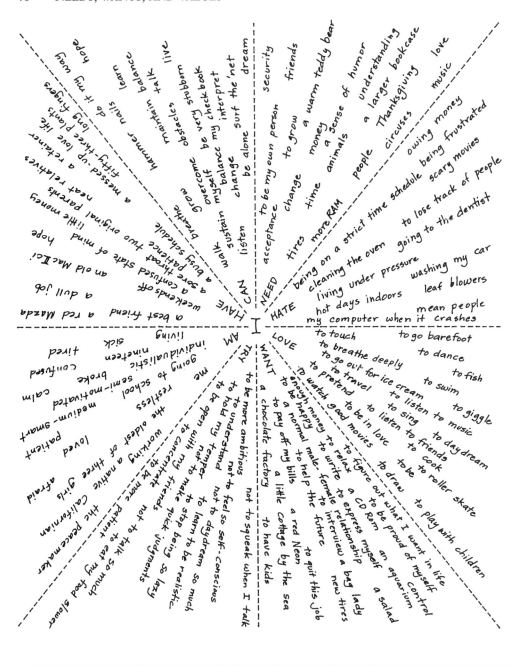

The I Wheel

    c. Name some of the many life roles you have seen yourself playing as you grew up. Describe your surroundings; tell what you were doing, what you were wearing.

    d. Do stereotypes about the roles you see yourself in now limit your chances for success? Explain.

7. Give as many answers as you can to this question: Why do we work?

8. What is your first memory? What advice your parents gave you do you recall most clearly? If your life keeps going the way it is, what will it be like in ten years? How would you like to be remembered at the end of your life?

9. Has this chapter clarified your image of the kind of person you are now and would like to be in the future; the kind of lifestyle you would like to lead? Using ideas from the exercises above, discuss points of interest to yourself with a group or write a short paper about yourself.

10. Has this chapter caused you to begin making some decisions that will bring you closer to your goals? How?

11. List as many principles as you can of good moral values. Do others in your group agree with you?

RÉSUMÉ WORDS

Identify words or phrases you gathered from this chapter that define you; jot down the ones you might use in a résumé.

2 | Personality and Performance

Pieces of the Puzzle

FOCUS

- *Assess your personality.*
- *Pinpoint your relationship to Data, People, Things, and Work Qualities.*
- *Identify your skills.*

*A*person is an intriguing mystery. All the themes that make up a personality can be likened to a stained glass window—a mosaic of light and color. A stained glass window is an enduring object of carefully chosen colors, yet it changes with the changing sun. In darkness it seems to disappear, but in the light it comes alive with color.

> It takes
> its life from light
>   it sleeps at night
>   and comes ablaze at dawn
>   it holds the day
>   'til shadows fade,
>   its brilliance strangely gone.
> —*Michelozzi*

You have surveyed your needs, wants, values, and important activities. You've begun to gather pieces of your own one-of-a-kind mosaic to create a portrait of a special person—*you*. The activities you've done and enjoyed so far will give you clues to the interests unique to your personality. These in turn will provide a base to help you discover your skills. You'll be ready to relate the assembled information to satisfying positions in the world of work. When you finally enter the workplace, you may have had to make some compromises, but the ideal is to minimize the compromises and maximize the match.

Areas of Interest: The Personality Mosaic

Psychologist and vocational counselor John Holland says that one of six major personality types—or perhaps a combination of two or more types—plays a highly important role in an individual's career choice.[1] We become interested in some areas more than others early in life. These areas become focal points, largely because of choices we make that stem from our needs, wants, and values.

Notice what interests draw individuals when family or friends get together. Sports and cars are a magnet to some; the lives and loves of people are a concern to others; participating in mind-bending discussions, plotting a financial move, or sharing creative endeavors can keep some members of a group going until all hours. Because each person notices and experiences things differently, *you* are unique in the combination of things that interest *you*. Those interests make up your predominant personality characteristics and are keys to your career satisfaction.

Becoming aware of your "lesser lights" can also provide some illumination and enrichment. We are all born with innumerable possibilities. Some of our talents may remain undeveloped for half a lifetime only to surface in the middle and senior years. Personal growth leads to the discovery of new dimensions of ourselves. Then there is that rare "Renaissance person" who seems able to be and to do all things with apparently equal ease, who is at home in all settings and with all people.

In this chapter, you can identify the predominant orientation of your personality with an inventory called the Personality Mosaic. It's important to take this inventory before reading the interpretation that follows. Then you can analyze the kinds of activities you've been enjoying all your life. Having reminded yourself of your interests, you will be ready to tie these data into the Job Group Chart in Chapter 3.

 ## Personality Mosaic

Circle the numbers of statements that clearly sound like something you might say or do or think—something that feels like *you*. Don't stop to analyze your responses too much. If you wish, put question marks (?) in front of doubtful items and X's on the numbers of statements that feel very unlike you.

1. It's important for me to have a strong, agile body.
2. I need to understand things thoroughly.
3. Music, color, writing, beauty of any kind can really affect my moods.
4. Relationships with people enrich my life and give it meaning.
5. I am confident that I'll be successful.
6. I need clear directions so I know exactly what to do.
7. I can usually carry/build/fix things myself.
8. I can get absorbed for hours in thinking something out.
9. I appreciate beautiful surroundings; color and design mean a lot to me.
10. I'll spend time finding ways to help people through personal crises.
11. I enjoy competing.
12. I prefer getting carefully organized before I start a project.
13. I enjoy making things with my hands.
14. It's satisfying to explore new ideas.
15. I always seem to be looking for new ways to express my creativity.
16. I value being able to share personal concerns with people.
17. Being a key person in a group is very stimulating to me.
18. I take pride in being very careful about all the details of my work.
19. I don't mind getting my hands dirty.
20. I see education as a lifelong process of developing and sharpening my mind.
21. I like to dress in unusual ways, try new colors and styles.
22. I can often sense when a person needs to talk to someone.

23. I enjoy getting people organized and on the move.
24. I'd rather be safe than adventurous in making decisions.
25. I like to buy sensible things I can make or work on myself.
26. Sometimes I can sit for long periods of time and work on problems or puzzles or read or just think.
27. I have a great imagination.
28. I like to help people develop their talents and abilities.
29. I like to be in charge of getting the job done.
30. I usually prepare carefully ahead of time if I have to handle a new situation.
31. I'd rather be on my own doing practical, hands-on activities.
32. I'm eager to read or think about any subject that arouses my curiosity.
33. I love to try creative new ideas.
34. If I have a problem with someone, I'll keep trying to resolve it peacefully.
35. To be successful, it's important to aim high.
36. I don't like to take responsibility for making big decisions.
37. I say what's on my mind and don't beat around the bush.
38. I need to analyze a problem pretty thoroughly before I act on it.
39. I like to rearrange my surroundings to make them unique and different.
40. I often solve my personal problems by talking them out with someone.
41. I get projects started and let others take care of details.
42. Being on time is very important to me.
43. I enjoy doing vigorous outdoor activities.
44. I keep asking, "Why?"
45. I like my work to be an expression of my moods and feelings.
46. I like to help people find ways to care more for each other.
47. It's exciting to take part in important decisions.
48. I am usually neat and orderly.
49. I like my surroundings to be plain and practical.
50. I need to stay with a problem until I figure out an answer.
51. The beauty of nature touches something deep inside me.
52. Close personal relationships are valuable to me.
53. Promotion and advancement are important to me.
54. I feel more secure when my day is well planned.
55. I'm not afraid of heavy physical work and usually know what needs to be done.
56. I enjoy books that make me think and give me new ideas.
57. I look forward to seeing art shows, plays, and good films.
58. I am very sensitive to people who are experiencing emotional upsets.
59. It's exciting for me to influence people.
60. When I say I'll do it, I do my best to follow through on every detail.
61. Good, hard manual labor never hurt anyone.
62. I'd like to learn all there is to know about subjects that interest me.

63. I don't want to be like everyone else; I like to do things differently.
64. I'll go out of my way to be caring of people with problems.
65. I'm willing to take some risks to get ahead.
66. I feel more secure when I follow rules.
67. One of the first things I look for in a car is a well-built engine.
68. I like a conversation to be intellectually stimulating/challenging.
69. When I'm creating, I tend to let everything else go.
70. I feel concerned that so many people in our society need help.
71. It's challenging to persuade people to follow a plan.
72. I'm very good about checking details.
73. I usually know how to take care of things in an emergency.
74. Reading about new discoveries is exciting.
75. I appreciate beautiful and unusual things.
76. I take time to pay attention to people who seem lonely and friendless.
77. I love to bargain.
78. I like to be very careful about spending money.
79. Exercise or sports are important to me in building a strong body.
80. I've always been curious about the way nature works.
81. It's fun to be in a mood to try something unusual.
82. I am a good listener when people talk about personal problems.
83. If I don't make it the first time, I usually bounce back with energy and enthusiasm.
84. I need to know exactly what people expect me to do.
85. I like to take things apart to see whether I can fix them.
86. I like to study all the facts and decide logically.
87. It would be hard to imagine my life without beauty around me.
88. People often seem to tell me their problems.
89. I can usually connect with people who get me in touch with a network of resources.
90. It's very satisfying to do a task carefully and completely.

Scoring Your Answers

To score, use the table on the following page and circle the same numbers that you circled on the Personality Mosaic.

Count the number of circles in each column and write the total number of circles in the spaces, 15 being the highest possible score:

R _____   I _____   A _____   S _____   E _____   C _____

List the letters R, I, A, S, E, and C, according to your scores, from highest to lowest:

1st _____   2nd _____   3rd _____   4th _____   5th _____   6th _____

R	I	A	S	E	C
1	2	3	4	5	6
7	8	9	10	11	12
13	14	15	16	17	18
19	20	21	22	23	24
25	26	27	28	29	30
31	32	33	34	35	36
37	38	39	40	41	42
43	44	45	46	47	48
49	50	51	52	53	54
55	56	57	58	59	60
61	62	63	64	65	66
67	68	69	70	71	72
73	74	75	76	77	78
79	80	81	82	83	84
85	86	87	88	89	90

Number of question marks:

R _____   I _____   A _____   S _____   E _____   C _____

Number of X's:

R _____   I _____   A _____   S _____   E _____   C _____

If you put question marks on the inventory, does adding them in change the order? _____ How? _____

Which areas have the most X's? _____

_____

In which areas do you have the most "unlike you" scores (X's)? _____

_____

Were you aware at any time of responding according to "shoulds"? _____

In what cases? _____

　　Do you have a tie score in two more or columns? If so, the remainder of this chapter will help you to decide which type is closest to the "real you."

To get more in touch with yourself, read aloud some of the statements for each orientation from the Personality Mosaic. *Be* that kind of person. Embellish and dramatize the statements to see how that kind of behavior feels. You may want to role-play this activity in a group.

Interpreting the Personality Mosaic

The inventory you have just taken is based on the six personality orientations identified by John Holland. As you can see from your score, you are not just one personality type—that is, you are not a person with fifteen circles in one area and no circles in any of the others. In most people, one or two characteristics are dominant, two or three are of medium intensity, and one or two may be of low intensity. A few people score high in each category because they have many interests. Others, who don't have many strong interests, score rather low in all areas.

Sometimes people experiencing emotional stress in their lives find it difficult to do this inventory. Finding a counselor or another trusted person to talk to may help before you continue your career exploration.

Here is an overview and discussion of the six personality types and their relationship to each other. Try to find yourself in the following descriptions.

Realistic Personality

Hands-on people who enjoy exploring things, fixing things, making things with their hands

Express themselves and achieve primarily through their bodies rather than through words, thoughts, feelings

Are usually independent, practical-minded, strong, well-coordinated, aggressive, conservative, rugged individualists

Like the challenge of physical risk, being outdoors, using tools and machinery

Prefer concrete problems to abstract ones

Solve problems by doing something physical

Realistic individuals are capable and confident when using their bodies to relate to the physical world. They focus on *things*, learn through their hands, and have little need for conversation. Because they are at ease with material objects, they are often good in physical emergencies. Their ability to deal with the material world often makes them very independent. Because these characteristics describe the stereotypical male, many women shrink from displaying any capability in this area, and even in this enlightened age, women are often still discouraged from doing so.

Investigative Personality

>   People who live very much "in their minds"
>
>   Are unconventional and independent thinkers, intellectually curious, very insightful, logical, persistent
>
>   Express themselves and achieve primarily through their minds rather than through association with people or involvement with things
>
>   Like to explore ideas through reading, discussing
>
>   Enjoy complex and abstract mental challenges
>
>   Solve problems by thinking and analyzing

The investigative type deals with the "real world" of things but at a distance. These individuals prefer to read, study, use books, charts, and other data instead of getting their hands on *things*. When involved with people, they tend to focus on ideas. Wherever they are, they collect information and analyze the situation before making a decision. If they enjoy the outdoors, it's because they are curious, not because they enjoy rugged, heavy, physical work.

Artistic Personality

>   People who are creative, sensitive, aesthetic, introspective, intuitive, visionary
>
>   See new possibilities and want to express them in creative ways
>
>   Are especially attuned to perception of color, form, sound, feeling
>
>   Prefer to work alone and independently rather than with others
>
>   Enjoy beauty, variety, the unusual in sight, sound, texture, people
>
>   Need a fairly unstructured environment to provide opportunities for creative expression
>
>   Solve problems by creating something new

Artistic people express creativity not only with paint and canvas but with ideas and systems as well. Those sensitive to sight, sound, and touch will be drawn to the fine arts such as art, drama, music, and literature. The weaver designs and makes fabric; the poet creates with words; the choreographer arranges dancers in flowing patterns; the architect creates with space. But the industrialist creates systems for the flow of goods; the program planner creates better delivery of services. Others will be content just to enjoy aesthetic experience.

Artistic types often love the beauty and power of the outdoors to inspire their creativity—but not its ability to make them perspire with heavy work. They would rather create ideas than study them. They like variety and are not afraid to experiment, often disregarding rules. Their ideas don't always please others, but opposition doesn't discourage them for long. Their irrepressible spirits and enthusiasm can often keep them focused on a creative project to the exclusion of all else, though plowing new ground can be lonely and agonizing. Not producing up to standard (their own) can plunge them to the depths of misery.

Social Personality

> People persons who "live" primarily in their feelings
>
> Are sensitive to others, genuine, humanistic, supportive, responsible, tactful, perceptive
>
> Focus on people and their concerns rather than on things or intellectual activity
>
> Enjoy closeness with others, sharing feelings, being in groups and in unstructured settings that allow for flexibility and caring
>
> Solve problems primarily by feeling and intuition, by helping others

The social personality focuses on people and their concerns. Sensitive to people's moods and feelings, these individuals may often enjoy company and make friends easily but not necessarily. Some, with a concern for people, may be shy individuals and even introverts who need time alone, although they focus on people's needs. Their level of caring may range from one person to the entire planet. Their relationships with people depend on their ability to communicate both verbally and nonverbally, listening as well as speaking and writing. Their empathy and ability to intuit emotional cues help them to solve people problems sometimes before others are even aware of them. They can pull people together and generate positive energy for the sake of others, but not for themselves. Because the social orientation seems to describe the "typical female," many men shrink from expressing or dealing with deep feelings. The social personality types sometimes focus on people concerns to the exclusion of all else. They sometimes appear "impractical," especially to the realistic types.

Enterprising Personality

> Project people who are thoroughly absorbed in their strategies
>
> Are energetic, enthusiastic, confident, dominant, political, verbal, assertive, quick decision makers
>
> Are self-motivated leaders who are talented at organizing, persuading, managing
>
> Achieve primarily by using these skills in dealing with people and projects
>
> Enjoy money, power, status, being in charge
>
> Solve problems by taking risks

The enterprising person is a leader who initiates projects but often gets others to carry them out. Instead of doing research, these people rely on hunches about what will work. They may strike an observer as restless and irresponsible because they often move on after a job is under way, but many activities would never get off the ground without their energizing influence. They need to be a leader of the "in crowd," but because their relationships center around tasks, they may focus so dynamically on the project that the personal concerns of others, and even their own, go unnoticed.

Conventional Personality

People who "live" primarily in their orderliness

Are quiet, careful, accurate, responsible, practical, persevering, well organized, task oriented

Have a strong need to feel secure and certain, get things finished, attend to every detail, follow a routine

Prefer to work for someone of power and status rather than be in such a position themselves

Solve problems by appealing to and following rules

The conventional person also is task oriented but prefers to carry out tasks initiated by others. Because these individuals are careful of detail, they keep the world's records and transmit its messages on time and accurately. They obey rules, and they value order in the world of data. They like to be well prepared ahead of time and prefer minimal changes. Getting tasks finished gives them immense satisfaction. Their sense of responsibility keeps the world going as they focus on details of the tasks at hand to the exclusion of all else.

> FOR THE MOST PART
> I do the thing which my
> own nature drives
> me to do.
> —*Albert Einstein*

The Personality Hexagon

The six personality types can be arranged in a hexagon. In the figure, "Personality Types: Similarities and Differences," the types next to one another are most similar. The words linking them indicate their shared traits or interests. For example, realistic and investigative people focus on things. The R person does something to or with the thing; the I person analyzes it. Investigative and artistic types are both "idea" people. The I explores and may develop ideas logically; the A invents them intuitively. Artistic and social people like to be in tune with their feelings—the A person with feelings about surroundings, the S person with feelings about people. Social and enterprising people are people leaders: the S person is concerned about people; the E person wants to get people motivated to undertake a task. The conventional person will carry out the details of the task to the last dot. Thus the E and C are both task oriented in different ways—the E person initiating and leading, and the C type carrying through to completion with the utmost responsibility. Both C and R types value order: the C values data/paper order; the R values physical order. People seek out work activities that enable them to be with others of like personality. Workplaces, too, tend to gather similar types and reflect the style of these workers.

The types opposite each other on the hexagon are most unlike. For example, the artistic personality is independent, doesn't mind disorder, and likes to try new things. The conventional person depends more on other people, likes order, and would prefer things to stay the same.

Two people who are strongly opposite in personality can improve their relationship by understanding the differences between them. A realistic person

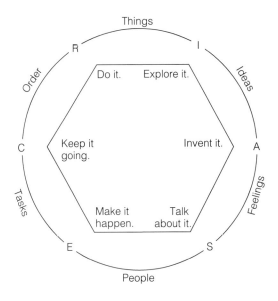

Personality Types: Similarities and Differences SOURCE: Reproduced by special permission of the publisher, Psychological Assessment Resources, Inc., from *Making Vocational Choices*, Third Edition. Copyright © 1973, 1985, 1992, 1997 by Psychological Assessment Resources, Inc. All rights reserved. Adapted from John Holland, *Making Vocational Choices: A Theory of Careers* (Englewood Cliffs, NJ: Prentice-Hall, 1973), copyright © 1970, by special permission of John Holland and Prentice-Hall, Inc. See also John Holland, *Self-Directed Search* (Palo Alto, CA: Consulting Psychologists Press), copyright © 1970.

doesn't deal much with people's feelings whereas a social person sees much of life through feelings. The introspective I person is amazed at the outgoing E person's ability to act without doing much research. Because opposites complement each other, it can be advantageous to see a radically different personality as a potential source of support and enrichment. Wise employers will hire those whose personality orientation is appropriate for the work to be done.

The strengths of each type can be weaknesses if taken to excess, giving each personality type a "down side." People who focus too narrowly may miss the nuances, the ways in which others' views and ways of doing things fit together to bring perspective to a situation. For example, attention to detail is a plus but can lead to such an extreme desire for perfection that a person can't finish a job lest it have a flaw, can't make a decision lest it be a mistake.

Imagine six people sitting around the hexagon. Each person is a strong representative of a personality type. Give the group an issue to discuss (such as lower taxes, in the figure "Personality Types: Typical Talk") and each person will look at it in a different way. A, I, R, C, and E types focus mainly on the tasks they do whereas the social personality is the one who focuses on the impact these tasks will have on people.

Sometimes we have personality conflicts within ourselves. We'd like to be creative and try something different, but our conventional nature tells us that's a "no-no." We'd like to take an enterprising risk, but our investigative side wants to gather all the facts before deciding. Realistic folks who mostly like to be alone dealing with physical objects need some people interaction, too. All personality types are surprised to learn that the characteristics of an opposite type can help make their own lives work better. The social personality

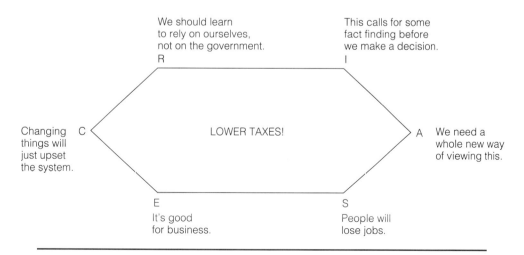

Personality Types: Typical Talk

PERSONALITY TYPES: AN EYE OPENER

An engineering manager is orienting a group of older women exploring careers in his company. The conversation turns to personal matters, and he shares with them his early difficulties in communicating with his wife. He found it hard to understand her continued wish that he would *talk* to her. When a divorce threatened, he sought some communications training and struggled with this strange new activity: sharing feelings he never knew he had. The women related well to this story. After a tour of the plant, they agreed that working with electronic circuits wasn't for them. Then the engineer replied that it would be as hard for them to work in his more realistic/investigative area as it was for him to learn the social skills of dealing with people and their feelings!

---

may need to learn a certain amount of independence from people; the enterprising one, to find out facts before acting; the artistic, to be careful of detail; the realistic person, to stay in touch with other people and their feelings; the investigative person, to take a risk; and the conventional person, to try something new!

You will likely find a job difficult if it lies in an area very different from the interests of your personality type. An engineer with thirteen years' experience in the field admitted that he had thought engineering would involve his hands and now wished to become a technician. An industrial arts teacher wished that his job didn't involve motivating people all the time. His industrial specialty was also "too clerical" because it dealt with safety and time studies. Both these people would have been more content with work that let them use machines and tools in some way.

A woman who works as an audiologist confides that after she obtained her degree in speech pathology and audiology she did remedial speech in a school setting. She felt that results were not very clear and successes difficult to pin down. She now finds that administering hearing tests and fitting people with hearing aids gives her a sense of definite accomplishment, enables her to use her hands, and gives her just the right amount of social interaction.

Rose Marie Dunphy, a realistic/artistic woman, illustrates what it feels like to be doing "what you are fitted for," as Maslow says. She says about her sewing, "Each time I touch a piece of fabric, magic occurs. I don't see corduroy or cotton but a dress, a shirt, curtains with tiebacks. Each time I sit on my chair facing the sewing machine, I disappear. I've gone into my hands . . . fabric, foot, and needle join hands to perform one function. In the process, they become one, and as in a chemical reaction, a totally different thing emerges. Not just a dress or curtain, but a new me."[2]

Wynne Busby describes the same sensation she observes happening in a young carpenter who puts in a window for her. "I could sense all the skill, years of experience, of loving handling of tools and wood, which was available to him even for such a simple task as this." And she sees the same absorption, the same intimacy of hand, mind, tool, materials in her calligraphy teacher. "Her hand remembers the shape of the pen. The ink flows and the letters curve, black and clean on the page. All the skill which her hand remembers is available for her work of creation."[3]

On a whimsical note that illustrates the differing approach of the investigative/idea, not-always-practical people and the realistic pragmatic ones, an old "Down-easter" said, "One of the things that struck me and other Maine people [was that] the bright young people had all the ideas about the way things should happen. The Maine people were more used to getting the hay in before it rained."[4]

At first you may not see yourself clearly in the results of the Personality Mosaic. One woman told her class that she was certain she was not investigative. Then she admitted to the delight of the group that her next thought was, "I wonder *why* it turned out that way!" Take time to study and understand each personality type and only then accept the data that really seem to fit you well.

Understanding your personality can help you make a good career decision. Understanding the personalities of others can improve your human relationships and ease your acceptance of the choices that others make. And note that we may act in each of these six modes more than we realize. They represent activities that we need and want to do.

Realistic: Physical Mode

Running on the beach

Eating a pizza

Cleaning the sink

Investigative: Mind Mode

Discussing politics

Reading *War and Peace*

Planning a trip to Europe

Artistic: Aesthetic Mode

Enjoying a sunset

Wearing complementary colors

Decorating a cake

Social: People Mode

Laughing with a friend

Hugging the baby

Listening to an aging person

Enterprising: Accomplishment Mode

Organizing a party

Saying "hello" first

Applying for a job

Conventional: Structure Mode

Stopping at a stop sign

Straightening your closet

Finishing a paper on time

Does growth mean allowing all these dimensions to surface and actualizing them to the best of your ability? Albert Einstein was not only a great scientist but also a creative visionary with concern for people. As you grow, will

Well, what have we here?

you feel more comfortable in all these areas? Your career decision may fall within the area of your highest personality type; it may reflect a blend of several types. Stop and take a good look at your personality; then discuss your dominant personality characteristics with someone and explain why they feel right to you.

Dealing with Data, People, and Things

The world around you has only three areas your personality can relate to: data (ideas and information), people, and things. We have organized much of the decision-making material that follows into these three areas.

Data

The human mind can take in and give out great quantities of information, or data, in the form of words, numbers, and symbols. All day long the mind clicks away, taking in and expressing thoughts and ideas, often creatively and always in a way unique to the individual. When you notice you are out of bread and jot it down on the grocery list, you've just processed some data. Reading, writing, speaking, and listening all deal with data. Every activity deals with data to some extent, from simple to complex. The cry of the new-born gives us data about how the baby feels. Lights blinking on your car dashboard can be saying, "Stop and get oil—now!" Some people think of data as complex numbers and computer spreadsheets. But data include all kinds of ideas and information: the words you speak, read, hear; the music you enjoy; the smiles of your friends; the colors of the sunset. Anything that is not a person or a concrete object is called data and we deal with it on various levels of complexity, from just noticing it to copying it to developing or creating it.

People

Another kind of activity depends on interaction with people. We deal with people at various levels of complexity, from greeting and waiting on them to dealing with their long-term personal growth. A rent-a-car clerk in an airport observed that she liked working with people, but not with the public! Conversely, a person who thought she wanted to be a counselor found the less-involved people contact she experienced as a bank teller to be just right. *We use a great deal of data when we deal with other humans.* We involve all sorts of body/mind perceptions and linguistic skills. The emotions, which are physical responses to sensory information, permeate our mental processes and influence our behavior and relationships with others. For example, managers find that people generally respond better to the people skills of genuine respect and affection, the basis for good human interaction, rather than to competition and control.

Things

We relate to physical objects in any number of ways: building, repairing, carrying, making things, running machines; tinkering with gadgets from food processors to power saws. The physical object that we use may be our bodies in such activities as sports and dance. Involvement with things can range from simple activities (putting up a picture) to complex ones (repairing a satellite). The body skills used require various degrees of strength, agility, and coordination in relating to other physical objects. The way the body fixes and builds things often requires creative ability. And, of course, we need the data required to deal with those things.

You learned to deal with data, people, and things at all levels early in life. Look again at your Candid Camera 3-D lists from Chapter l. How many times have you planned events, organized people, or repaired objects in your lifetime? Using data, people, and/or things, individuals do tasks that range

A FEW ACTION WORDS DEALING WITH DATA, PEOPLE, AND THINGS

DATA	PEOPLE	THINGS
Analyze	Appoint	Assemble
Budget	Assist/advise	Clean
Compare	Communicate with	Cut
Compile	Counsel	Decorate
Compute	Direct	Demonstrate
Decide	Encourage	Drive
Design/develop	Entertain	Fit
Evaluate	Evaluate	Guard
Illustrate	Hire	Inspect
Learn	Interview	Install
Organize	Manage	Lift
Plan	Motivate	Measure
Process	Negotiate with	Mix
Read	Organize/coordinate	Move
Record	Refer	Operate
Research	Represent	Process
Schedule	Sell	Repair
Synthesize	Serve	Set up
Visualize	Supervise	Tend
Write	Teach/Train	Test

from repairing clocks and computers to creating music, art, literature, and scientific and technical wonders. And amazingly, every day—using your body, emotions, mind, and spirit—*you* create your life.

Activity Analysis

In the Candid Camera-3D exercise in Chapter 1, you listed every activity you could think of that you've done in your life: jobs, community and extracurricular activities, education, and other projects, along with all the things you had to do to accomplish each activity. This expanded activity list gave you background that helped you determine your personality orientation. Now you will use it to choose satisfying life activities.

It's important to analyze activities in detail. A woman says she is realistic because she likes to garden. Her notebook shows that she obviously loves collecting, organizing, and analyzing data as she had a list of seeds, a planting schedule, a layout of her garden. Asked how her garden was, she said, "Not so good!" She didn't get out there very much. Her personality type and then her activity analysis showed that she was much more investigative than realistic and that data were more interesting than things. So study your lists to be sure that you have broken down each activity into as many specific component activities as possible. And check to be sure that you have coded them D, P, and/or T for their involvement with data, people, or things. These lists will be important for the skills identification exercises that follow.

Skills

If you actually listed all the activities you've ever done, your list would be enormous. Now here is one of the most important connections for you to make. When you've *done* any activity, that means you *can* do it! You've shown you have the ability, and that ability is a *skill!* Many people think they have no skills because they can't play the oboe or dance up a storm. But in reality they have been accomplishing things successfully for many years and have the capacity to accomplish much more. One factor is confidence. If you *think* you can, then you are well on the way to accomplishment. At least you can probably do something that has some of the satisfiers of your dream job.

For example, a teacher completed an interest inventory that suggested a career in the performing arts. Acting seemed intriguing, but not likely to provide much income for a beginner. It suddenly dawned on the teacher how much she loved "appearing" in a class or workshop, making people laugh and appreciate her. When she first became a teacher, she found teaching difficult and, as a result, tended either to over- or under-discipline her classes. Her confidence grew with her realization that she could teach and have fun doing it. Now she rarely misses a chance to talk with a group.

So instead of groaning at your "lack of talent," think of all the talents you've used in a life filled with data, people, and things. And because the majority of workers have only average skills—most workers can do *many* jobs. And that includes you! Part of using skills effectively is having confidence in yourself. The question is, then, of all the skills you possess, which do you enjoy using? And more important, which would you like to use in a work setting? For having skills is only one part of the puzzle. Do you prefer to work primarily with data, people, or things? Of all the jobs you *can* do, which would you *like* to do? Then knowing when and where to use those skills wisely takes growth.

> If you like what you are doing,
> you will likely excel at it!
> —*Ironworker Clif Signor*

All activities flow from just ten basic aptitudes or skills that are listed here and grouped according to their interaction with data, people, and things

TEN BASIC SKILLS

THE ABILITY TO USE OR DEVELOP:

Data Skills[5]

I   1. Logical intelligence: Think, observe, plan, analyze, evaluate, understand, solve problems. Put ideas and information together to deal with complex operations, or plan and organize work. Keep track of verbal and numerical information in an orderly way; make decisions using common sense based on practical experience.

A   2. Intuitive intelligence: Imagine, compare, see things holistically, decide based on best guesses and intuitive common sense rather than rules or measurements. Use words, numbers, or symbols creatively, develop new ideas, new processes, new combinations.

E/S   3. Verbal ability: Use words to read, research, write, listen, record, discuss, direct, instruct, communicate, motivate.

I   4. Numerical ability: Use numbers and symbols to figure, calculate, estimate, keep books, budget, analyze. Measure, using instruments to determine such factors as length, mass, time, temperature, electric charge.

C   5. Exactness with detail: Follow directions exactly, make decisions based on set rules or measurements; attend to small details in proofreading words or numbers or examining lines and shapes of products.

A   6. Facility with multidimensional forms: Understand, visualize, relate, two- or three-dimensional lines or shapes, spaces, shadings—sometimes in color.

People Skills

E/S   7. Facility in businesslike contact with people: Manage, supervise, organize, motivate, entertain, train, serve, negotiate, cooperate with people.

E/S   8. Ability to influence people: Persuade/inspire others to think or behave in certain ways. Teach, exchange, interpret ideas/facts/feelings, help solve personal problems.

Thing Skills

RIAC 9. Finger/hand agility: Use fingers/hands to make, repair, process, test, assemble, operate various products/machines/tools using special, sometimes highly complex techniques.

RIAC 10. Whole-body agility: Use the whole body to handle, carry, lift, move, balance, or coordinate itself or other physical objects.

and coded as to their basic personality type. Though most people can operate in all these areas reasonably well, they will be more comfortable in some than in others based on their personality types.

As you can see, these ten skill areas range from almost invisible activities of the mind to very visible activities of the body. The interests you have been listing are usually a good clue to your skills. Most people acquire skills in areas they enjoy, and they tend to neglect other areas. If you like something, you spend time doing it, get better at it and like it more, and spend more time doing it. And it's comforting to remember that most jobs, by definition, require only average skills.

We came into this world already well equipped for action. Unless a serious defect exists, human growth and potential for growth are phenomenal. Look at a six-month-old and be amazed at the complexity of skills he or she has acquired compared with those of a newborn infant. Compare with a six-year-old and be further astounded! Educator and author Peter Kline says that we are all budding "everyday geniuses" when we are born. But we express that genius in different ways.[6] Sometimes, somewhere along the line, confidence and energy may begin to lag. Brain researcher Jean Houston says that by age seventeen we are using only 17 percent of our body's potential for flexible movement, compared to what we used at age three. She says that as the body goes, so does the mind. Houston finds that even the very elderly, with correct exercise, can "remake" their bodies in six months, and their mental and emotional powers are greatly enhanced at the same time.[7]

Dividing the self into "mind" and "body" is only an exercise about concepts that are very difficult to define. Because our educational system stresses mental activities, we sometimes infer that men and women who work with their hands are not "using their heads." In reality, the two cannot be separated; they can only be examined separately as two different modes of living and learning. Life experiences help us develop innumerable skills of both mind and body.

The Skills Trio

There are three kinds of skills: transferable, work specific, and personal responsibility skills.[8] The ten basic aptitudes and their related skills are called *transferable* skills because they can be used in many kinds of activities and transferred from one job to another. For example, planning, which draws on logical intelligence, can involve the following steps: (1) determine/establish objectives for a program; (2) set policies, procedures; (3) do long- and short-range forecasts; (4) schedule strategies; and (5) evaluate/revise the program. We take steps like these almost unconsciously as we learn to make decisions and plan to accomplish some task.

Every job requires transferable skills, with communications skills in writing and speaking highly important to many positions and often the key to getting a job and advancement on the job. For example, engineers find they must often write up and present proposals for projects and then report their results. Education has tended to over-emphasize "intelligence," usually meaning ability in logical intelligence, language, and math so that those who do not excel in those areas often feel that they have *no* ability. Yet we know people who were not at the top of the class who have managed to go far in life using other basic skills. Perhaps 80 to 90 percent of the content of most jobs requires transferable skills—those you already have *to some degree.*

The other 10 to 20 percent may require on-the-job training (OJT), further formal education, or both. A general salesperson, for example, depends largely on transferable skills and can learn the needed *work-specific skills* quickly. More and more jobs require special training, especially in science, technical fields, and the arts. This training develops work-specific skills, such as those used by electronics technicians, business managers, doctors, and ballerinas. For example, job seekers who are knowledgeable and at ease with computers will have a major advantage over those who are not. But everyone needs a base of transferable skills, too.

Personal responsibility skills reflect the ways you manage *yourself* in relation to data, people, and things; they reflect the ways you express your transferable and work-specific skills. They are the traits that parents and teachers often stress: common sense; responsibility; dedication; willingness to learn, to work hard, and to finish what you begin; careful use of others' property; working well with people including the ability to understand your own feelings and those of others and to handle them well; working without undue anxiety; acceptance of criticism; good grooming; courtesy; kindness; honesty; humor; optimism; promptness. Every skill area is greatly enhanced by personal responsibility skills.

The ability to deal well with oneself in relationship to other people is an aspect of personal responsibility skills that is a strong predictor of success. You may have noticed that the brainiest kids in your class may not always be the most adept at getting along with people. Now researchers are beginning to measure this important area of ability which they call emotional intelligence (EQ—Emotional Quotient); it is quite distinct from intelligence (measured in the past by IQ—Intelligence Quotient.)[9] Some people develop such skills at an early age, often independent of formal education. Others must learn them by encountering and solving difficulties in their interpersonal relationships. Review the statements and the qualities of the social personality from the Personality Mosaic to gain more insights about emotional intelligence.

Negative interpersonal habits *can* be changed by taking an unprejudiced look at the "trouble spots" you experience with others. Assess how much of the problem is your responsibility without unduly blaming yourself. Learn to sense what you and other people are feeling and don't blame them for what you experience. For example, no one can *make* you angry, even though it seems that way. To improve his or her EQ, a person can work at being sensitive, caring, and kind to others; to see the positive side of events; to be persistent and enthusiastic; to learn to delay gratification; to give credit to others when it is due.

Employee recruiters often remark that the ability to get along with people is one skill they look for above all others. In management positions, the ability to motivate, encourage, and respect others is a giant plus. Acquiring all the personal responsibility skills is more vital than ever for career and life success as workplaces downsize their managerial ranks, require more education of new hires, and use more technology, depending on each employee to "self-manage"—that is, take more responsibility on the job.

It's great to be intelligent, to be proficient with data and things, but without good people skills success is often hard to achieve. Using well-developed interrelational skills can even help return "civility to our streets and caring to our communal life," says Harvard psychobiologist Daniel Goleman, author of *Emotional Intelligence*.[10] Generally, we would much rather work with, play with, and marry someone with good people skills.

You have survived modern life so far. Your physical, mental, emotional, social, and financial well-being have depended on your abilities. You *must* possess a good measure of skills in all areas *and be able to build on this foundation.*

Work Qualities[11]

You use your skills in four different modes called work qualities:

- **Repetition:** Duties involve a set way of doing things, sometimes over and over again.
- **Variety:** Duties change frequently, requiring a flexible response, different knowledge and skills.
- **Physical Risk:** Duties involve pressure in stressful, dangerous situations but sometimes provide adventure and excitement.
- **Status:** Duties involve recognition that you are someone important or in authority.

Getting an Edge on the Job Hunt Process

People often underestimate what they have done in life. Both career searching and job hunting require that you know what you have done so you can apply it to what you want to do. When a high school graduate was asked to make a list of her job activities in a drive-in, she replied that she had done nothing of importance. "All I did was make hamburgers." But speaking informally, she was able to describe what she did in more detail. That became her list. She then coded each activity with a P (dealing directly with people), T (dealing directly with things or material objects), or D (dealing with data): she noticed when supplies were running low, and ordered (D) and put them away (T). She took charge when the owners were away (D). She showed new clerks what to do (P, D). Sometimes she did minor repairs on kitchen equipment (T). She made all the sauces (T). She settled disagreements about orders (P). She could always tell when a new clerk wasn't going to work out (D).

After a great deal of polishing, her list looked like this:

Human Relations (People, Data)
Worked well with customers/employers, coworkers (good teamwork)
Oriented, trained, evaluated employees
Settled customer/employee disagreements

Materials Maintenance (Things, Data)
Inventoried, ordered, stored, prepared materials
Did maintenance/repair
Opened and closed business
Handled cash/cash register

Data without People or Things
Organized/scheduled work

Her job activities drew on many of the ten basic skills to a modest degree, especially logical intelligence, verbal ability, businesslike contact with people, finger/hand agility, and occasionally intuitive intelligence, numerical ability, and exactness with detail. Her work had a great deal of variety, also. Knowing what she had done enabled her to make a better career decision.

A section of her résumé, developed for a management trainee position in a small restaurant, summarized her experience as a supervisor/cook:

Inventoried, ordered, prepared, and stocked food supplies.
Settled employee and customer problems and complaints.
Oriented/trained new employees, informally evaluated performance.
Did minor repairs/maintenance.
As occasional acting manager, opened and closed shop, handled cash/cash register.

She also included a personal section—an "I" section that says, "I am . . . ," "I can . . . ," and so on. It pointed out these abilities:

Demonstrates good teamwork with customers, employees, and coworkers.

Reprinted with permission from Mal Hancock.

Notice and take care of details.
Am reliable.

With her additional training in food and restaurant management, she was qualified for the position she was seeking.

Observe yourself. What skills do you want to acquire and develop to get where you would like to be? In what ways would you like to focus your transferable skills to gain those that are more work specific? If you have good finger dexterity, for example, would you prefer to become adept at the guitar, the computer keyboard, brain surgery, or all three? Are you willing to devote some time to further training and education to acquire these work-specific skills? Which personal responsibility skills are your strengths? Which will you work to improve? These are important questions to answer when you are making career decisions.

In this chapter, then, you've discovered your very own Personality Mosaic. You have identified skills that have motivated you to act successfully in the past and will carry you into the future. And you are putting together some extremely valuable pieces of the career decision puzzle. In short, you have been gathering important words to describe the one and only YOU! In the next chapter we will relate this information to careers.

 *Self-Assessment Exercises*

1. Six Personality Types

a. Circle the personality types that describe you best: realistic, investigative, artistic, social, enterprising, conventional.

b. Discuss the ways in which the strengths of each personality type can become weaknesses. _____

_____

2. Data, People, Things Indicator

To determine your most important orientations in regard to data, people, and things, consult the Activity Lists you have been working on from Chapter l, Candid Camera 3-D. Be sure that the lists are as long as you can make them, that you have broken down your activities into specific component activities, and that you have coded all these activities with a P, T, or D as follows:

P = interacting directly with people

T = interacting directly with things

D = using ideas and information (data) without interacting with people or things

Now, check the following: (No check means "little or no involvement.")

Data: I want to get involved with data on my job:

_____ at a modest level with data that are easy to learn or that I simply keep track of while others direct my work.

_____ at a high level by putting ideas and information together to plan/organize work and perhaps develop new ideas and ways to do things.

People: I want to get involved with people on my job:

_____ at a modest level by being friendly and cooperative, greeting and serving them, discussing simple problems with them.

_____ at a high level by leading/influencing/organizing/motivating them, teaching/entertaining them, negotiating, or exchanging ideas with them, counseling them.

Things: I want to get involved with things on my job:

_____ at a modest level by following simple procedures set up by others.

_____ at a high level by working with more complex procedures/equipment that allow my own input.

3. *Identifying Important and Enjoyable Skill Areas*

If you are uncertain of your important key qualities, write ten to fifteen of your favorite activities as specifically as possible in the Favorite Activities Chart from your expanded activity list. Then check (✓) the numbers of the basic skills you used to perform each favorite activity. For example, if you ordered supplies by phone, you would check 4, 5, and 7. If you arranged food attractively on a plate, you would check 6 and 9.

Activity	1. Logical intelligence	2. Intuitive intelligence	3. Verbal ability	4. Numerical ability	5. Exactness with detail	6. Facility with multidimensional forms	7. Businesslike contact with people	8. Ability to influence people	9. Finger/hand agility	10. Whole-body agility

Which of the basic ten activities do you like to do the most? _____

4. *The Key Qualities Indicator*

- Check those qualities below that are important for you in your career. It is not necessary that the *entire* description of each quality apply to you. (You may wish to circle those words that *do* apply to you.)
- Now go back and place an H in front of those skills you want to use at a high level of ability. Place an M in front of those skills you want to use at a modest level of ability.

Data Skills

_____ **Logical intelligence:** Think, observe, plan, analyze, evaluate, understand, solve problems; put ideas and information together to deal with complex operations; plan and organize work; keep track of verbal and numerical information in an orderly way, make decisions using common sense based on practical experience.

_____ **Intuitive intelligence:** Imagine, compare, see things holistically, decide based on best guesses and intuitive common sense rather than rules or measurements; use words, numbers, or symbols creatively; develop new ideas, new processes, new combinations.

_____ **Verbal ability:** Use words to read, research, write, listen, record, discuss, direct, instruct, communicate, motivate.

_____ **Numerical ability:** Use numbers and symbols to measure, figure, calculate, estimate, keep books, budget, analyze.

_____ **Exactness with detail:** Follow directions exactly; make decisions based on set rules or measurements; attend to small details in proofreading words, numbers, symbols, and/or diagrams or in examining lines and shapes of products.

_____ **Facility with multidimensional form:** Understand, visualize, relate together two- or three-dimensional lines or shapes, spaces, shading— sometimes in color.

People Skills

_____ **Facility in businesslike contact with people:** Manage, supervise, organize, motivate, entertain, train, serve, negotiate with, cooperate with people.

_____ **Ability to influence people:** Persuade/inspire others to think or behave in certain ways; teach, exchange, interpret ideas/facts/feelings, help solve personal problems.

Thing Skills

_____ **Finger/hand agility:** Use fingers/hands to make, repair, process, test, assemble, operate various products/machines/tools using special techniques—sometimes very complex.

_____ **Whole-body agility:** Use the whole body to handle, carry, lift, move, balance, or coordinate itself or physical objects.

Work Qualities

Circle the names of those qualities that are important for you in a job.

Repetition: Duties that involve a set way of doing things, sometimes over and over again.

Variety: Duties that change frequently, requiring a flexible response and different knowledge and skills.

Physical risk: Duties that involve pressure in stressful, dangerous situations but sometimes provide adventure and excitement.

Status: Duties that bring recognition that you are someone important or in authority.

5. Personal Responsibility Skills

Evaluate yourself and your ability to handle data, people, and things. Check (✓) "Good" or "Could improve" after each statement.

- Evaluate YOURSELF

	Good	Could improve
I usually		
work hard, with persistence	_____	_____
use common sense	_____	_____
show enthusiasm	_____	_____
have a sense of humor	_____	_____
am aware of and handle my feelings and moods well	_____	_____
dress appropriately for work	_____	_____

- Evaluate your interaction with PEOPLE

	Good	Could improve
I usually		
balance my needs and wants with those of others	_____	_____
respond with tact and courtesy	_____	_____
accept criticism without anger and learn from others	_____	_____
communicate assertively without attacking or blaming others	_____	_____

admit mistakes; apologize   _____   _____

respect and compliment the ideas and good   _____   _____
work of others

share with and assist others; enjoy teamwork   _____   _____

▪ Evaluate your interaction with DATA and THINGS

I usually

follow rules and also work to make them   _____   _____
more reasonable

am willing to learn, asking for help only   _____   _____
when necessary

am flexible, willing to try new and unfamiliar   _____   _____
tasks

carry through with difficult or pressured   _____   _____
work on time, without excuses

take care of property and equipment   _____   _____

6. Work-Specific Skills

List your work-specific skills—those acquired by education or training
to do a particular job:

_____   _____

_____   _____

_____   _____

7. Sharing Your Discoveries

In the space that follows (or on a separate sheet of paper), you may find it
helpful to write an enthusiastic paragraph or letter about yourself and your
abilities to a potential employer (or friend). Use as many of the skill words as
possible from this chapter to describe yourself and show that you would be an
effective worker. Later you will be able to use the data gathered in this chapter to write an effective résumé.

3/

The Career Connection

Finding Your Job Satisfiers

 FOCUS

- *Identify your satisfying job areas.*
- *Survey the entire U.S. job market.*
- *Learn to research jobs.*

Career Focus: Job Chart Inventory

The data you collected on your personality and your skills in Chapter 2 will be helpful background for using the Job Chart Inventory that follows. This inventory will help you see which of the twelve major career interest areas[1] in the U.S. job market might suit you.

Find satisfying job groups by answering these questions about personality types in the job market:

Realistic   Things/Body: The World of Matter

Interest areas = *Mechanical, Industrial, Nature, Protective, Physical Performance*

Y   N   1. Do you like using your hands, e.g., to make, repair, "tinker with" physical objects?
Y   N   2. Do you like being physically active?
Y   N   3. Do you generally prefer working with physical objects rather than with people?
Y   N   4. Do you like doing physically daring things?

   Do you wish to explore *Realistic* Interest Areas (the world of matter)?

   NO = Go on to Mind: *Investigative and Artistic* Job Groups
   YES = Continue here

   Jobs in the *Realistic* Interest Areas are involved with things, from simple to complex; they require little contact with people unless they involve supervising, teaching, or managing; use of data depends on complexity of the job. The skills needed are finger/hand to whole-body agility, coordination, strength, along with moderate intelligence, some multidimensional awareness, and ability with numbers. The world of matter (or things) is associated with the realistic personality, which gravitates toward jobs that deal with mechanical systems; factory or production jobs; heavy outdoor work with nature; police work, firefighting, or other protective types of employment; and activities requiring physical performance such as sports and acrobatics.

Answer the following to help select *Realistic* Interest Areas:

Mechanical
Y   N   1. Do you like large, mechanical systems?
Y   N   2. Do you like working with machines and tools?

Industrial
Y   N   1. Do you like to use your hands doing factory-type production work?
Y   N   2. Would you like being directly involved with large-scale production?

Nature
Y   N   1. Do you like heavy, physical, outdoor work?
Y   N   2. Do you like working with plants or animals?

Protective
Y   N   1. Does protecting people's lives and properties interest you?
Y   N   2. Would you like doing police work, firefighting, or other jobs that may involve physical risk?

Physical Performance
Y   N   1. Have you been actively involved in sports or other displays of physical ability?
Y   N   2. Do you keep physically fit?

YES answers indicate interest in one or more of the *Realistic* Interest Areas.
NO answers indicate little or no interest in the five *Realistic* Interest Areas.
Regardless of your answers, do you wish to explore Job Groups in these areas?
YES = Explore *Realistic* Job Groups on the Job Group Chart.
NO = Goodbye *Realistic*! Go on to *Investigative* and *Artistic* Job Groups.

R—REALISTIC JOB GROUPS

	1. Logical Intelligence	2. Intuitive Intelligence	3. Verbal Ability	4. Numerical Ability	5. Exactness with Detail	6. Facility with Multidimensional Forms	7. Businesslike Contact with People	8. Ability to Influence People	9. Finger/Hand Agility	10. Whole-Body Agility	11. Repetition	12. Variety	13. Physical Risk	14. Status
MECHANICAL														
1. 05.01 Engineering: Applying research of science and math to design of new products and systems.	H	H	H	H	M	H	M	M	M			•		
2. 05.02 Managerial Work–Mechanical: Managing technical plants or systems.	H	H	H	H	M	H	H	M	M			•		•
3. 05.03 Engineering Technology: Collecting, recording, coordinating technical information.	H	H	M	H	H	H			H					
4. 05.04 Air and Water Vehicle Operations: Operating planes/ships to carry freight/passengers.	H	H	H	H	H	H	H		M	M			•	•
5. 05.05 Craft Technology: Doing highly skilled hand/machine custom work.	M	M		M	H	H			H	M		•		
6. 05.06 Systems Operation: Caring for large, complicated mechanical systems like heating/power.	M		M	M	H	M	M		M			•		
7. 05.07 Quality Control: Checking/testing materials/products in nonfactory situations.	M	M		M	H	M			M		•			
8. 05.08 Land Vehicle Operation: Operating/driving vehicles that haul freight.	M				M	M			M	M	•			
9. 05.09 Materials Control: Keeping records of flow/storage of materials and products.	M		M	M			M				•			
10. 05.10 Skilled Hand and Machine Work: Doing moderately skilled hand/machine work.					M	H			M		•			
11. 05.11 Equipment Operation: Operating/driving heavy equipment such as in construction, mining.	M				H	M			M	M	•			
12. 05.12 Manual Labor–Mechanical: Doing nonfactory manual labor with machines, tools.					H	M			M	M	•			
INDUSTRIAL	1.	2.	3.	4.	5.	6.	7.	8.	9.	10.	11.	12.	13.	14.
13. 06.01 Production Technology: Setting up/operating machines to produce goods in specific ways.	M			M	H	M	H		M					
14. 06.02 Production Work: Doing hand/machine work to make a product: supervising/inspecting.	M			M	H	M	H		M		•			
15. 06.03 Quality Control: Testing, weighing, inspecting, measuring products to meet standards.	M				H	M			M		•			
16. 06.04 Manual Labor–Industrial: Basic manual labor in production requiring little training.						M			M	M	•			
NATURE	1.	2.	3.	4.	5.	6.	7.	8.	9.	10.	11.	12.	13.	14.
17. 03.01 Managerial Work–Nature: Planning work for farming, fisheries, logging, horticulture.	H	H	M	M	M	M	M	M	M			•		
18. 03.02 General Supervision–Nature: Supervising on farms, in forests, fisheries, nurseries, parks.	M	M	M	M	M	M	H		M			•		•
19. 03.03 Animal Training/Care: Training, breeding, raising, showing, caring for nonfarm animals.	M	M	M		M	M			M	M	•	•		
20. 03.04 Manual Labor–Nature: Doing basic physical labor related to farming, fishing, gardening.						M			M	M	•			
PROTECTIVE	1.	2.	3.	4.	5.	6.	7.	8.	9.	10.	11.	12.	13.	14.
21. 04.01 Safety/Law Enforcement: Administration, enforcement of laws/regulations.	H	H	H		M	M	H	H	M			•	•	•
22. 04.02 Security Services: Protecting people and property from crime, fire, other hazards.	M	M	M			M	M		M	M	•		•	
PHYSICAL PERFORMANCE	1.	2.	3.	4.	5.	6.	7.	8.	9.	10.	11.	12.	13.	14.
23. 12.01 Sports: Of all sorts; playing, training, coaching, and officiating.	M	M	M		M	M	M	M	H	H			•	•
24. 12.02 Physical Feats: Amusing/entertaining people with special physical skills/strengths.	M	M	M		M	H	M		H	H			•	•

Investigative and Artistic   Ideas/Intellect: The World of the Mind

Interest areas = *Scientific/analytic* and *Artistic/creative*

Y N   1. Do you like to think or read about or discuss new ideas?
Y N   2. Do you like solving problems and puzzles?
Y N   3. Do you like to create new things?
Y N   4. Do you like to work alone?

Do you wish to explore *Investigative/Artistic* Interest Areas (the world of the mind)?

NO = Go on to People: *Social and Enterprising* Job Groups
YES = Continue here

The *Mind* world attracts scientific/investigative people with a logical/rational personality who like to explore ideas; it also includes the artistic/intuitives who like to create them. These jobs usually involve high to medium use of data and little involvement with people (except in the field of medicine); they often require dealing with things or thinking about things and creating solutions to problems. Skills required are generally above-average logical and/or intuitive intelligence, good verbal skills and—in the scientific area—numerical ability; in some cases you will need a well-developed sense of multidimensional awareness and color.

Those investigative types who pursue the physical/biological sciences or engineering need to have some sense of the *Matter/Realistic* world. Purely investigative people with little interest in the physical world usually take their inquiring minds into areas such as theoretical math or they may research people, the arts, industry, or business—that is, any area that requires little direct interaction with things or people.

Artistic people are generally very intuitive and may find satisfaction in painting, sculpture, or crafts, if they have a facility with things. The more investigative artistic types deal with music and writing. Some artistic people with little specific "talent" give creative expression to their many ideas in a variety of other environments—for example, the innovative side of engineering or the innovative worlds of the classroom, the office, or the factory.

Answer the following to help select *Investigative* or *Artistic* Interest Areas:

Scientific
Y N   1. Do you enjoy using your mind to analyze or solve various kinds of problems?
Y N   2. Do you enjoy researching and exploring the physical world?

Artistic
Y N   1. Do you enjoy and have you been involved with the fine arts: art, drama, dance, music, or literature?
Y N   2. Would you be willing to make a long-term commitment to a fine arts area?

YES answers indicate interest in the *Investigative* or *Artistic* Interest Areas.
NO answers indicate little or no interest in the *Investigative* or *Artistic* Interest Areas.
Regardless of your answers, do you wish to explore the *Investigative* or *Artistic* Interest Areas further?
YES = Explore *Investigative/Scientific* and/or *Artistic* Job Groups on the Job Group Chart.
NO = Goodbye *Investigative/Artistic* Job Groups! Go on to *Social/Enterprising* Job Groups.

Column key:
1. Logical Intelligence
2. Intuitive Intelligence
3. Verbal Ability
4. Numerical Ability
5. Exactness with Detail
6. Facility with Multidimensional Forms
7. Businesslike Contact with People
8. Ability to Influence People
9. Finger/Hand Agility
10. Whole-Body Agility
11. Repetition
12. Variety
13. Physical Risk
14. Status

I—INVESTIGATIVE JOB GROUPS

SCIENTIFIC/ANALYTIC

	Job Group	1	2	3	4	5	6	7	8	9	10	11	12	13	14
25. 02.01	Physical Sciences: Research/development in physics, chemistry, geology, computer science.	H	H	H	H	M	H		M	M					
26. 02.02	Life Sciences: Studying functions of living things/ways they relate to environments.	H	H	H	H	M	H		M	H					
27. 02.03	Medical Sciences: Practicing medicine to prevent, diagnose, cure illnesses of people or animals.	H	H	H	H	M	H	M	H	H			•		•
(1) 05.01	Engineering: Applying research of science and math to design of new products and systems.	H	H	H	H	M	H	M	M	M			•		
28. 02.04	Laboratory Technology: Doing laboratory work to carry out studies of various researchers.	H			H	M	H			M					
29. 11.01	Mathematics/Statistics: Using numbers and computers to analyze and solve problems.	H	M	H	H	H	H	M	M	M					

A—ARTISTIC JOB GROUPS

ARTISTIC/CREATIVE

	Job Group	1	2	3	4	5	6	7	8	9	10	11	12	13	14
30. 01.01	Literary Arts: Producing creative pieces from writing to publishing for print, TV, films.	H	H	H				M	M						•
31. 01.02	Visual Arts: Doing artistic work (paintings, designs, photographs) for sale or for media.	H	H				H	M	M	H					
32. 01.03	Performing Arts–Drama: Performing, directing, teaching for stage, radio, TV, film.	H	H	H				H	M		M				•
33. 01.04	Performing Arts–Music: Playing an instrument, singing, arranging, composing, conducting music.	H	H	H			H	H	H	M	H	H			•
34. 01.05	Performing Arts–Dance: Performing, teaching, choreographing dance routines.	H	H	M			M	H	H	M	H	H			•
35. 01.06	Craft Arts: Producing handcrafts, graphics, decorative products.	M	M			H	H			H					
36. 01.07	Amusement Arts: Entertaining/doing novel routines at carnivals, circuses, fairs.	M	M	M			M	H	M		M	•			
37. 01.08	Modeling: Posing for artists; displaying clothing, accessories, other products.	M							M		M	•			•

Social and Enterprising   Helping/Motivating: The World of People

Interest Areas = *Human services, Accommodating, Leading/influencing, Persuading/selling*

Y N   1. Do you enjoy having a friendly conversation with someone?
Y N   2. Do you like to talk people into doing a project and get them organized?
Y N   3. Are you concerned about the welfare of others?
Y N   4. Do you like to influence people and their opinions?

> Do you wish to explore the *Social/Enterprising* People Helping/Motivating Interest Areas (the world of people)?
>
> NO = Go on to Paper/Data: *Conventional* Job Groups
> YES = Continue here

The world of *People* generally requires ongoing involvement with people; the level of data increases with complexity of the work; there is usually little or no involvement with things except in jobs requiring physical contact. Skills required are generally a range of "people skills": facility dealing with and communicating with people, solving people problems, and providing human services. The world of people includes four interest areas: (1) human services, (2) accommodating (the social personality), (3) leading/influencing, and (4) persuading (the enterprising personality). Jobs in these areas involve helping or motivating people. For career seekers who would love to work with people, opportunities range from waiter to psychiatrist, from manager to mortician! Such jobs involve being with people all day: greeting people, waiting on them, taking charge of a group, solving business or personal problems. These jobs often require leadership to organize groups, show people what to do, and direct projects. If you wish to work with people at a high level, consider earning a degree in business or one of the behavioral sciences. You will need creativity and intuition to work with people on any but the simplest level.

Answer the following to help select *Social* and/or *Enterprising* Interest Areas:

People Helping: *Human Services*
Y N   1. Do you wish to deal with people's personal concerns, their personal growth/care?
Y N   2. Do you like fairly steady involvement with people who have problems or needs?

People Helping: *Accommodating*
Y N   1. Do you enjoy waiting on people, serving them in some way?
Y N   2. Would you like dealing with the public in a nonpersonal way?

People Motivating: *Leading/Influencing*
Y N   1. Do you like to be a key person in a group?
Y N   2. Do you enjoy encouraging people to try new ways of thinking or doing things?

People Motivating: *Persuading/Selling*
Y N   1. Are you confident and persistent, with enough energy to get things done?
Y N   2. Do you enjoy persuading people to accept an idea, service, or product?

YES answers indicate an interest in the *Social* and *Enterprising* Interest Areas.
NO answers indicate little or no interest in the *Social* and *Enterprising* Interest Areas.
Regardless of your answers, do you wish to explore the *Social* and/or *Enterprising* Interest Areas further?

YES = Explore *Social* and/or *Enterprising* Job Groups on the Job Group Chart.
NO = Goodbye *Social* and/*Enterprising* Job Groups! Continue to *Conventional* Job Groups.

S—SOCIAL JOB GROUPS

HUMAN SERVICES

		1. Logical Intelligence	2. Intuitive Intelligence	3. Verbal Ability	4. Numerical Ability	5. Exactness with Detail	6. Facility with Multidimensional Forms	7. Businesslike Contact with People	8. Ability to Influence People	9. Finger/Hand Agility	10. Whole-Body Agility	11. Repetition	12. Variety	13. Physical Risk	14. Status
38. 10.01	Social Services: Helping people deal with personal, vocational, educational, religious concerns.	H	H	H	M			H	H				•		•
39. 10.02	Nursing/Therapy Services: Providing diagnosis and therapy to help people get well.	H	H	H	H	H	M	H	H	M	M		•		
40. 10.03	Child/Adult Care: Assisting with medical/physical care/services.	M	M	M		H		M	M	M	M	•	•		

ACCOMMODATING

		1.	2.	3.	4.	5.	6.	7.	8.	9.	10.	11.	12.	13.	14.
41. 09.01	Hospitality Services: Touring, guiding, greeting, serving people to help them feel comfortable.	M	M	M		M		H	M	M			•		•
42. 09.02	Barber/Beauty Services: Hair/skin care to help people with personal appearances.	M	M	M		M	H	M	M	H			•		
43. 09.03	Passenger Services: Transporting people by vehicle; also instructing/supervising.	M	M		M	M	M	M			M	M	•		
44. 09.04	Customer Services: Waiting on people in a routine way in business settings.	M		M	M	M		M			M		•		
45. 09.05	Attendant Services: Providing personal services to people at home or when traveling.	M		M				M		M	M	M	•		

S/E—SOCIAL/ENTERPRISING JOB GROUPS

LEADING/INFLUENCING

		1.	2.	3.	4.	5.	6.	7.	8.	9.	10.	11.	12.	13.	14
46. 11.02	Educational/Library Services: Teaching, providing library services.	H	H	H	M	H		H	H				•		•
47. 11.03	Social Research: Studying people of various backgrounds both past and present.	H	H	H	H	H			M				•		
48. 11.04	Law: Counseling, advising, representing people, businesses regarding legal matters.	H	H	H	M	M		H	H				•		•
49. 11.05	Business Administration: Designing procedures, solving problems, supervising people in business.	H	H	H	H	M		H	H				•		•
50. 11.06	Finance: Setting up financial systems; controlling, analyzing financial records.	H	H	H	H	H		H	M				•		•
51. 11.07	Services Administration: Designing procedures, solving problems, supervising people in business.	H	H	M	M	M		H	H				•		•
52. 11.08	Communications: Writing, editing, translating information for media—radio, print, and TV.	H	H	H	M	M		M	M				•		•
53. 11.09	Promotion: Advertising, fundraising, sales, and public relations.	H	H	H	M			H	H				•		•
54. 11.10	Regulations Enforcement: Checking/enforcing government regulations, company policies, procedures.	H	H	H	M	M	M	M	M				•		
55. 11.11	Business Management: Taking responsibility for operation and supervision of a business.	H	H	H	M	M	M	H					•		•
56. 11.12	Contracts and Claims: Negotiating contracts, investigating claims.	H	H	H	M	M		H	H				•		•

E—ENTERPRISING JOB GROUPS

PERSUADING

		1.	2.	3.	4.	5.	6.	7.	8.	9.	10.	11.	12.	13.	14.
57. 08.01	Sales Technology: Selling technical equipment or services including insurance. Also clerical work.	H	H	H	M	M	M	H	M						•
58. 08.02	General Sales: Selling goods and services, wholesale/retail to individuals, business, or industry.	M	M	M	M		H	M							
59. 08.03	Vending: Peddling, promoting items in public settings.				M			H	M	M		•			

Conventional   Words/Numbers/Symbols: The World of Paper/Data

Interest area = *Business detail*

Business Detail
Y N   1. Do you enjoy organizing papers, files, and notebooks?
Y N   2. Do you enjoy working with office machines?
Y N   3. Are you generally prompt, very accurate, and orderly with detail?
Y N   4. Do you prefer to follow a set routine with established guidelines?

The *Paper* or *Conventional* World involves consistent use of data or business detail: words, numbers, and symbols; there is usually little involvement with people beyond what is required to process business details or other tasks; things dealt with are often office machines. Required skills are moderate intelligence in most cases; verbal and numerical ability; an eye for detail; and, in some cases, finger/hand agility. The world of *paper* (which now includes the paperless virtual world) attracts *Conventional* personalities who are careful about detail and valued for their contribution in keeping track of the many transactions that go on in any work setting. If your interests lie in the world of paper and your present job does not include this, look for ways to handle the data of your work environment.

YES answers indicate interest in the *Conventional* Business Detail Interest Area.
NO answers indicate little or no interest in the *Conventional* Business Detail Interest Area.

Regardless of your answers, do you wish to explore Business Detail Job Groups further?

YES = Explore *Conventional* Business Detail Job Groups on the Job Group Chart and then go on to Combinations and Other Considerations.
NO = Goodbye *Conventional* Business Detail Job Groups! Next, explore Some Combinations and Other Considerations.

C—CONVENTIONAL JOB GROUPS

BUSINESS DETAIL

	1. Logical Intelligence	2. Intuitive Intelligence	3. Verbal Ability	4. Numerical Ability	5. Exactness with Detail	6. Facility with Multidimensional Forms	7. Businesslike Contact with People	8. Ability to Influence People	9. Finger/Hand Agility	10. Whole-Body Agility	11. Repetition	12. Variety	13. Physical Risk	14. Status
60. Administrative Detail: Doing secretarial/technical clerical work. 07.01	H	H	H	M	H		H	M	M			•		
61. Mathematical Detail: Keeping numerical records, 07.02 doing basic figuring.	M		M	M	H		M		M		•			
62. Financial Detail: Keeping track of money flow to and from 07.03 the public.	M		M	M	H		M		M		•			
63. Oral Communications: Giving information in person or by 07.04 communication systems.	M		M	M	M		M	M	M		•	•		
64. Records Processing: Putting records together and keeping 07.05 them up to date.	M		M	M	H		M		M		•			
65. Clerical Machine Operation: Using various machines to record, 07.06 process, and compute data.	M				H		M		H		•			
66. Clerical Handling: Keeping data in order by filing, copying, 07.07 sorting, delivering.	M		M		M				M		•			

Some Combinations and Other Considerations

People are attracted to jobs for all sorts of reasons besides interest in the job itself. They want people to like them. They'd like to feel important. They want to avoid competition, to please parents, to look like the stereotypical successful male or female, to earn more money. We are all influenced by the convenience and availability of jobs. All these reasons tap into our value system. But can you find long-term satisfaction in a career field that doesn't interest you? This all-important question must be answered in a way that is consistent with your values. If you pay attention to your strong interests, you will probably find that you have fewer conflicts with your value system. Also, people often have an interest in more than one area and would like a career that will use those interests. While many jobs tend to reflect a single interest, most jobs, just like people, will have significant qualities of more than one interest area.

A person who enjoys physical activity and doesn't mind working with mechanical systems but would also like to work with people and follow set guidelines (the Realistic, Social, and Conventional personality) may enjoy one of more than 300 careers in health care. A person who is mechanically adept and enjoys persuading people about a product may find technical sales or service an interesting area (the Realistic, Enterprising, Conventional personality) whereas the mechanically inclined person with an investigative bent may like research and development in industry (Realistic and Investigative personality). The Realistic and Conventional personality would find satisfiers in safety and time studies and other data-keeping tasks as well as with data processing equipment; the more creative person may enjoy product/process design, crafts, model building, or graphics (Realistic and Artistic personality).

The investigative person can also research and analyze people, the arts, and business—in fact, this individual can find satisfiers in almost any workplace. Likewise artistic/creative people can innovate new systems in many job settings that are flexible enough to allow for their creativity. And social personalities can find people to supervise, manage, train, and develop in almost any place they work.

Remember, many Social, Investigative, Artistic persons enjoy working with people to solve problems by creating new systems! This is important in just about every workplace.

Understanding these interests can sometimes save people from jobs where they will feel quite uncomfortable. For example, realistic personalities with few social characteristics often find that a promotion to management status brings headaches they'd rather do without. And an artistic person may feel stifled doing routine work all day.

Perhaps none of those combinations and considerations interest you right now. For the present, you feel you simply want to consider an entry-level job in an enjoyable place that will allow for advancement. But as you travel on through the career search process, you will have the opportunity to look at

"Your son has made a career choice, Mildred. He's going to win the lottery and travel a lot."

a variety of creative as well as traditional career ideas that could expand your view of what is available down the road. You will see how alternative work schedules, a change of work environment, an involvement with a different product or service, or a new slant on an old challenge may be the trick that will turn the tide toward satisfaction in your present career or even launch you in an entirely new direction.

You may want to review this career focus material with a counselor or teacher if you still feel uncertain about which interest area is of greatest importance to you. You may wish to explore the Job Group Chart in more detail by using the following material, or skip on to Library Research. Whichever you choose, your future career will turn up somewhere on this chart in some way.[2]

Exploring the Job Chart Further

Just choosing one of the twelve major career interest areas is a significant step in choosing a career. It can help you to zero in on an educational path or college major. Then, if you wish, you can explore the sixty-six job groups or subdivisions of these twelve interest areas in more detail. Next you will learn how to explore the 20,000 different occupations identified, defined, and arranged into these groups by the U.S. Department of Labor. Twelve major interest areas representing sixty-six job groups with 20,000 jobs—there must be a job for you!

You may feel that you have already chosen a career and that you know exactly why that career fits you. It still can be an interesting exercise to learn something about the whole U.S. job market and how it attracts people from all backgrounds into jobs with such a wide variety of characteristics. You will be working with many different people over a lifetime. Understanding their personalities, interests, and skills can be a plus in most any field you choose.

Job Groups   The numbers 1 through 66 in the left-hand column refer to the sixty-six job groups identified by the Department of Labor. With some small exceptions, all jobs in a group have similar characteristics and call for similar preferences regarding the key qualities. They also call for similar preferences regarding involvement with data, people, and things; they have the same key qualities; and they use the same skills.

Decimal Code   Decimal numbers such as 05.01 refer to the numbered items in the Department of Labor's *Guide for Occupational Exploration,* available in many libraries and state employment offices. The second two digits, 01 through 12, designate the twelve interest areas.

Key Qualities   In each of the fourteen columns following the job group, the symbol H means there is a need at a higher-than-average level and the symbol M means there is need for an average level of the key qualities in that particular group of jobs. A dot (•) means that the quality is needed, with no degree of need indicated.

Do you wish to explore your interest areas further on the Job Group Chart?

NO = Goodbye Interest Areas and Job Group Chart! Continue on to Library Research.

YES = Do the Following Activities.

Directions: Finding Your Satisfiers

1. Read the description of each job group in your top three or more interest areas. Circle the numbers of any groups that interest you.
2. If you wish to go further, locate the Key Qualities at the top of each column that match those you circled on the Key Qualities Indicator in Chapter 2, Exercise 4. Using a colored pencil, go down the columns and circle the symbols that indicate your satisfiers. For example, if you wish to use the skill "logical intelligence" at a modest level, circle the M's down the column in the interest areas you wish to explore further. When you have finished, you may discover job groups that have many of your satisfiers.
3. Study the Job Group Chart in your interest areas (or even throughout the whole chart) line by line to find groups that look interesting. Some of your satisfiers may be more important than others. Try to be as flexible

PEANUTS reprinted by permission of United Feature Syndicate, Inc.

as possible. Maybe you have indicated that physical activity related to whole-body agility is an important quality for you, but in looking at the other qualities required in such jobs, you find that most would not suit you.

4. Double star (**) any job group that has all your satisfiers. If you choose a job group that is not listed under any of your top three personality types, you may still be able to find ways to express your personality in some jobs in the group. Be aware that the Job Group Chart is only an imperfect summary of the qualities to be found in thousands of jobs. An individual company can change a job title, alter the job duties at will, and come up with something that no job chart could describe in one line! It's important not to force the data about yourself to make it fit the Job Group Chart. It's also important to be open to possibilities that may be hidden there.

Many people are dismayed to find themselves at sea in an ocean of many choices. If you don't have a nice, neat job title in hand by the time you finish this chapter, much less this book, you may be tempted to give up. But if you keep searching, you will have a great chance to learn more about yourself and the work world. You may become more willing to explore important, supporting factors that go into a career choice, and you may also have the joy of learning that many enjoyable careers would suit you equally well. All in all, the career search process is a confidence builder. Even those with a clear-cut career choice can find it valuable to learn about the job market and how to connect with it.

Library Research: Looking In

Library research enables you to survey the whole job market and eliminate those areas that would not work for you while you zero in on those that are important. Here are some resources to make that task easier. The Department of Labor has listed every job title in a monumental work called the *Dictionary of Occupational Titles* (DOT).[3] The book is a gold mine of information—if you know how to dig for the gold. Because there are sometimes several different titles for the same job, the 20,000 occupations result in about 40,000 listings. Job titles are listed both alphabetically and by industry. The alphabetical listings give the code number needed to find a short description of each job, located among descriptions grouped by occupational area.

The DOT supplement, the *Guide for Occupational Exploration,* is a much simpler book, classifying jobs into the same sixty-six job groups that you found on the Job Group Chart.[4] You can find these books in career centers, library reference rooms, and state employment offices.

Before you go to the library, list the job groups you would like to explore. Use the decimal code number from the Job Group Chart for easy reference. At the library, look up those numbers in the *Guide for Occupational Exploration.* As you explore the job groups, make a list of all the job titles included in each group of interest to you so you can investigate them further.

Suppose you are interested in Job Group 55, Business Management, code number 11.11. In the *Guide for Occupational Exploration* you will find this information:

> Workers in this group manage a business, such as a store or cemetery, a branch of a large company, such as a local office for a credit corporation, or a department within a company, such as a warehouse. They usually carry out operating policies and procedures determined by administration workers, such as presidents, vice-presidents, and directors. Some managers own their own businesses and are considered self-employed. Managers find employment in all kinds of businesses as well as government agencies.[5]

This paragraph is followed by answers to some important questions: What kind of work would you do as a business manager? What skill and abilities do you need for this kind of work? How do you know whether you would like or could learn to do this kind of work? How can you prepare for and enter this kind of work? What else should you consider about these jobs? This information is followed by a list of all the job categories in the Business Management group:

11.11.01 Lodging

11.11.02 Recreation and Amusement

11.11.03 Transportation

11.11.04 Services

11.11.05 Wholesale–Retail

Each of these listings is subdivided into specific job titles and identified by a nine-digit number. Under Wholesale–Retail, for example, you will find

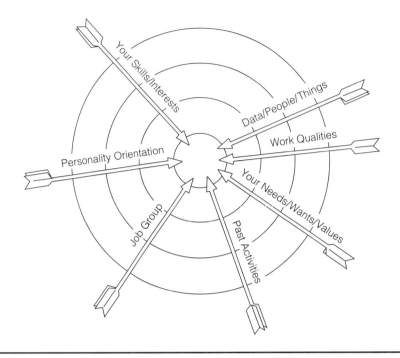

The Career Target

Manager, Retail Store 185.167.046. If this particular job interests you, you can find a description of it in the *Dictionary of Occupational Titles* by looking up the nine digit number, 185.167.046. The section includes other similar job titles so you can explore a variety of jobs with like characteristics.

Remember that titles for the same job may differ from one company to another. You may find the most accurate information about a job title in the job description developed by companies when they advertise a position. Continue to develop a list of general functions you'd like to perform so that you'll recognize the ideal job when it comes your way.

By now, if you've marked your areas of interest on the Job Chart, you have noticed which of the sixty-six job groups offer your most important satisfiers. Whenever many of your likes and skills point toward the same job group, you've hit the bullseye on the career target.

At this point you might be feeling a little scared, anxious, or confused. These are all normal feelings for anyone on the verge of a *great discovery!* Keep going! Don't be overwhelmed if you find that several career areas look good to you. Some people are comfortable in more than one. Sometimes a person needs more work experience before making a decision. Give yourself more time if you need it. Don't decide to decide without seeing clearly.

There are still other activities that will help you zero in on a career. The next chapter will lead you to reflect on major societal challenges and the ways people are dealing with them as part of their work. This will give you perspective when you take the next step—researching workplaces. After an in-depth study of companies and alternative workplaces and workstyles, you will be ready to look at the elements necessary for the job hunt. Although you will have been making many decisions throughout the process, you will then have a chance to review a structured decision-making process. Making a good career decision is a growth process, and growth takes patience. You can't make a flower grow by pulling on it!

 Self-Assessment Exercises

1. Interest Areas

Rank the twelve interest areas of the Job Chart in order of importance to you.

_____ 01 **Artistic** (Artistic Personality Type—Creative/Data): An interest in creative expression of feelings/ideas.

_____ 02 **Scientific** (Investigative Personality Type—Researching Data): An interest in discovering, collecting, analyzing information about the natural world, and applying scientific research findings to problems in medicine, the life sciences, and the natural sciences.

_____ 03 **Nature/Plants and Animals** (Realistic Personality Type—Outdoor/Things): An interest in working with plants and animals, usually in an outdoor setting.

_____ 04 **Protective** (Realistic Personality Type—Protecting People and Property/Things): An interest in the use of authority to protect people and property.

_____ 05 **Mechanical** (Realistic Personality Type—Machine/Things): An interest in applying mechanical principles to practical situations by use of machines or tools.

_____ 06 **Industrial** (Realistic Personality Type—Factory/Things): An interest in repetitive, concrete, organized activities done in a factory setting.

_____ 07 **Business detail** (Conventional Personality Type—Office/Data): An interest in organized, clearly defined activities requiring accuracy and attention to details, primarily in an office setting.

_____ 08 **Selling** (Enterprising Personality Type—People/Persuading): An interest in bringing others to a particular point of view by personal persuasion, using sales promotion techniques.

_____ 09 **Accommodating** (Social Personality Type—People/Waiting On): An interest in catering to the wants and needs of others, usually on a one-to-one basis.

_____ 10 **Human services** (Social Personality Type—People/Development): An interest in helping others with their mental, spiritual, social, physical, or vocational needs.

_____ 11 **Leading/influencing** (Enterprising/Social Personality Type—People/Leading, Influencing): An interest in leading and influencing others by using high-level verbal or numerical abilities.

_____ 12 **Physical performance** (Realistic Personality Type—Thing/Body Performance): An interest in physical activities performed before an audience.[6]

2. Job Group Expanded

The following list of the sixty-six job groups and their subcategories may help you to further zero in on job groups of interest to you. They are in a somewhat different order than found in the Job Group Chart. Circle those of interest to you at this time. Note those job groups with the most circles.

SUMMARY LIST OF INTEREST AREAS, JOB GROUPS, AND SUBGROUPS

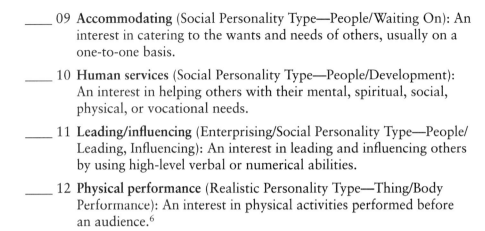

01	ARTISTIC/CREATIVE
01.01	**Literary Arts**
01.01-01	Editing
01.01-02	Creative Writing
01.01-03	Critiquing
01.02	**Visual Arts**
01.02-01	Instructing and Appraising
01.02-02	Studio Art
01.02-03	Commercial Art
01.03	**Performing Arts: Drama**
01.03-01	Instructing and Directing
01.03-02	Performing
01.03-03	Narrating and Announcing
01.04	**Performing Arts: Music**
01.04-01	Instructing and Directing
01.04-02	Composing and Arranging
01.04-03	Vocal Performing
01.04-04	Instrumental Performing

01.05	Performing Arts: Dance
01.05-01	Instructing and Choreography
01.05-02	Performing
01.06	**Craft Arts**
01.06-01	Graphic Arts and Related Crafts
01.06-02	Arts and Crafts
01.06-03	Hand Lettering, Painting, and Decorating
01.07	**Elemental Arts**
01.07-01	Psychic Science
01.07-02	Announcing
01.07-03	Entertaining
01.08	**Modeling**
01.08-01	Personal Appearance
02	**SCIENTIFIC/ ANALYTIC**
02.01	**Physical Sciences**
02.01-01	Theoretical Research
02.01-02	Technology

02.02	Life Sciences
02.02-01	Animal Specialization
02.02-02	Plant Specialization
02.02-03	Plant and Animal Specialization
02.02-04	Food Research
02.03	**Medical Sciences**
02.03-01	Medicine and Surgery
02.03-02	Dentistry
02.03-03	Veterinary Medicine
02.03-04	Health Specialties
02.04	**Laboratory Technology**
02.04-01	Physical Sciences
02.04-02	Life Sciences
03	**NATURE (PLANTS, ANIMALS)**
03.01	**Managerial Work: Plants and Animals**
03.01-01	Farming
03.01-02	Specialty Breeding
03.01-03	Specialty Cropping
03.01-04	Forestry and Logging

(continued)

05	MECHANICAL *(continued)*
05.12.04	Hoisting, Conveying
05.12.05	Braking, Switching, and Coupling
05.12.06	Pumping
05.12.07	Crushing, Mixing, Separating, and Chipping
05.12.08	Lubricating
05.12.09	Masonry
05.12.10	Heating and Melting
05.12.11	Welding
05.12.12	Structural Work
05.12.13	Cutting and Finishing
05.12.14	Painting, Caulking, and Coating
05.12.15	Mechanical Work
05.12.16	Electrical Work
05.12.17	Food Preparation
05.12.18	Cleaning and Maintenance
05.12.19	Reproduction Services
05.12.20	Signaling

06	**INDUSTRIAL**
06.01	**Production Technology**
06.01-01	Supervision and Instruction
06.01-02	Machine Set-Up
06.01-03	Machine Set-Up and Operation
06.01-04	Precision Hand Work
06.01-05	Inspection

06.02	**Production Work**
06.02-01	Supervision
06.02-02	Machine Work, Metal and Plastics
06.02-03	Machine Work, Wood
06.02-04	Machine Work, Paper
06.02-05	Machine Work, Leather and Fabrics
06.02-06	Machine Work, Textiles
06.02-07	Machine Work, Rubber
06.02-08	Machine Work, Stone, Clay, and Glass
06.02-09	Machine Work, Assorted Materials
06.02-10	Equipment Operation, Metal Processing
06.02-11	Equipment Operation, Chemical Processing
06.02-12	Equipment Operation, Petroleum Processing
06.02-13	Equipment Operation, Rubber, Plastics, and Glass Processing
06.02-14	Equipment Operation, Paper and Paper Products Processing
06.02-15	Equipment Operation, Food Processing
06.02-16	Equipment Operation, Textile, Fabric, and Leather Processing
06.02-17	Equipment Operation, Clay and Coke Processing
06.02-18	Equipment Operation, Assorted Materials Processing
06.02-19	Equipment Operation, Welding, Brazing, and Soldering
06.02-20	Machine Assembling
06.02-21	Coating and Plating
06.02-22	Manual Work, Assembly Large Parts
06.02-23	Manual Work, Assembly Small Parts
06.02-24	Manual Work, Metal and Plastics
06.02-25	Manual Work, Wood
06.02-26	Manual Work, Paper
06.02-27	Manual Work, Textile, Fabric, and Leather
06.02-28	Manual Work, Food Processing
06.02-29	Manual Work, Rubber
06.02-30	Manual Work, Stone, Glass, and Clay
06.02-31	Manual Work, Laying Out and Marking
06.02-32	Manual Work, Assorted Materials

06.03	**Quality Control**
06.03-01	Inspecting, Testing, and Repairing
06.03-02	Inspecting, Grading, Sorting, Weighing, and Recording

06.04	**Elemental Work: Industrial**
06.04-01	Supervision
06.04-02	Machine Work, Metal and Plastics
06.04-03	Machine Work, Wood
06.04-04	Machine Work, Paper
06.04-05	Machine Work, Fabric and Leather
06.04-06	Machine Work, Textiles
06.04-07	Machine Work, Rubber
06.04-08	Machine Work, Stone, Glass, and Clay
06.04-09	Machine Work, Assorted Materials
06.04-10	Equipment Operation, Metal Processing
06.04-11	Equipment Operation, Chemical Processing
06.04-12	Equipment Operation, Petroleum, Gas, and Coal Processing
06.04-13	Equipment Operation, Rubber, Plastics, and Glass Processing
06.04-14	Equipment Operation, Paper Making
06.04-15	Equipment Operation, Food Processing
06.04-16	Equipment Operation, Textile, Fabric, and Leather Processing
06.04-17	Equipment Operation, Clay Processing
06.04-18	Equipment Operation, Wood Processing
06.04-19	Equipment Operation, Assorted Materials Processing
06.04-20	Machine Assembly
06.04-21	Machine Work, Brushing, Spraying, and Coating
06.04-22	Manual Work, Assembly Large Parts
06.04-23	Manual Work, Assembly Small Parts
06.04-24	Manual Work, Metal and Plastics
06.04-25	Manual Work, Wood
06.04-26	Manual Work, Paper
06.04-27	Manual Work, Textile, Fabric, and Leather
06.04-28	Manual Work, Food Processing
06.04-29	Manual Work, Rubber
06.04-30	Manual Work, Stone, Glass, and Clay
06.04-31	Manual Work, Welding and Flame Cutting
06.04-32	Manual Work, Casting and Molding
06.04-33	Manual Work, Brushing, Spraying, and Coating
06.04-34	Manual Work, Assorted Materials
06.04-35	Laundering, Dry Cleaning

06.04-36 Filling
06.04-37 Manual Work,
        Stamping, Marking,
        Labeling, and
        Ticketing
06.04-38 Wrapping and Packing
06.04-39 Cleaning
06.04-40 Loading, Moving,
        Hoisting, and
        Conveying

07   **BUSINESS DETAIL**

07.01   **Administrative Detail**
07.01-01 Interviewing
07.01-02 Administration
07.01-03 Secretarial Work
07.01-04 Financial Work
07.01-05 Certifying
07.01-06 Investigating
07.01-07 Test Administration

07.02   **Mathematical Detail**
07.02-01 Bookkeeping and
        Auditing
07.02-02 Accounting
07.02-03 Statistical Reporting and
        Analysis
07.02-04 Billing and Rate
        Computation
07.02-05 Payroll and Timekeeping

07.03   **Financial Detail**
07.03-01 Paying and Receiving

07.04   **Oral Communications**
07.04-01 Interviewing
07.04-02 Order, Complaint, and
        Claims Handling
07.04-03 Registration
07.04-04 Reception and
        Information Giving
07.04-05 Information
        Transmitting and
        Receiving
07.04-06 Switchboard Services

07.05   **Records Processing**
07.05-01 Coordinating and
        Scheduling
07.05-02 Record Verification and
        Proofing
07.05-03 Record Preparation and
        Maintenance
07.05-04 Routing and
        Distribution

07.06   **Clerical Machine**
        Operation
07.06-01 Computer Operation
07.06-02 Keyboard Machine
        Operation

07.07   **Clerical Handling**
07.07-01 Filing
07.07-02 Sorting and Distribution
07.07-03 General Clerical Work

08   **PERSUADING/**
         SELLING

08.01   **Sales Technology**
08.01-01 Technical Sales
08.01-02 Intangible Sales
08.01-03 General Clerical Work

08.02   **General Sales**
08.02-01 Wholesale
08.02-02 Retail
08.02-03 Wholesale and Retail
08.02-04 Real Estate
08.02-05 Demonstration and Sales
08.02-06 Services
08.02-07 Driving/Selling
08.02-08 Soliciting, Selling

08.03   **Vending**
08.03-01 Peddling and Hawking
08.03-02 Promoting

09   **ACCOMMODATING**

09.01   **Hospitality Services**
09.01-01 Social and Recreational
        Activities
09.01-02 Guide Services
09.01-03 Food Services
09.01-04 Safety and Comfort
        Services

09.02   **Barber and Beauty**
        Services
09.02-01 Cosmetology
09.02-02 Barbering

09.03   **Passenger Services**
09.03-01 Group Transportation
09.03-02 Individual
        Transportation
09.03-03 Instruction and
        Supervision

09.04   **Customer Services**
09.04-01 Food Services
09.04-02 Sales Services

09.05   **Attendant Services**
09.05-01 Physical Conditioning
09.05-02 Food Services
09.05-03 Portering and Baggage
        Services
09.05-04 Doorkeeping Services
09.05-05 Card and Game Room
        Services
09.05-06 Individualized Services
09.05-07 General Wardrobe
        Services
09.05-08 Ticket Taking, Ushering

10   **HUMAN SERVICES**

10.01   **Social Services**
10.01-01 Religious
10.01-02 Counseling and Social
        Work

10.02   **Nursing, Therapy, and**
        Specialized Teaching
        Services
10.02-01 Nursing
10.02-02 Therapy and
        Rehabilitation
10.02-03 Specialized Teaching

10.03   **Child and Adult Care**
10.03-01 Data Collection
10.03-02 Patient Care
10.03-03 Care of Others

11   **LEADING/**
         INFLUENCING

11.01   **Mathematics and**
        Statistics
11.01-01 Data Processing Design
11.01-02 Data Analysis

11.02   **Educational and Library**
        Services
11.02-01 Teaching and
        Instructing, General
11.02-02 Vocational and
        Industrial Teaching
11.02-03 Teaching Home
        Economics,
        Agriculture, and
        Related
11.02-04 Library Services

(continued)

11	LEADING/ INFLUENCING (continued)

11.03	Social Research
11.03-01	Psychological
11.03-02	Sociological
11.03-03	Historical
11.03-04	Occupational
11.03-05	Economic

11.04	Law
11.04-01	Justice Administration
11.04-02	Legal Practice
11.04-03	Abstracting, Document Preparation

11.05	Business Administration
11.05-01	Management Services: Nongovernment
11.05-02	Administrative Specialization
11.05-03	Management Services: Government
11.05-04	Sales and Purchasing Management

11.06	Finance
11.06-01	Accounting and Auditing
11.06-02	Records Systems Analysis
11.06-03	Risk and Profit Analysis
11.06-04	Brokering
11.06-05	Budget and Financial Control

11.07	Service Administration
11.07-01	Social Services
11.07-02	Health and Safety Services
11.07-03	Educational Services
11.07-04	Recreational Services

11.08	Communications
11.08-01	Editing
11.08-02	Writing
11.08-03	Writing and Broadcasting
11.08-04	Translating and Interpreting

11.09	Promotion
11.09-01	Sales
11.09-02	Funds and Membership Solicitation
11.09-03	Public Relations

11.10	Regulations Enforcement
11.10-01	Finance
11.10-02	Individual Rights
11.10-03	Health and Safety
11.10-04	Immigration and Customs
11.10-05	Company Policy

11.11	Business Management
11.11-01	Lodging
11.11-02	Recreation and Amusement
11.11-03	Transportation
11.11-04	Service
11.11-05	Wholesale/Retail

11.12	Contracts and Claims
11.12-01	Claims Settlement
11.12-02	Rental and Leasing
11.12-03	Booking
11.12-04	Procurement Negotiations

12	PHYSICAL PERFORMANCE

12.01	Sports
12.01-01	Coaching and Instructing
12.01-02	Officiating
12.01-03	Performing

12.02	Physical Feats
12.02-01	Performing

3. Job Group Choice

Now, of the sixty-six job groups, list the top three job group choices you might consider at this time, in order of importance. Use the four-digit number and name, beginning with 01.01 Artistic:

1. _____   2. _____   3. _____

4. Match Analyzer

a. To analyze your choice(s) further, fill in the following information about your top job group choice:

Number   Decimal code   Title

_____   _____   _____

b. Check below all the qualities from l to 14 required by that job group as they appear on the Job Group Chart on pp. 73–78. Then, using your colored pencil, circle the same qualities you circled in the Key Qualities

Indicator in Chapter 2, Exercise 4, as being important to you. This will give you a comparison between the qualities the job group requires and the qualities you would like in your job.

__ M __ H 1. Logical intelligence   __ M __ H 8. Ability to influence people

__ M __ H 2. Intuitive intelligence   __ M __ H 9. Finger/hand agility

__ M __ H 3. Verbal ability   __ M __ H 10. Whole-body agility

__ M __ H 4. Numerical ability   __   11. Repetition

__ M __ H 5. Exactness with detail   __   12. Variety

__ M __ H 6. Facility with multi-   __   13. Physical risk
                dimensional forms

__ M __ H 7. Businesslike contact   __   14. Status
                with people

c. Is there a perfect match between qualities the job group requires and those you would like to use on the job? ___ Yes ___ No

d. Explain how you could overcome each quality that does not match.

_____

_____

_____

e. You can repeat this analysis for any other job group of interest to you.

5. Researching a Job Group

Look up your top job group in the *Guide for Occupational Exploration*. Find the answers to the following questions.

■ Summarize the kind of work you would do.

_____

_____

_____

■ Summarize the skills and abilities needed for this kind of work.

_____

_____

_____

- Summarize clues that tell whether you would like or could learn this work.

  _____

  _____

  _____

- Summarize the training needed and the methods of entry into this field.

  _____

  _____

  _____

- List job titles you'd like to explore further.

  _____

  _____

  _____

6. Researching Job Titles

Identify one job title from your top job group. Look it up in the _Dictionary of Occupational Titles,_ using the nine-digit number. Summarize what you find there.

Job Title: _____   Nine-digit code: _____

_____

_____

_____

_____

7. Confirm Career Choice

If you have already made your career choice, ask yourself these questions.

- Is this career clearly your own choice?
- Are you afraid to look at alternatives?
- Are you willing to be open to important factors that may change your decision?
- Can you support your choice with facts about your skills, interests, and values?

8. Blocks and Barriers

At this point, what could be holding you back from completing the career search process?

___ In too much of a hurry to take time to explore

___ Have done some exercises (or pieces of the puzzle) but left others out

___ Experiencing personal/painful traumas

___ Afraid to look at myself; low/no self-confidence

___ Afraid to make a commitment

___ What else? _____

9. Filling in the Lines

Discuss with a group or in writing the decisions you have made so far in regard to your career/life choices and how they feel to you.

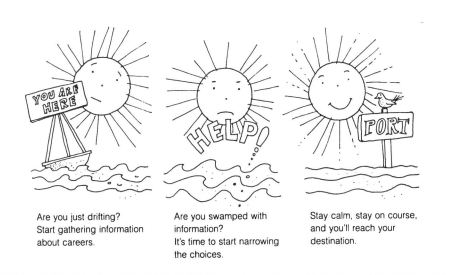

Are you just drifting?
Start gathering information
about careers.

Are you swamped with
information?
It's time to start narrowing
the choices.

Stay calm, stay on course,
and you'll reach your
destination.

Where are you now on the Career Choice Continuum?

4/

Work

Challenges, Options, and Opportunities

 FOCUS

- *Reflect on the meaning of work.*

- *Explore challenges and options for the twenty-first century.*

- *Relate personality types to job market opportunities.*

Y̲ou have assessed your needs, wants, and most cherished values. You know your personality orientation and your interests and abilities. You have identified qualities that represent the unique person you are. And you have seen how, by identifying these qualities, you can find your satisfiers in the job market. By now, you may also have an inkling that self-discovery is a lifetime process.

Next, either to firm up or facilitate a career decision, wise career searchers will do well to acquire a broader, deeper understanding of work in the global village that looms on the horizon. This chapter considers the meaning of work and looks at some of the many positive and hopeful options and opportunities we have for responding to the societal challenges we face. You will look at ways people with your personality type can relate to the job market of the future. As you continue deepening your understanding of work, you'll also realize your need for a set of enduring values and a hopeful outlook that will enable you to maintain a broad sense of direction without being swept away by fads or predictions of gloom and doom. In short, you'll be ready to face the fast-paced, fast-changing world of the twenty-first century.

> The trouble with the future
> is that it arrives before we're ready for it.
> —Andy Capp

Charting the Future: A Global Philosophic View of Work

The Time of No Time

The pace of change seems to accelerate daily. The speed of change is captured by John Peers, founder of Silicon Valley's Robotics Institute, who said, "We live three days in a day compared to the 1950s. We do in one day what couldn't be done in a week in 1900, in a lifetime in the 1600s."[1] As this is being written, California bulldozers can be seen literally moving mountains to repair the state's coast highway, damaged by El Niño storms—a task that couldn't have been done in the 1600s.

In an instant, with a process unknown a few years ago, we can e-mail our computer thoughts to Guam or Guatemala and overnight see them turn into prototypes or procedures. Such speedy decisions affect both the economy and the environment and have an ethical impact on the life of individuals and communities, often in far-reaching and unforeseen ways. Like a riddle, we save time and yet have none of the time we saved. What an uncertain moment in which to be making a career decision, but also what an exciting time this is.

> We live in the time of no room . . .
> the time when everyone is obsessed with lack of time, with saving
> time, conquering space, projecting into time and space the anguish
> produced in them by the technological furies of size, volume,
> quantity, speed, number, price, power, and acceleration.
> —*Thomas Merton*[2]

Jeremy Rifkin suggests as a motto for the twenty-first century, "Slow is beautiful."[3] It seems that we need to slow down and reflect very seriously and creatively on the future and how our choices can contribute in a positive way to that great adventure called life. If we rush to get ahead without clarifying our direction, we may be rushing behind!

Work Past and Present

We can roughly divide jobs into two categories: those that produce goods and those that supply services. From the beginning of time until very recently, most work produced goods that supplied basic needs: farming, construction, mining, and manufacturing. As late as the early 1900s, over one-third of the workers in the U.S. labor force were still farmers.[4] Such work was often brutally hard, done at or close to home. As the industrial revolution accelerated, it brought dramatic change to many of the slow-paced, self-sufficient communities of the world; the entire goods-producing world changed.

The Global Panorama

Picture the entire world at work. Day and night it hums with the sounds of people and machines producing goods for one another. Mines and forests, oceans and fields yield raw substances to make mountains of *things*. Wood and metal, coal and cotton, giant and motley masses of materials are baked and baled, pounded and pummeled, mixed and milled, cut and checked, piled and packed for delivery to the world. Trucks and trains, ships and planes move endlessly, huffing and hauling it all to factories and farms, stores, and homes. Things! They are bought, sold, used, recycled, worn out, and finally discarded to become heaps of debris—some of it to return to the earth, some of it to pollute and plague us.

Today less than one-fifth of U.S. workers are employed in product-oriented industries.[5] For example, the farming population has decreased markedly in this past half century—only 2 percent still live on farms[6]—yet the food and fiber industry is the single largest industry in the United States.[7]

The other parts of the job world include transactions, interactions, communications, deals, those intangible "services rendered," which mingle with the flow of goods. Orders are taken, food served, children taught, cases tried, patients treated. Many services that used to be done with modest training and common sense now require more and more education and a continuous supply of information. For example, firefighters have became explosives and toxics experts, bomb defusers, and structural engineers. They get degrees in fire science, chemistry, engineering, and human relations.

We are all becoming *information* mills. We create it, collect it, evaluate it, manipulate it, control it, and pass it on to the twenty-four-hour-a-day world. Screens glow, faxes beep, copiers click, computers talk to computers, and modems squeak and squawk to each other while we sleep. Vast webs of information "technet" around the world at the stroke of a key, bringing us online and in line. The piles of data grow too fast to be absorbed and comprehended. Bombarded with so much information, we feel that we know less and less. Even so, we need to respond more quickly than ever. In the cyber world, information is called the product and power of the future.

Information is like a child's riddle: it's not only renewable, it's also expandable; it's never scarce, uses few resources, and takes little energy to produce; it can be kept while being given away. It has changed the way we live and work in ways we have barely begun to understand. We call all this *work!*

Once a mysterious shuffling of papers, work is now an even more mysterious shuffling of electronic impulses. The silicon chip is king, computers reign, and robots rule. James Burke, host of the PBS series *Connections,* feels we have rushed into a technology trap.[8] When the power goes out or your computer crashes, you understand what he means. We are left more and more to our own devices to find our way through the techno thicket.

Some years ago, in a paper for one of his classes, drafter and student Scott Ellner summed up his feelings:

> A feeling of being overwhelmed by this technological juggernaut. A yearning to get away from it all and return to a simpler way of life. Walking into any bookstore and being filled with a sense of dread. "So much information! How can I possibly even know just a tiny fraction of all this?" As a drafter, not having kept up with the technological advances in my field and feeling that I'm being left behind. A feeling against technological developments not understood.

Futurist and author Alvin Toffler called this feeling "future shock." José Ortega y Gasset wrote in *The Revolt of the Masses,* "Modern man is becoming more primitive. He understands as little about the technology that serves him as primitive people understood about lightning and air."[9]

Stephen J. Kline defines technology as a sociotechnical system in which people meld with machines, resources, processes, and legal, economic, political, and physical environments. He says that without this system, we humans now might not exist as a species, and if we did we should be relatively power-less, few in number, and of little import on the planet.[10]

What has happened to the people component of the data-people-things trio in this information age? Some are running mightily to stay in place; some are falling by the wayside in future shock; and some are at night classes, delving into the mysterious machinations at work in the belly of the computer beast.

Though most of the world, and indeed, many people in the United States, have not gone high tech, the assumption is that everyone must do so or be left behind. Some people question that assumption. Nevertheless, schools are "teching" up. Students have plunged in; they e-mail their professors, listen to lectures, observe intricate science experiments, and solve problems via videos and the Internet. Sometimes they spend more time in their dorm rooms or at home in front of a computer monitor than in a lecture hall or lab.

Jeremy Rifkin's book, *The End of Work,* predicts a trend toward highly skilled "knowledge workers" and fewer low-skilled, low-paid, easily replaced others, mostly due to automation. Among his many examples is his prediction that an automobile will be produced in eight hours. A bike can now be ordered and made in three hours. At the Victor plant in Japan, two humans manage sixty-four robots making camcorders where 150 people worked before. Priscilla Enriquez of the Food Institute feels that there is an unnecessary trend toward "downgrading of work." With automation, fast-food clerks, for example, hardly need to know any math or even how to read.[11]

Henry Ford once asked Walter Reuther of the United Auto Workers Union, "What are you going to do with your union when all of your men are replaced by robots?" Reuther answered: "Who are you going to sell your cars to, if nobody's working?"[12] Someone once suggested letting workers buy a share in the robots that replaced them and then collect the robot's pay.

In a humorous vein, a University of Miami aeronautics professor described an aircraft of the future to the International Airline Pilots Association: "The crew will consist of one pilot and one dog. The pilot's job will be to nurture, care for, and feed the dog. The dog's job will be to bite the pilot if he tries to touch anything."[13]

In the tech world, this service/information sector now accounts for over four-fifths of all workers and includes federal/state/local government, education, health services, law, entertainment/the arts, and repair services as well as wholesale/retail trade, finance/banking, insurance, real estate, management, and marketing. Service/information continues to grow rapidly. Note that although the giant technology industry deals with the tools of information, it is still an industry, manufacturing everything from computers to cell phones. Its pristine image as clean and its sites in manicured industrial parks can make us forget that it depends upon dangerous chemicals that often find their way into the environment. Also, it has been a voracious user of prime agricultural land.

Reprinted with permission of Mal Hancock.

While this new world can be see as a world of hazards, it is also one of possibilities and hopes. In newly technological societies of this past half century, and in the United States in particular, work and life choices have multiplied beyond anything our elders could have dreamed. A cornucopia of abundance has spilled forth and the "good life" has become a reality for countless numbers of people.

Despite the view in the United States from the top of the tech heap, most of the world's people still make their living at low-tech, goods-producing activities, as well as some service enterprises so small as to be unnoticed. In tiny courtyards and on dusty country roads and city streets, people from little children to the elderly work in this informal sector. They are marginalized people, often displaced from their land and their villages by large-scale enterprises such as logging, mining, and agribusiness. Their work is not counted, taxed, or noted in important statistics. They do small-scale farming; shuck and grind corn; cook; care for children; make small items by hand such as clay pots, straw mats, belts, and twine; do piecework for apparel makers; weave fabric. In public squares, they squeeze oranges, make tortillas, roast chickens, sell apparel and any other salable object, buy in bulk and sell to villagers, and guide tourists. They carry products to market—vegetables, fruit, chickens, pigs, and articles of clothing—on buses or trucks or on foot over many miles.

We see increasing contrasts between a small, highly sophisticated work force and an increasingly, marginalized global majority. Former Soviet President Mikhail Gorbachev said,

> We are facing a sweeping crisis that challenges our entire civilization. It has expended most of its resources, its patterns of life are fading. We are in dire need of redefining the parameters of our society's economic, political, and social development. . . . [T]he conflict between man and the rest of nature carries the risk of truly catastrophic consequences. We are seeing a crisis in public life, in international relations, and in the loss of fundamental spiritual values, the anchors that are indispensable for normal life worthy of human nature . . . and finally a crisis of ideas. The prevailing ideologies have proven to be incapable of either clarifying this situation or offering ways of dealing with it.[14]

Work impacts not only your own life but the planet as well. It can be rewarding, exciting, fulfilling, exasperating, enriching, exhausting, and dreadful—sometimes all at once. Work is often hard work, and in this time, it presents considerable challenges as well!

Societal Perspectives: Challenges and Options

As a career seeker, you are told to find a need and fill it. Finding the needs is the easy part. The media are filled with overwhelming problems. But seeing these problems as *challenges* can be invigorating, especially when we begin to see that there are innumerable, real, hopeful, *and* socially responsible *options* for every challenge, not just *a* solution to *a* problem. Stop here for a moment and brainstorm/list the global challenges that you see happening.

The areas of major challenges we will consider—economics, environment, and ethics—are all closely connected to work and lifestyle choices. The hopeful options that follow are only the tip of the iceberg of thousands of socially responsible activities being developed and actually being done as paid work around the globe. They are charting courses into the future job market, are certain to grow, and are designed to make the world a better place. As you read about the challenges of today's work world, think about your values and your job satisfiers. Ask yourself, "Which of these challenges challenge *me*?"

Economics Oversimplified

The word *economy,* from the ancient Greek *household,* still means the system by which we exchange goods and services with each other. Paul Reynolds, Coleman Foundation chair holder in entrepreneurial studies at Marquette

University, says, "The major objective [of economics] is to have a livable, just society with an acceptable level of economic efficiency and adaptability."[15] As simple as this sounds, the challenges facing us in the new global economy are formidable.

Work, in the economies of the industrial/technical nations, is tightly connected to the dramatic science/technological explosion of the twentieth century and the globalization of business. The business of industry is the production of goods. The business of business is facilitating the movement of goods and services from manufacturer to entrepreneur to consumer. All career areas—including such human service fields as health care and education as well as the arts—have increasingly become businesses that are oriented toward and dependent on technology, looking to the bottom line for value.

As this partnership among science, technology, industry, and business creates marvels, it creates monsters as well. It saves us from disease, it creates disease; it creates jobs, it eliminates jobs; it rescues us from tedious and boring work, it generates work that is tedious and boring; it makes wealth, it leaves many people behind in poverty; it preserves life, it destroys life; it has given us better, warmer, healthier shelters and abundant food and medicine as it destroys farmland and draws down resources to do so; it increases longevity and shortens lives; it both cleans and pollutes; it saves time and consumes time; it brings us education, it entertains us with trivia; it brings us new information, but not always truth and wisdom.

The challenges that face us indeed seem formidable. As the economy heats up and goes global, using earth resources in increasing amounts, the environment seems to be increasingly threatened and ethical decisions hard to come by. Renowned "world watchers" Lester R. Brown, Christopher Flavin, and Sandra Postel write in "A Planet in Jeopardy" that we are as slow to come to grips with the potential disaster in earth functions as were passengers on the Titanic.[16]

> Although its strictly economic implications
> have still not been worked out,
> it should be clear:
> an exhausted planet is an exhausted economy.
> —*Thomas Berry*[17]

State of the Ark People: Worldwide

Without doubt, while wealth multiplies, gaps between the income and lives of the rich and the poor grow wider. It seems amazing that the richest 20 percent of the world's population increased its share of world income from thirty times greater than the poorest to sixty times greater between 1960 and 1990, according to the United Nations Development Program report, 1992.[18] We

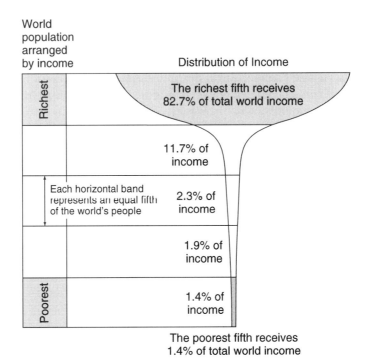

Global Income Distribution SOURCE: From *Human Development Report 1992* by United Nations Development Programme. Copyright © 1992 by United Nations Development Programme. Used by permission of Oxford University Press, Inc.

were told by Acción International, an organization that lends money to the very poor, that half the world's population (three billion people) live on less than $2 a day; the global economy barely touches them.[19]

- 25 percent of the world—increasingly women as single parents or elderly—and children do not have housing, clean water, health care, or education.[20]

- Between 6 million and 7 million children die every year of malnutrition, leaving millions more stunted both physically and intellectually.[21]

State of the Ark People: United States

There are people and places in the United States that are so poor they could qualify for "Third World" status. Many full-time workers in this country live below the poverty level, which in 1996 was $16,036 for a household of four.[22] The current minimum wage of $5.15 an hour—$10,712 a year—is not enough to support a family with children.[23] Even triple that amount is not

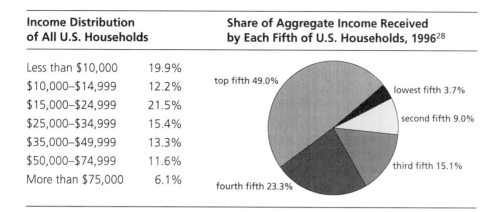

Income Distribution of All U.S. Households		Share of Aggregate Income Received by Each Fifth of U.S. Households, 1996[28]
Less than $10,000	19.9%	
$10,000–$14,999	12.2%	
$15,000–$24,999	21.5%	
$25,000–$34,999	15.4%	
$35,000–$49,999	13.3%	
$50,000–$74,999	11.6%	
More than $75,000	6.1%	

Pie chart labels: top fifth 49.0%, lowest fifth 3.7%, second fifth 9.0%, third fifth 15.1%, fourth fifth 23.3%

enough to rent or own a home in some parts of the country. Single mothers are the most likely of any group to be living in poverty, especially if they are minorities.

On any given night in the United States, as many as 700,00 people are homeless, 27 percent of them children.[24] One in four children under twelve does not get enough food.[25]

Since 1980, worker productivity has gone up 24 percent, corporate profits have increased 64 percent, and executive compensation has increased 360 percent.[26] Twenty years ago the typical chief executive officer of a large American company earned about forty times as much as a typical worker did. Now *he* earns 326 times as much.[27]

It's very difficult for the average American to fathom the plight of most of the world's people, yet voices are being raised in remarkable places regarding these economic trends. Richard Longworth, author of *Global Squeeze,* questions whether democracy and social stability can flourish when so many people are excluded from the global economy.[29] Multibillionaire and international financier George Soros says on this topic, "The arch enemy of an open society is no longer the Communist threat but the capitalist."[30]

Even William J. McDonough, the sixty-one-year-old president of the Federal Reserve Bank of New York, made this amazing statement about what he feels is a critical issue facing our country, "the growing disparity in wages earned by different segments of our labor force. These issues of equity and social cohesion affect the very temperament of the country. Can we go forward as a unified society with a confident outlook or [will we be] a society of diverse economic groups suspicious of both the future and each other?"[31]

> There is enough
> for everyone's need;
> But not enough
> for everyone's greed.

Buy Now, Pay Later: The Consumer Society Goes Global

After World War II, retailers easily followed the thinking of retailing analyst, Victor Lebow, who declared, "Our enormously productive economy . . . demands that we make consumption our way of life, that we convert the buying and use of goods into rituals, that we seek our spiritual and ego satisfaction in consumption. . . . We need things consumed, burned up, worn out, replaced, and discarded at an ever-increasing rate."[32]

The values expressed by the electronic media—television and computers—are often the values we "learn" simply from repeated exposure. As competition in the marketplace overheats, the urge to urge people to consume grows apace. Media messages are so strong that young people who live in the most remote villages of the world, who do not even have enough to eat or shoes to wear, will buy U.S. consumer goods that do not always represent the healthiest aspects of our society. Technology in this information age is a mixed bag—it has extraordinary value in bringing the wonders of the world to the world; it can also bring messages that are harmful to our long-term welfare.

To keep the affluent supplied with consumer goods, poor people in many ways subsidize them/us by their labor. In developing countries, people, including very young children, earn less than $10 per week making brand-name clothes, athletic shoes or equipment, and other products that sell for many times that in the United States. Famous athletes earn millions advertising them.[33] The poor often live in inadequate shelters and sometimes go without food and medicine for themselves and their children as they work for us.[34]

- The United States, with less than 5 percent of the world's population, uses a third of the world's resources and causes almost half of its industrial pollution.[35]

- If everyone lived an American lifestyle, we would need two more planets the size of earth to live sustainably.[36]

We build a 34,000-square-foot store in the United States every hour, yet have a half-billion square feet of store space sitting empty. In the 1980s, while the U.S. population increased by 10 percent, superstores increased by 80 percent. We have enough retail stores to service almost twice our population.[37] Often large chains cause small businesses to close; create low-wage, low-skill jobs; increase the need for such city services as roads and fire and police protection; and send revenues out of the local economy. A survey found that one well-known superstore adds 140 low-paying jobs in a town and destroys 230 higher-paying jobs.[38]

In the United States, advertising costs run about $500 per person per year.[39] And we continue to fill our waking hours with more and more ads. An eighteen-year-old will have spent 20,000 hours watching TV compared to

11,000 hours in a classroom and much less on homework and reading. In a lifetime, the average American spends thirteen years as a couch potato. Many people would argue that ads do not influence them, but 89 percent of women and 79 percent of men admit to buying more than they need,[40] with the ratio of nonjunk to junk in the typical American household estimated at roughly 1:10.[41] The natural resources consumed would fill 300 shopping bags per week for each American.[42] Lance Morrow once wrote in *Time* Magazine that "whole nations could live comfortably on [our] leftovers."[43]

Megacorporations are forces to be reckoned with, amassing more power and money than most governments, often operating without respect to national boundaries or laws. The Fortune 500 firms control 70 percent of world trade and 25 percent of the world's economic output, yet they employ only one-twentieth of one percent of the world's population.[44]

> We often forget that the price of never-ending economic growth and material prosperity has been spiritual and social impoverishment, psychological insecurity, and the loss of cultural vitality.
> —*Helena Norberg-Hodge*[45]

Energy Fires Up the Industrial/Technical World

Just about everything we use involves energy—in production, use, and maintenance. Despite severe pollution, the specter of global warming, and threats that "the oil is running out," energy use is increasing in developing countries as well as in affluent countries, as everyone struggles to obtain many of the amenities they see others enjoying. Energy consumption is expected to grow, perhaps to double its current use by 2025.

Think of all the ways you use energy. How does the United States as a whole use it? As much as 25 percent of U.S. energy goes to maintain buildings,[46] much of it unnecessary. Cars, giant energy guzzlers, leave no part of the environment untouched from the materials they use; the land for roads and parking they take up; the earth, air, water they pollute; to the huge amounts of fuel they consume every day.

Nuclear power, once thought to be the key to unlimited energy, has not lived up to expectations; its waste products are dangerous for centuries, and states are unwilling to provide a storage place for them. Even though it is becoming clearer that their time is running out, fossil fuel interests are unwilling to lose profits to alternative fuels.

Military Security

Wars are fought for many reasons but often over wealth-producing resources, including land and energy, and of course over personal and political power.

More than any other activity, war destroys infrastructure; millions of dollars and many years are required to restore the results of its devastation on lives, property, and the environment. The tools of war become more deadly; violence at home, school, and the workplace seems to escalate.

> Every gun that is made, every warship launched, every rocket fired,
> signifies in a final sense, a theft from those who hunger and are not fed,
> those who are cold and not clothed.
> —*Former U.S. president and general Dwight Eisenhower*[47]

Our economy—ever expanding and heating up and needing protection—is affecting the environment in ways that seem to threaten life on the planet. Without question, economics meets the environment at the factory gate and the office door.

Economy Meets the Environment

Spotted owls! Who needs them? In reality, we all do. The truth is that we are all environmentalists—at least, those of us who breathe, eat and drink, wear clothing, live in shelters. We all depend on the earth. The loss of the spotted owl signals the loss of an entire ecosystem and the irreparable loss of old-growth forests that house a vast array of plant and animal species. We often destroy a system before we understand it. Lt. Dick Lawrence, director of a wildlife program that dealt with alligators in Florida, asked, "Why do we always kill what we do not understand?"[48]

Prominent zoologist Jane Lubchenco, says, "[M]ore and more ecologists . . . are becoming convinced that the systems they have known and loved and studied for years are changing . . . in ways they wouldn't have believed possible. And they are feeling . . . frustrated that the information that they think they have to share has not been heard or sought."[49]

> Trees can live without people,
> but people cannot live without trees.[50]

As these words fall on the page, a nearby tree is slowly dying—one of many Monterey pines in the Monterey Bay area being attacked by a disease. Why it should happen is a mystery. We still understand very little about our fragile and interconnected ecosystems. Many species keep other destructive species in check.[51] Slight changes in overall temperature bring new predator insects to vulnerable plants. Many magnificent specimens of species that are strong, graceful, and beautiful as well as those that are lowly, cumbersome, and ugly—though useful—are becoming scarce.

Our Basic Needs

Air: Breathing Life   We know now that damage to the ozone layer has gone global. Pollution chokes cities, threatening health and causing the shutdown of many activities.

Climate: A Closed System   Emissions of greenhouse gases into the atmosphere include six billion tons of carbon dioxide per year (the main greenhouse gas), largely from burning fossil fuels.[52] Burning just one gallon of gasoline releases twenty pounds of carbon dioxide into the atmosphere.[53] Many elements make up the world's climate, but global warming does seem to be increasing. Storms are growing in frequency and force. The insurance industry is alarmed because this increase is overwhelming them with natural disaster claims. They have begun to work against the burning of fossil fuels.[54] Our economic activities seem to be having many unforeseen effects on the environment. A computer simulation of the Sahel in Africa showed that activities such as clearing forests reduce humidity, favorable winds, cloud formation, and rainfall.[55]

Fresh Water: Drinking Life   After air, water is the most important basic need. Like the earth with its oceans, our bodies largely consist of water, which keeps our systems running. In times past, outside cities, fresh clear water was abundant. Today, few people would dare to drink out of a stream in the wilderness. One-fifth of Americans are said to be drinking dangerous, dirty tap water.[56] Bottled water and home water purifier systems are becoming ever-more common. Worldwide, water wars are already in process, notably in the Middle East where oil flows. By 2025, two-thirds of the world could live in countries facing moderate or severe water stress.[57] California, the country's largest grower of produce, is a prime example. While we struggle with shortages, we still do not fully understand how water works in earth/air systems.

Earth Systems: Land's End   A nation's ultimate health—physical, economic, emotional, and spiritual—is said to depend on the health of its land. Ancient civilizations probably failed because they abused their land. We would like to believe that we could take the land under our feet for granted, but in the United States, we lose six billion acres of soil a year through erosion and by building roads and shopping malls, often on prime agricultural land.[58] Soil erosion has exceeded soil formation by 26 billion tons worldwide.[59] We are told that artificial fertilizers, pesticides, and their overuse are depleting soil fertility. Soil is the source of most of our food and fiber as well as countless other products necessary for life.

Forests: Earth's Lungs   Hardly anyone could be against forests, intriguing symbols of mystery and abundance. Yet worldwide we are losing 168 square kilometers of forests per year.[60] Deforestation takes more than 17 million hectares through clearing, burning, and cutting, an area about the size of

Arkansas.[61] As of 1993, 55 percent of the world's richest species habitat, the tropical forest, had already been destroyed.[62] In 1998, Central American forest fires filled cities in the United States with polluting smoke.[63]

Species: Our Companion Creatures   Most people are intrigued by a trip to an aquarium or a zoo. When no one is looking, many of us may find ourselves conversing with a brightly colored parrot, a cat, or a dog if one is in the vicinity. Like the earth under our feet, we take these companion creatures for granted, too. Species have always disappeared, as the dinosaurs tell us. But in the 68 million years prior to the industrial age, it took 10,000 years for 50,000 species to disappear.[64] Today, due to massive human causes, an estimated 50,000 plant and animal species are lost *each year.*[65] The numbers of bees are decreasing rapidly, a fact that may not move you until you realize that bees are a vital link in the food chain. The waters of the earth, especially oceans, also a symbol of mystery and abundance, are at risk. Sixty percent of fish stocks, once a low-cost food for millions, especially the poor, are being overfished or are depleted, while an estimated 100,000 fishers have been put out of work.[66] Pollution is found in the most distant parts of the oceans.

Food/Farming: The Most Basic of Needs   Air, water, then food make up the very necessities of life. Yet worldwide, some 65,000 human beings die from starvation every twenty-four hours.[67] Satellite observation and weather analysis by the World Agricultural Outlook Board assembled at the U.S. Department of Agriculture confirmed that the world's supply of essential grain is falling as the population of the world grows dramatically.[68] In many poor countries, the need for grain is greater than the land and water available to grow it.[69] We might think that famine is due solely to food shortages, but in reality, poverty, poor farming methods, bad weather, military buildups, war, inadequate transportation, politics, and ecological devastation are more likely the causes.

Americans consume very expensive food, shipped an average of 1,300 miles before it reaches them, processed and packaged, using great amounts of energy.[70] It may not be fresh; its vitality, nutrients, minerals, and vitamins are often reduced; frequently, it is treated with pesticides, covered with wax, and picked before it is ripe.[71] Some 20 percent of all the food produced in the United States each year is wasted or lost, enough to feed all the country's hungry people.[72]

Overall, unsustainable food systems can cause more harm than good. Once thought to be the answer to food shortages, factory farms that breed and feed livestock are accused of animal cruelty and massive pollution. Tropical biologist Christopher Uhl of Pennsylvania State University calculates that every hamburger imported to the United States requires the clearing of five square meters of jungle. A pound of U.S. feed-lot steak costs five pounds of grain, 2,500 gallons of water, and about thirty-five pounds of eroded topsoil.[73]

Health   It's often pointed out that no amount of money can buy good health, but access to help in a health crisis can go a long way toward that goal. In the United States, about 41.7 million people lack health coverage,[74] and many people do not take advantage of the abundant information available that would lead to improved health. The excellent U.S. health care systems are threatened by shrinking dollars. New diseases stalk us, transmitted through rapid global transportation.

Pollution   A pollution stew of pesticides, toxic and hazardous wastes, and just plain junk mix with air, water, soil, and the products of these in ways we do not understand.

Population: Planet People Increasing and Multiplying   As many species disappear, there seems to be no shortage of people on the planet, their numbers increasing dramatically every day. The world population has passed the five billion mark, with six billion on the horizon and possibly an increase anywhere from eight to eleven billion sometime after the mid-twenty-first century. While fertility rates are decreasing more than expected, population is still increasing faster than some believe we have resources to support it. People, especially the poor, are crowding into the world's cities, outpacing services and employment.[75]

**Years Needed for Human Population
to Reach Successive Billions[76]**

First billion = 2,000,000 years

Second billion = 105 years

Third billion = 30 years

Fourth billion = 15 years

Fifth billion = 12 years

Sixth billion = 11 years

Options Banish Gloom and Doom

By now, you may be having nightmares over the formidable challenges that face us, but there are many more reasons to be positive. We may feel helpless, but author and monk Brother David Steindl-Rast said, "We know enough." We know enough to bring health and beauty to the earth and its people. Designer Buckminster Fuller realized very early that we were the first generation to be aware that we are affecting the universe with our every act. He saw by the 1970s that we had the capability to produce and sustain, within ten years' time, a higher standard of living than ever imagined for all humanity, using fewer resources and already existing technologies.[77] We *do* know what to do.

As the technological revolution has taken root, our global consciousness, or awareness of the interconnectedness of life on this planet, has grown. Viewing the earth from space, astronaut Russell Schweickart said:

> It is so small and so fragile, such a precious little spot in the universe . . . you realize that everything that means anything to you—all of history and art and death and birth and love, tears and joys, all of it—is on that little blue and white spot out there, which you can cover with your thumb.[78]

The challenge, rather than getting discouraged or looking for another planet, is to catch the options that put us on the right side of change here and now.

The natural world, sometimes frightening, is intensely beautiful. There *is* a growing consciousness that we can tame science and technology for human need. We understand the necessity for pure air and water and for systems that do not pollute; for renewable energy; for healthy, vigorous soil and environmentally friendly food production; for biodegradable products and packaging; for hazardous waste cleanup; for shelter and clothing made of alternative and/or recycled materials. We already know many ways to use technology without causing undue harm to the planet.

The Office of Technology Assessment, the analytical arm of the U.S. Congress, as well as many government and private groups, has identified hundreds of earth-friendly options in every area of challenge, including those involving buildings, transportation, manufacturing, electricity generation, forestry, and food. Although these options are sometimes expensive in initial outlay, they require no major technological breakthroughs. Their long-run savings far outweigh the expense. For example, with technologies and methods available today, industry and agriculture could cut air and water pollution significantly. Farmers could cut water needs 10 percent to 50 percent, industries by 40 percent to 90 percent, and cities by 33 percent—with no sacrifice of economic output or quality of life.[79] We are learning to live in harmony with nature. One Alaska governor said, "You just can't let nature run wild."[80] Not everyone would agree!

As the old millennium fades away and as the new millennium winds up, some people are seeing a different kind of economy. Sharron Cordaro of *In Context,* says, "Hopefully, with the growing interest in voluntary simplicity, more people are choosing to ignore the commercial clamor of the media and are opting out of this lifestyle. They have discovered not only financial relief, but a sense of freedom, joy, and harmony with the earth, with others, and within themselves."[81] We can begin to see that we can live very well with less in a sustainable way. In the first century B.C., the Roman poet Horace said, "This was what I prayed for: a piece of land, not so very large where there would be a garden, and near the house a spring of ever-flowing water, and besides these a bit of woodland . . . more and better than this have the gods done for me. I am content."[82]

Sustainable Systems Defined

In the past, the systems that supplied basic necessities were sustainable—that is, they were largely self-renewing. For example, if we grow tomatoes, save the seeds, fertilize the soil with vegetable and other plant scraps and mulch the soil so that we use little water, and sometimes let the soil rest, we can continue growing tomatoes with little outside input for a very long time. Because fresh food is fragile, selling locally will minimize transportation and storage costs and will increase the sustainability of the process. Land in some parts of the world, such as China, has been farmed this way for many centuries. The Worldwatch Institute provides a yearly report on progress toward a sustainable society, and their research shows innumerable ways of charting a path to a sustainable future.

Robert Rodale of Rodale Press pioneered the concept of regenerating towns that have failing economies. By working with the forces of nature instead of trying to overcome them, restoring nature instead of destroying it, and avoiding centralization and monopolization, a regenerated community uses local renewable resources and energy sources so that they do not need to be transported from far away. Cleaner, healthier, prosperous networks of caring neighborhoods develop. The arts as well as businesses flourish. The local economy becomes both self-generating and self-improving; the worker base is kept intact, and people's health and welfare count more than monetary wealth as a measure of success.[83] Income is spent locally, energy is saved, health and the environment are enhanced, and people get involved with each other and have time to celebrate.

> The concerns for man and his destiny must always be
> the chief interest of all technical efforts.
> Never forget this among your diagrams and equations.
> —*Albert Einstein*[84]

If people indigenous to tropical rainforests are left to harvest the products of their lands and if they are encouraged by new markets, they *and* the forests can survive well in sustainable harmony. Harvesting quick-growing and sturdy parts of rain-forest cactus for twine and domesticating animals for food—thus saving the wild variety—are just two examples of viable businesses that can help save the natural environment.[85] People produce, market, and use jewelry, art, and furniture that does not exploit forests or wildlife. Rubber tapper Chico Mendes, who was murdered while working to preserve an area of rainforests in Brazil, said, "A rubber tree can live up to one hundred years if you tap it right, *affectionately*."[86]

Mining metals and other products to make cars, computers, plastic gadgets and toys, and then discarding them when they are too old to use—these are nonsustainable processes. Recycling, using sunlight for energy, using alternative transportation like bicycles and mass transit are a few examples of systems that come closer to being sustainable. There are many viable options to help create a healthy planet. Solutions will come, often slowly, drop by drop. For example, a project in Chile uses huge nets to catch enough "fog drops" to provide a nearby village of 450 people with twenty liters of water per day for each person.[87] A group of inventors and visionaries have created a sustainable community called Gaviotas in one of the most barren and difficult places in Colombia.[88]

How Do They Work?

Air and Water: Cleansing the Systems   Many industries as well as individuals are cleaning up and polluting less, recycling more, trying to create user friendly products. CO-OP America's *Green Pages* directory highlights these businesses. Some cities are saving valuable nutrients, using partially purified wastewater as fertilizer instead of chemical materials. John and Nancy Todd, founders of the Center for the Restoration of Waters at Ocean Arks International, use sewage-eating plants or bacteria they call "living machines" to bring sewage water back to pristine purity; it can then be used to produce food and fish as well as nonfood items.[89] David Packard, co-founder of Hewlett-Packard Company in Silicon Valley, has helped to fund the impressive Monterey Bay Aquarium and Research Center that aims to deepen our understanding of the sea and its creatures.

Swampy wetlands, now rightly seen as powerful water cleansers as well as rich wildlife habitats, are being protected and restored. Use of drip irrigation, delivering tiny amounts of water where it is needed, is increasing. Mulching and conditioning soil is recognized as lessening its need for water. Low-flow showers and toilets are mandated in some places to conserve water and the energy used in purifying and pumping it. "Composting" toilets that compost waste using little or no water are viable water and resource savers.

> *Big Buck$*
> *Keeping air and water clean*
> *puts money in the bank for all of us and creates new jobs.*

Trees Support Life   We are beginning to understand more clearly that trees refresh and cool the air as well as bring beauty to a landscape. Trees supply us with many resources such as building materials, food, and medicine. Beyond that, one tree will eventually remove twenty-six pounds of carbon dioxide from the air every year.[90] Urban trees also save Americans an estimated $4 billion a year in air conditioning expenses.[91]

Lislott Harberts, founder of Forest Care, teaches careful logging methods to loggers so they can create healthier and longer lasting forests.[92] Rogue Community College in Oregon has a "Jobs in the Woods" program to teach former loggers environmental restoration of the forests.[93] EcoTimber sells thousands of board feet of "certified" lumber—that is, lumber that has been logged in an environmentally sound and sustainable way.[94] Many jobs are opening up that bring people to better appreciation of natural and beautiful areas as they also work to preserve and restore them or lead groups on eco-vacations.

Big Bucks
Conserving trees
creates beauty, conserves water, energy, and soil,
provides economically sound resources—a money saver for all—
putting money in your pocket and creating new and interesting careers.

Food/Farming: Planting the Planet   New and old food systems are coming online. A giant food processor, seeing the demand for more natural food, calls people to make one of the nation's most productive agricultural areas totally organic. Rodale Research Institute in Pennsylvania, promoters of organic food production, have shown that crops grow better and are pest free in healthy soil using organic compost and natural fertilizers. Natural pest control is being used successfully to grow organic crops. The number of certified organic farms tripled between 1988 and 1990 and continues to grow across the country. Some companies are researching, developing, and selling organic pesticides. Here are some examples of these systems:

- Organically farmed since the 1940s, Walnut Acres in Pennsylvania grosses more than $5 million annually through local and catalog sales.[95]

- Dennis Tamura, a graduate of the Agricology Program at the University of California, Santa Cruz, grows and sells elegant produce throughout the San Francisco Bay Area on land called Blue Heron Farms "never touched by pesticides."

- Eliot Coleman finds that one-half to five acres is a highly productive scale for organic vegetable growing, using simple tools and no chemicals.[96]

- Rooftop gardens, driveway gardens, prosperous greenhouses in the ghetto, gardening without soil, gardening in hay bales, gardening in gravel, or even gardening in a bed of crushed soft drink cans—it's all been done successfully.

- At least 40 percent of Americans are gardeners,[97] supplying a great deal of their own food, saving energy and water, and lessening or eliminating pesticide use.

- Urban agriculture is a growing phenomenon and the best way to ensure fresh food with the least cost of resources; about 15 percent of food is grown in cities, according to the United Nations Development Program.[98]

- John Kuhn uses the biointensive method of Alan Chadwick and John Jeavons, gardening to provide at-home vegetable gardens for people too busy to do their own. His profits in 1996 were $62,000.[99]

- Farmers' markets are growing everywhere, many of them featuring organic produce.

- Gray Bears, a volunteer organization, gleans food left over in fields after harvesting to provide meals for poor elderly people.

- People reduce meat consumption when they realize that every 10 percent reduction in consumption of grain-fed livestock products frees up 64 million tons of grain for direct human consumption—and this diet is healthier.

- Farmer Bob Cannard grows gourmet, organic vegetables for upscale restaurants in Berkeley, California, and they in turn send back their food waste for compost on his farm, forming a circle of community.[100]

- Seeds of Change company founder Kenny Ausubel says, "It's taken the planet millions of years to slowly assemble and evolve its intricate cellular opera and there are still at least 50,000 known edible plants still left on earth. Yet only three of those—rice, corn, and wheat—account for half of everything we eat."[101] So Santa Cruz organic farmer, Mark Love, as well as others, grows heirloom/heritage seeds to preserve genetic diversity. Food specialists are discovering easily grown, nutritious food plants and developing alternative diets; health and environmentally conscious restaurants and supermarkets are increasing.

- Alida Stevens, founder/owner of Smith and Vandiver, manufactures personal care products using such natural substances as almond meal, apricots, honey, sea salt, sesame oil, and mint, and she prefers local, agricultural products. Her firm employs ninety people,[102] markets to 6,000 stores in fourteen countries, and recorded $8.5 million in sales in 1993.[103]

- In the United States, the Food Security Act encouraged farmers to cut excessive soil erosion by one-third in the five years from 1985 to 1990. Planting wind breaks, multicropping, using mulch, planting marginal land with grass or trees or letting it return to a native state, and contour plowing all reduce erosion.

Big Buck$
Eating a healthier diet
—especially home-grown—
is good for both people and planet, saves money,
and develops new careers.

Preserving Planet People   We are appalled when we hear of population control methods that use force to make people limit their families. Population control is a contentious issue as it touches on people's deepest religious, social, and personal values. Yet statistics show that one of the best means of cutting population is educating women. There is "no social indicator that correlates more closely with the shift to smaller families than the level of female education," and this holds across all cultures.[104] Educated women marry later; often involved in careers, they opt to have fewer children. It helps also to educate men to realize that they are still worthwhile even though they may have fewer children. People can be taught systems of birth control that fit even the strictest ideologies. It's possible that the world of 2030 could have a population of eight billion people that's heading downward to a number the earth can support comfortably.[105]

Looking simply at the population's well-being, the United States has some of the best and most abundant food sources in the world and some of the healthiest living/working spaces. We are aware of the need to exercise, avoid drugs and alcohol, and eat a healthy diet. We have the latest technology and pharmaceuticals, and research facilities seeking to combat new diseases that arise. People are questioning their doctors, asking for second opinions, and spending billions on alternative health care like relaxation techniques, herbal medicine, chiropractic, acupuncture, and homeopathy—more than they spend on primary care physicians.[106] Health food stores have become upscale markets with upscale profits as the food industry races to keep up with people's desire for good, toxin-free food.

People consult with businesses to develop cost-containing health plans; others are becoming ombudspersons and inspectors to ensure proper care for patients in health care institutions; still others are opening health care centers. Fitness spas and recreational sports centers flourish. In-home health care grows, a comfortable, viable, money-saving alternative to hospitals. People are taking more and more advantage of education, including lifelong learning, to create a sense of well-being as well as career enhancement.

Safety/Security Although there still seem to be threats around us, we also have many hopeful signs that safety and security are increasing. New methods of law enforcement, firefighting, and military strategy are being developed constantly to protect our lives and property. Community policing cuts crime and strengthens neighborhoods. The protection of civil rights and human rights spreads slowly across the globe with focus on reducing child and spousal abuse and prosecuting war crimes and other violent practices against humanity. Arms control stays on the world agenda, making progress slowly. Note that Jodi Williams, coordinator of the International Campaign to Ban Landmines won the Nobel Peace Prize in 1997.

> How much more delightful to an undebauched mind
> is the task of making improvements on the earth,
> than all the vain glory which can be acquired from ravaging it.
> —*George Washington, shortly after the Revolutionary War*[107]

Mediation, anticipating conflicts before they happen, is being taught in schools and has been used successfully to avoid armed conflict; observers often see ways that many wars could have been avoided. Jim Wallis, the editor of *Sojourners,* urges us to foster a "culture of nonviolence." We hear voices raised asking us to redefine national security as a state when people's basic needs and enriching wants are sufficient. Michael Clossen has worked for years to facilitate "economic conversion," the smooth transition from weapons production to a full-employment peace economy[108]—for example, rotor blade engineers in the attack helicopter industry now make rotor blades for electricity-generating wind farms.[109]

Big Buck$
Staying healthy, getting a good education, and resolving conflicts peacefully are all cost-effective and human-effective systems as well as a way for individuals and nations to get a raise in salary! Vibrant and new careers result, too.

Cooling the Planet: Energy Savings   Concerned over global warming, energy giants British Petroleum and Royal Dutch Shell are cutting back emissions at their plants and increasing their investments in solar energy.[110] This transition in transportation, heating, and electricity is moving forward, although slowly.

About 8 percent of the energy used in this country in 1992 came from renewable energy sources.[111] The stores of renewable and safe energy resources in the United States and globally are enormous. Here are some specifics.

The sun shines everywhere, in some places over long periods of time. Researchers at the U.S. Department of Energy estimate that if PV (photovoltaic) panels—panels that produce electricity from light—were mounted atop 5,000 square kilometers of roof space, they could generate 25 percent of the electricity used in the United States.[112] Globally, sunlight on rooftop solar panels/collectors could supply much needed electricity and heat for residential and business buildings. Homes in the coldest parts of the country can be heated by the sun and kept within five degrees plus or minus of 70 degrees all year long without a furnace or woodstove.[113] Such simple technologies as super insulation and thermal-pane windows and draperies can save energy. Straw-bale or rammed earth homes can both heat shelters and keep them cool.[114] Deciduous shade trees can cool shelters considerably in the summer. Construction oriented to the sun, thermal mass heat collectors such as stone floors and walls, containers of water (either glass or black-coated) as well as attached greenhouses (which can also provide food) keep or release heat into shelters. Solar power can run water pumps and other small machines. Solar water heaters provide hot water. Solar ovens as well as more efficient stoves are usable, especially in developing countries, for cooking, heating and purifying water.[115]

The sun produces the temperature differential that creates wind. California has 17,000 wind turbines in place, and the state gets a sizable amount of its electricity from renewable energy. Wind power has been the fastest growing energy market in the 1990s.[116] In 1993, the school district in Spirit Lake, Iowa, powered its schools with a wind turbine that now generates about $25,000 of electrical energy annually.[117]

Plants also grow by sun power. Biomass—vegetable and animal by-products such as manure, corn husks, bagasse from sugar cane, and other decaying biological materials—is being converted into clean-burning fuels such as methane and alcohol.

Heat generated from copiers and other machinery and even bodies is being recycled/used in commercial buildings! Cogeneration recycles heat from industrial processes to heat homes, offices, and other industrial sites instead of letting it escape.

Big Buck$
Living in a home that uses little energy
and few resources is equivalent to another salary raise
—and creates jobs, too!

Transportation New developments have multiplied the speed and ease of movement in this past century. Now, automakers are speeding into a new market with "hybrid cars" that can run alternately on electricity or gasoline. They have developed electric cars with motors four and five times as efficient as internal combustion engines with lower battery weight, shorter recharging time, and longer drive range.[118] Cars have been run successfully with both hydrogen fuel cells and solar cells with no pollution.

If U.S. cars had an average gas mileage of forty miles to the gallon, that would save 2.8 million barrels of oil a day by 2005, even with several million more vehicles on the road. This saving represents about ten times the amount of oil produced in the fragile Arctic National Wildlife Refuge and almost four times the oil imported from Iraq and Kuwait prior to the Gulf War.[119] Add conservation by using mass transit, van pools, car pooling, and many energy conserving devices and systems, and the results can be impressive.

Bicycles are used mostly for utilitarian purposes by many of the world's people and are the principal means of transport other than walking.[120] Some cities have developed safe bike lanes and encourage the use of bikes to haul and deliver goods.[121] Many more bicycles are produced worldwide than cars each year, and their production is increasing.[122] For some people in developing countries, having a bike is a giant step up to an easier and profitable lifestyle.

Efficient, comfortable, affordable, flexible mass transit is being developed with community input. Municipalities explore clean, comfortable, efficient rail service: per passenger mile, trains use one-third the energy of an airplane and one-sixth that of a driver-only auto and cost as little as 10 percent of the price of freeway construction.[123] A two-track right of way for a rail system can carry as much traffic as sixteen lanes of highway.

We might look down on the use of draft animals, but some communities in the United States employ them—for example, the Amish settlements—and worldwide they are a huge energy saver. They can navigate tough terrain and provide fertilizer for crops or heating, saving fossil fuel.[124]

Telecommuting is becoming ever-more popular and can be a great energy, resource, and time saver.

Big Buck$
The average adult spends as much as 18 percent of income on a car—
more if a child's car is included. That's over two months of work
a year that a person could be on vacation.[125]
Saving money on transportation costs is money in the bank!
There are many energy-conserving careers in transportation.

Conservation   Amory and L. Hunter Lovins of the Rocky Mountain Institute have told U.S. officials, "America's energy bill could shed $300 billion a year using conservation with existing technologies rather than building and maintaining traditional energy systems, that are profitable at today's prices." This can be done with no sacrifice in our present lifestyle or standard of living. [126]

If all U.S. households replaced their regular bulbs with fluorescent bulbs, we would save $30 billion a year, use 20 percent to 25 percent less electricity, and shut down 120 thousand-megawatt nuclear power plants.

Energy can be saved in innumerable ways from large to small. One family practices energy efficiency and has a utility bill at least 75 percent lower than those of its neighbors with little or no sacrifice of comfort. They turn off lights, TVs, and other appliances when not in use. They use heat only when and where necessary; their lights are compact fluorescent; they use a solar clothes dryer, otherwise known as a clothes line.

Big Buck$
And for the individual,
saving energy and other resources
is like getting a raise in salary![127]
Careers in energy alternatives are growing, too.

Shelter/Community   From cabins to condos, people have managed to create a wondrous array of shelters. Whether it's a home or a workplace, the best structure is a beautiful one that gives its inhabitants a sense of belonging and a sense of safety, at reasonable cost in a human-scale community. Bob Berkebile, a principal in one of Kansas City's leading architectural firms, says that "we are waking up to the fact that our buildings and our communities are part of nature rather than an environment apart."[128] Oberlin College has recently developed a sustainable environmental studies building that aims to show just that and to educate by its very design. It incorporates state-of-the-art technologies in water, energy, and resource use.[129] The savings will be considerable.

Former mayor of Davis, California, Michael Corbett not only wrote about a new "village" concept but he also developed one at Village Homes.[130] More such villages, even within cities, are on the drawing boards, creating, as Sarah van Gelder calls them, cities of exuberance.[131] In these communities, trees and gardens flourish. Rainwater can be preserved in cisterns and also moves naturally along streambeds to nourish the groundwater. The automobile is deemphasized; walking and biking are encouraged. Shops and other workplaces are nearby. Community is strengthened.

Many abandoned inner cities are finding new life. Old, well-built housing stock is being remodeled for energy efficiency. Transportation and cultural, social, and educational amenities are being developed in convenient locations. Locally owned and operated stores flourish as do their support staff and suppliers. This generally ensures that money is recycled over and over right in town, not hundreds of miles away. Urban gardens can be used to provide organic food, save energy, and strengthen community. When urban development takes place, outlying open space and farmland are preserved. Wherever a sense of community develops, crime and pollution are lessened.

Another innovative approach to living is called co-housing, which saves resources by blending private space with shared facilities. Some groups including municipalities are using community land trusts to keep land costs from escalating; here, the land is not sold but only rented for a small yearly fee.

Big Buck$
Affordable shelter built on affordable land
also adds money to your bank account.
People are developing many new careers in the design,
construction, and maintenance of sustainable shelters.

Recycling: A Sustainable Option   At the time of the first Earthday in April of 1970, did *anyone* know *anyone* who recycled? At that time someone posed the question, "What if you had to keep all your discards on your own property?" It brought the problem home at once: there *is* no "away." In a giant burst of higher consciousness, mainstream Americans began to recycle.

Now local governments are setting up curbside pickup to recycle cans, bottles, newspapers, and cardboard. Companies are springing up to make treasures out of trash, others to find use for and market these treasures. In Naperville, Illinois, a company turns plastic milk bottles into building and fencing material that looks like wood and can be sawed and nailed. Plastic bottles turn into warm sweaters, jackets, and blankets. Recycled asphalt as well as the millions of discarded tires and even old ceramic toilets are ground up and mixed with new asphalt to become an excellent road surface. German automakers are required to take back discarded autos and reuse or recycle the parts.[132] Composting is becoming mainstream as municipalities look for ways to reduce material going into their landfills. The new motto is reduce and reuse while recycling what is left.

Sweden has inaugurated a comprehensive plan for a sustainable economy called "The Natural Step," involving everyone from the king to school children. From manufacturers to innkeepers, everyone is looking for nonpolluting, energy-efficient materials and systems.[133]

Big Buck$
Reusing, conserving, and recycling save money
for people and the planet.
There are many new jobs developing in the recycling industry.

Hope on the Economic Horizon: Business As Unusual

Howell Hurst, principal of Strategic Asset Management in San Francisco, says, "We face a multitude of social problems that cry out for creative business solutions. . . . *I am interested in new businesses built on innovative concepts that contribute to the improvement of our society.*"[134]

Former Secretary of Labor Robert B. Reich urges a "new social contract between business, government, and citizens" that will help people survive global competition.[135] And *Business Week* says that "there are only two kinds of organizations: those that have embraced the global standards process, such as that found in the corporate environmental code CERES Principles, and those that will."[136]

Companies are marketing environmentally safe products, using recyclables, developing biodegradable packaging in ever-greater numbers, and creating jobs in the process. By their ecological concern, such publications as *World Watch* make us aware of the effects of business and personal activities on the planet. CO-OP America lists "Green Businesses" that support the environment by their work.[137]

Microlending: An Idea Whose Time Has Come

Economist Muhammad Yunus developed the concept of microlending to provide money for people without credit in one of the poorest countries on earth: Bangladesh. This Grameen (or Village) Bank in 1997 had close to 36,000 branches lending to two million borrowers, of whom 94 percent are women;

the bank has made over $2 billion in loans over twenty years. It's ret
repayment is 98 percent![138]

> The poor need capital, not charity;
> a hand up, not a handout.
> —*Millard Fuller*
> *Founder of Habitat for Humanity*

Microlending peer groups meet now from ghetto basements in Chicago
to tiny shacks in Bolivia to make loan decisions, apply peer pressure for
repayments, and support their members.[139] Since 1973, the staff of South
Shore Bank in a ghetto area of Chicago has successfully financed over 8,000
multifamily units with small loans, placed 3,500 individuals in jobs through
its employment-training programs, and assisted over 156 new firms.[140] Their
nonprofit housing corporation has assisted residents in rehabilitating a 265-
square-block ghetto area, helping many to become homeowners. It is more
effective for business to support poor entrepreneurs in the inner cities than for
government to supply them with endless public subsidies.[141]

As of 1997, small lending institutions plan to reach 100 million of the
world's poorest families with microcredit and financial advice by the year
2005. They do this by leveraging money loaned by affluent people through
large banks. A ten thousand dollar loan in the mysterious world of international finance can end up providing $87,000 in loans in one year. Purchase of
a sewing machine, a dozen chickens, equipment for a fish pond, a corn
grinder, material to bake small amounts of bread, or hair clippers may mean
the difference between a life of grinding poverty and one in which families
prosper and children can be fed, clothed, educated, and given health care.

These economic institutions range from successful cooperative businesses
of Mondragon in the poor Basque section of Spain to the Women's World
Bank,[142] to Trickle Up (TUP) for low-income people worldwide,[143] to the nonprofit Institute for Community Economics in Springfield, Massachusetts, to
the Heifer Project of Arkansas, which provides food-supplying animals to
poor people. Acción International says that the process of microlending is "an
essential element within viable development programs";[144] U.S. banks, the
World Bank, and US AID agree and are joining them.

> *Big Buck$*
> *When money is available to*
> *small entrepreneurs at reasonable cost,*
> *the economy flourishes*
> *and more people have money in the bank.*
> *There are many new careers in the socially*
> *responsible money world.*

The Real Economy

The old axiom says that money makes the world go 'round and it *is* certainly a giant motivator, but money pays for less than half of all the work that is done in society. The money part of the economy includes the private sector, which rests on and depends on the tax-generated money of the public sector. It is surprising, however, to find that over half our production, consumption, and investment consists of unpaid activities such as volunteering, community work, family gardening, and child and elder care.

Fifty-one percent of Americans volunteer an average of 4.2 hours per week, a contribution equivalent to 9 million full-time employees and $176 billion. There are more than 1,400,000 nonprofit organizations in the United States, *many of whom do have paid staff.*[145]

This third sector encompasses all types of work; it is that group of activities that enhances the life of the community and is independent of the marketplace and the public sector. Habitat for Humanity is one such example. It is a worldwide organization that builds homes for people too poor to afford a conventional loan. Habitat keeps the house affordable by seeking donated land and materials and using volunteer labor where possible. The organization charges no interest and makes no profit. A family makes a "down payment" of as much as 500 hours of sweat equity by working on the building, then pays back such costs as building materials, permits, and fees. Everyone wins. As of 1998, Habitat had built over 70,000 homes worldwide.

Futurist Hazel Henderson says this "layer cake" of private, public, and nonmonetized sectors rests and depends on Mother Nature for all its resources.[146] The economy cannot function without the environment.

Putting it all together, the White Earth Land Recovery Project in western Minnesota reclaims land that belonged to the Anishinabeg Native American reservation. The tribe's cultural and economic development now includes production of various food products, medicinal plants, and baskets. Project participants are pursuing a sustainable agricultural program, researching a wind-power project, partnering with a local financial institution in a micro-lending program, starting a reservation radio station, and developing jobs and a healthy community.[147]

Although there are many things that money cannot buy—true friendship and love, good health, a sunrise on a spring day—a basic money supply is generally essential. More and more people are using their time, energy, and talents to find careers in business or industry that promote a vital local community. Some people feel that if everyone played fair on the world economic field, everyone would win. Founder of the Institute for Community Economics, Chuck Matthei, writes:

> There is nothing more personal than economics. It is, fundamentally, a moral and spiritual field, in a sense, the outward manifestation of our spiritual relationship, our moral and social relationships with one another.

If we look at how we respond to others economically, we will also find out, despite our illusions and pretensions, how we really do regard one another.[148]

The Ethical Perspective: Time for a Change

Both our economic and our environmental decisions have moral and ethical implications. We have access to enormous amounts of information, the best education and health care, excellent food, and stores full of wonderful gadgets; yet we must ask, Are we wiser and better people for all this—that is, are we ethical? We are all confronted daily with ethical dilemmas. Here are a few:

- To cheat or not on assignments or taxes
- To use others' property without permission or to ask first
- To lie or not when in a tight spot
- To treat others with respect or to treat them poorly

Workplaces are also presented with ethical decisions daily. One ad urges its customers to "Play Smart, Not Fair."[149] In the next chapter, we discuss the qualities of socially responsible or ethical businesses. Needless to say, with the help of the media, the corruption of people in high and low places is brought to our attention daily. At an international conference, "The Future of Intellectual Property Protection for Biotechnology," an eminent speaker said he hoped others would not have to face "environmentalists and those who would bring ethics and other irrational considerations to the table."[150] But most people think that ethics is a very rational subject and that the Golden Rule is still a good one: "Do unto others as you would have them do unto you," or its variant, "Bring no harm to anyone." But in a complex society, the lines become blurred when people can use loopholes in laws to do what really does harm, and large institutions make decisions far from the places where the decisions will be implemented. People can say, "That's business!" But the question is this: Is what is legal, profitable, and seemingly efficient always ethical? Must business be cruel, as business-management guru Peter Drucker says it sometimes is?

Lending institutions, the guardians of our money supply, were a startling example of poor ethical decisions in the 1970s and 1980s. They overextended themselves on loans, especially to foreign governments, and helped to mastermind financially shaky buyouts. In some cases, downright fraud resulted in closures, loss of people's investments, government intervention, legal prosecution, and people suffering from their government's misuse of loaned funds. Heads of corporations have gone to prison for disregarding public safety, and high government officials have joined them for fraud and dishonesty.

We have seen the enemy and he is us.

—Pogo

Being Good: Ethics for a New Age

> Work is the way that we tend the world,
> the way people connect.
> It is the most vigorous, vivid sign of life—
> in individuals and civilization.
> —*Lance Morrow*

In the long run, those who gain the respect and trust of others, who are most admired, are those who have lived ethically. We make many ethical choices within the borders of our own jobs and lives, and those decisions, that often seem so small and hidden, will have an impact on ourselves and on everyone whose lives we touch. In fact, they will touch many whom we will never see.

People are finding that ethics is good business. Some industries are hiring ethics consultants. Business schools are reinstating ethics courses. There is a growing awareness that choices have consequences, whether they are made by private individuals or by people acting as businesses. Actions that people think are hidden become front page news.

Many people are longing to deal with businesses where they *know* people and feel both trusting and trusted. In rural areas, a family will sometimes leave a table with bags of fruit out by the road with a sign giving the cost and a can for buyers to drop the money in. The amounts usually tally at the end of the day! Such entrepreneurs will order items for you, trust you to pay later, and often donate to your special causes. They are friends and neighbors as well as businesspeople.

Being socially responsible, however, doesn't mean being stupid. To use good social practices does not make businesses competition proof. Business practice must be both wise and prudent. There is no question that economics meets ethics and the environment at the factory gate and the office door.

> The opposite of social responsibility
> is social irresponsibility.

Global Consciousness: Thinking the Unthinkable, Doing the Undoable

People need time to get used to new ideas. A first reaction is often to ridicule them as unworkable. An old Chinese proverb tells us,

> Person who says it cannot be done,
> should not interrupt person doing it!

Albert Einstein wrote, "The unleashed power of the atom has changed everything except our way of thinking." And never underestimate how difficult it is for people to change the way they think. Even the "experts," positive they are right, are sometimes wrong.

- In 1865, an editorial in the *Boston Post* assured its readers that "it is impossible to transmit the voice over wires and that were it possible to do so, the thing would be of no practical value."
- Early in the 1900s, Simon Newcomb said, "No possible combination of known substances, known forms of machinery and known forms of force can be united in a practical machine by which men shall fly long distances through the air."
- Dr. Richard van der Riet Wolley, British Astronomer Royal, stated in 1956: "Space travel is utter bilge!"[151]
- Then President Grover Cleveland said in 1905, "Sensible and responsible women do not want to vote."
- Harry M. Warner of Warner Bros. Pictures said of proposed movies with sound in 1927, "Who the hell wants to hear actors talk?"[152]

We tend to resist strongly those people who give us unpleasant messages about changing our attitudes and our ways. We say they do not understand the environment or the economic systems or ethics in the real world. But such visionaries are often proven correct in the long run. People predicted all sorts of dire results to the economy if the slaves were freed or women could vote and own property and businesses. Since those events have happened, the United States has become an economic giant! The alternative: Aldo Leopold says, "We strive for safety, prosperity, comfort, long life—and dullness!"[153]

> The fact that everyone
> doesn't want to believe something
> doesn't mean it's not true.
> —*Arlene Goetz*[154]

People Power

Sometimes it takes years for new concepts to become trends, and the path is seldom a straight line. Someone estimated that it takes about 15 percent of the population, which they call a critical mass, to act on something for it to become mainstream. It seems that many people feel that the work they do has little meaning in the larger scheme of things, and they are looking for more meaningful alternatives to business as usual. Someone wrote humorously that Americans spend $30 billion a year to keep their approximately 50,000 square miles of lawn from doing what lawns would do if left untended.[155]

But people *are* "voting" at the checkstand of the global marketplace, choosing socially responsible products. They seem ready to challenge companies that do not follow ethical principles in the economic and environmental areas. They are putting money in this direction. Socially responsible investing topped $1 trillion in 1997 in the United States and is growing fast.[156]

After 33,455 letters and calls prompted by Working Assets Long Distance phone service, one maker of athletic shoes agreed to pay its Asian factory workers a living wage and institute a comprehensive third-party monitoring system to interview workers and assess working conditions.[157] Pepsico withdrew its marketing from Burma because of that country's brutal dictatorship. Apartheid fell in South Africa largely because of consumer pressure for companies to withdraw their investments and operations there.

It seemed that overnight people came to realize the harm being done by tobacco, not only to the health of individuals, especially young people, but also to the economy that had to pay the huge health care costs of smoking. A once-invincible industry showed itself vulnerable to the public's growing awareness.

Oscar Arias, former president of Costa Rica and winner of the 1987 Nobel Peace Prize, says that since Costa Rica abolished its army in 1948, it has achieved a level of human development that is the envy of Latin America. In his acceptance speech for the Global Citizen Award, he suggests the unthinkable: that nations disarm and use the funds they save to address human needs.[158] Other unthinkable ideas have become reality:

- People *are* conserving water.
- Meat consumption has shown a 14 percent reduction, down from seventy-nine pounds per person per year in 1986 to sixty-eight pounds four years later.[159]
- Recycling has become a mainstream activity.
- Organic produce is being sold in supermarkets, and people's demand that the definition of organic not be diluted was accepted.[160]
- Two-thirds of Americans consider themselves actively pro-environment, whereas only 4 percent were found to be "unsympathetic to environmental concerns."[161]
- More "green" buildings (energy saving) are appearing.
- Insurance companies are encouraging alternative health options as well as energy-saving strategies.
- Military spending has fallen worldwide.
- Nuclear stockpiles have dropped considerably.
- Production of ozone-depleting chemicals has fallen.
- Energy-conserving power use is up significantly; cigarette smoking is down.[162]

- In a period of six months, four historic agreements were signed by world governments: the Law of the Sea, the Biodiversity Convention, the Climate Convention, and the Ban on Hazardous Waste Exports.[163]

- A group of wealthy people called "Responsible Wealth" urges the government to change tax laws that favor the wealthy at the expense of the poor. They suggest donating the money saved in taxes to a worthy cause or returning it to the government.[164]

- Billionaire Ted Turner gave a billion dollars to the UN for poverty programs, and others are joining him.

- The percentage of Americans who agree with the statement, "Most of us buy and consume far more than we need" is 82 percent. The percentage of Americans who say they have downshifted or voluntarily cut back on their income in some way over the last five years is 28 percent.[165]

- The *Tightwad Gazette,* a newsletter that has helped people live frugally and sustainably, was launched from a kitchen table in 1990 at $12 per year for a monthly copy. In twenty months subscriptions rose to 50,000![166]

- Journals and books promoting a simpler, less consuming lifestyle are flourishing—for example, *Yes, a Journal of Positive Futures* and *The New Road Map Foundation Newsletter.*

- An international campaign called Jubilee 2000 is calling for forgiveness of the debt held by Third World countries, especially in Africa.[167]

- A third of mainstream medical schools are teaching meditation and other alternative forms of healing.[168]

And absolutely unthinkable is this idea: it is quite possible that a small percentage of the world's population could work—or that everyone could work a small percentage of the time—and satisfy all needs and wants for everyone, with a modest expenditure of resources, energy, and burden on the planet. Or is it?

In our rush to the future, we sometimes lose our way and forget why we do what we do and where we are headed. An American businessman and aged multibillionaire continued to clear-cut enormous amounts of Brazilian rainforest to amass yet more profits. His manager agreed that they didn't waste time with research. He said, "Naturally we make a lot of mistakes, but we also get things done a lot faster."[169] Acquiring profit and the power and prestige that come with money becomes the main goal and—besides the environmental devastation—the enrichment that life can bring is lost. Many people find that a time-out can put them back on track.

> Never doubt that a small group of
> thoughtful committed citizens can change the world;
> indeed, it's the only thing that ever has.
> —*Margaret Mead*

Jobs Lost and Gained

One argument often presented to avoid different ways of doing things is that certain changes will take away jobs. There are, however, many arguments to refute this—like the following:

- Recycling produces more jobs per ton of solid waste than either landfills or incinerators.[170]

- Public transit and light rail investments produce 50 percent more jobs per dollar spent than new highway construction.[171]

- Increasing the recycling rate of aluminum to 75 percent would create 350,000 new jobs.[172]

- Some two million Americans in over 65,000 companies earn their living doing some kind of environmental clean-up work.[173]

- Urban Ore, a recycling company in Berkeley, California, contributes over $300,000 to the local tax base each year by salvaging, cleaning, repairing, and reselling items from the municipal waste.[174]

- Weapons industries create far fewer jobs than would the same amount of investment in other areas.[175] The U.S. Bureau of Labor Statistics says that an expenditure of $1 billion could create 76,000 jobs in the military versus 92,000 jobs in transport, 100,000 jobs in construction, 139,000 jobs in health, or 187,000 jobs in education.[176]

- In the area of energy, "Creating a less carbib-intensive energy system would create hundreds of billions of dollars of business, and millions of jobs—most of them in making and installing devices that cleanly and efficiently turn renewable resources into useful forms of energy."[177]

- "The Wisconsin Energy Bureau found that the use of renewable energy generates about three times more jobs, earnings, and sales than does the same level of imported fossil fuels. A 75 percent increase in the use of renewable energy would result in more than 62,000 jobs, $1.2 billion in new wages, and $4.6 billion in new sales for Wisconsin businesses."[178]

- Some years ago, James Benson of the Council of Economic Priorities estimated that in the Nassau-Suffolk area of Long Island, New York, a low-cost energy package aimed at installing insulation, storm windows, and solar hot water systems could provide 270 percent more employment and 206 percent more energy over a thirty-year period than would the same amount of money spent to construct and maintain nuclear power plants.[179]

- The Organization for Economic Cooperation and Development estimates that the worldwide market for environmental goods and services in 1990 was some $200 billion, projected to grow 50 percent by the year 2000, making environment-related businesses one of the world's fastest-growing sectors.

- Former CIA director William Colby said, "We can cut military spending by 50 percent and meet our national security needs."[180]

According to the United Nations Center for Disarmament, in the early 1980s:

> The money required to provide adequate food, water, education, health and housing for everyone in the world has been estimated at about $18.5 billion a year. It is a huge sum of money . . . about as much as the world spends on arms every two weeks.[181] The U.S. share would be $2 billion per year—we spend that amount on beer *each month!*[182]

Now those are really Big Buck$.

David Korten, conservative Stanford Business School Ph.D., military officer, professor at Harvard's School of Business, senior adviser for the U.S. Agency for International Development and other international organizations, wrote *When Corporations Rule the World* when he realized some of the harmful practices of corporations. He suggests barring companies from all forms of political activity; eliminating subsidies for big business; a guaranteed income for workers; and a twenty-hour workweek. He feels that our focus on money and material goods is a "quest to fill a void in our lives created by a lack of love . . . a loss of our sense of spiritual connection as the foundation of our culture values and relationships."[183] He is saying the unsayable.

Job Market Outlook and Opportunities: Realities and Balance

How do you fit yourself and your values into a world crowded with challenges and overflowing with options and opportunities? The best way is to be true to yourself, know your strengths, accept your limits, and find those challenges, options, and opportunities that "charge you up." You no doubt want a better world. The difficult part is to avoid being a part of systems that will make it worse, to avoid staying with old, worn-out options, but to be open to change. Then make choices that will connect you with others like yourself who are likely to hire you, or do business with you, or start a business with you. Your wise choices will definitely put you on the side of positive and hopeful change. Your good example will inspire others. You can choose to be an artist or a zoologist and do it responsibly and creatively.

Despite images of the general affluence of this country, a major concern for most people is to make enough money to live on at any job they can live with. But ethical, satisfying work does not have to be a luxury for the lucky few, though finding work that fits their values may take extra time and persistence! Luis Samoyoa, executive director of Habitat for Humanity, Guatemala, tells of his struggle between accepting a less-well-paying job with Habitat and a very lucrative one that would involve a great deal of time away from

"I had the dream about meaningful employment again last night."

home. At a family meeting his younger son opted for the job that would buy more toys while his eight-year-old son said, "I want you, Daddy." His wife concurred.

Ask yourself: Which of the challenges discussed in this chapter captures your attention, your energy, your concern? Which options seem to speak to your personality type, to your values? Remember, the content of work remains basically the same whether you are helping to create more problems for the world or finding solutions. You can produce, manage, repair, compute, sell, cure, or create in almost any type of workplace.

No matter what your career is, you will be working in an economy that affects the environment and is guided by ethics. The challenges are formidable, but the options are exciting. We need to see ourselves as dynamic pioneers, looking beyond ourselves, and moving into a new century. A father used to tell his children, "The person who is all wrapped up in himself is overdressed."

We have a choice. Yes, the problems are considerable and people often act without concern for the common good. People seem to be losing confidence in established institutions. But there are also many people working for the common good and creating hopeful, positive alternatives, relying on their innate sense of what is right to do what is right. They are thinking the unthinkable, doing the undoable.

Personality Types in the Job Market

Realistic Type

Realistic personalities provide food, clothing, shelter, transportation, repair, and maintenance—jobs that are basic, necessary, and highly visible. They are also at home in the world of physical performance. Careers in sports, of course, are extremely competitive and limited to the most talented. Increased automation and cheap imports have cut employment for many realistic jobs. Large-scale farming, fishing, and forestry now use more technology and fewer people. Mining has decreased because of resource depletion, cheaper imports, and use of alternative materials. The employment outlook in specialized areas is good, however, especially for workers who are service oriented or do highly skilled and specialized work.

You might consider indoor or outdoor jobs in industry or with public utility companies. Vocational training, on-the-job training, or an apprenticeship in a construction union is sometimes necessary. With increased emphasis on protecting against crime—providing security to companies, their computers, and individuals is a growing possibility. Government cutbacks have limited the number of outdoor jobs available to people who like to work with nature, but ecological awareness is helping to slow that trend and even create such jobs in the industrial area. Realistic people are valuable because they can handle the practical needs of any workplace. Further training can be a plus.

Investigative Type

Most investigative jobs, except for some technical areas, require at least a four-year college degree. Many jobs in the sciences are not "productive" because they deal with "pure research," so funding is limited even though research is necessary for future development. The growth of the information society is tailor-made for the person who is investigative: new kinds of artificial intelligence and new ways of putting information together are there to challenge the mind person. Vast amounts of data that formerly took years to work with can now be crunched in seconds. Computers can tell marketers the likes, dislikes, and activities of just about anyone. Engineers and medical researchers who research practical problems find jobs more available and are generally well paid because their work earns company profits. Because few women and minorities go into math and science, those who do should find jobs readily available in more gender- and race-neutral workplaces.

With its electronic network, the information world provides service jobs for multimedia content developers, services marketers, and all sorts of computer specialists, systems analysts, and software programmers. In general, the investigative job outlook (except for scientific research) is good. Investigative types who are not scientifically or technologically oriented can apply their investigative talents to other areas. Many work settings can profit from the research and analytical skills of the investigative person.

Artistic Type

Most jobs for the artistic type require special talent along with special training. They tend to be highly competitive, so the artistic persons should plan alternatives. Although the work of the artistic individual enriches everyone, Americans generally do not place high value on fine arts and artists in their lives.

New developments in electronic media will provide increasing opportunities for some creative people. Packaging information using computerized layouts can be a rewarding outlet for the creative person. Technical writing would fit the scientifically minded creative person, and that area is growing. Decision makers in many businesses and industries are slowly realizing that workers on the front line often have better ideas about how to do their jobs than the people in the front offices. Creativity is useful in just about every career and workplace.

Social Type

Social personality careers involve caring for people. There is great need here, especially in social service jobs, often in government; but these most often are still underfunded and thus scarce. Workers in some settings are drained by responsibilities for large numbers of clients, many of whom have serious and chronic problems. With little support, few resources, and yards of red tape, a worker needs strong motivation to succeed. People with good business sense and enough funding sometimes start private practices or community organizations. Because our society is committed to building many more prisons, prison work is a growing field.

The health care industry is experiencing significant restructuring, with certain careers showing promise. Fewer people are using hospitals, as out-patient care offers a cheaper and often more desirable alternative, and healthier lifestyles are becoming mainstream. Medical practice has achieved dramatic breakthroughs such as imaging techniques, transplants, and genetic discoveries. Although there are periodic shortages of workers, admission to training programs is often limited. With the growing population of the elderly, geriatric care managers and physical therapists should be able to find a well-paying niche. Although they are not paid well, home health aides, medical assistants, and child care workers will be in demand.

Employee assistance programs are growing as industry sees the need to help its workers with personal problems, and human resources managers guide employees through the maze of personnel demands. The desire to share some of their profits with nonprofit organizations has prompted some companies to hire "planned-giving officers" who review proposals from the community and fund those that meet certain criteria. Teachers such as those in special education are on almost every state's critical shortage list. People with social concerns find that their special talents can be used in a variety of settings, however, because all employers hire people and need to solve employee and customer problems.

Enterprising Type

Enterprising personalities have the inner drive to connect with the people and events that help them get involved, though they do not always see that in themselves. And there is always a need to organize and sell goods and services in the world of things and data. Marketing financial services and doing financial planning with investors are two hot career areas. Hotel managers, tourism promoters, law firm marketers, paralegal/legal assistants, labor/employment lawyers, intellectual property lawyers, environmental attorneys, and engineers are other professionals whose jobs are likely to be satisfying to the enterprising person.

The most effective person for an enterprising job achieves a balance between courage and confidence and commitment to people's concerns. Enterprising jobs are mostly high-data jobs requiring intelligence and good verbal skills. They are readily available for the go-getter.

Conventional Type

Conventional personality careers require steadiness, order, and tolerance for data/paperwork. At times they involve business contact with people and the use of office machines. Experience may build the conventional person's confidence and the courage to advance, but generally such types prefer supportive roles. Now that we have become a nation of datakeepers and processors, jobs in this area are abundant, visible, usually easy to find, and can pay well in the right setting.

Social-Investigative-Artistic (SIAs) and Other Combinations: The Hard Cases

The realistic, conventional, and enterprising types and various combinations of these have the easiest time starting careers: the realistic, because their jobs are concrete and visible; the conventional, because they tend to follow established patterns; and the enterprising, because they are willing to take risks. Generally speaking, the SIA personalities—social, investigative, artistic, or some combination of these—have a harder time choosing and launching a career. People who work with ideas or feelings often have no tangible product to show their employers.

SIA personalities gravitate toward work in which they can deal with people to solve problems by creating new systems, a need that may arise in just about any work setting. Information systems require these SIA qualities: intelligence, analytical and communication skills, autonomy, sensitivity, responsibility, commitment, flexibility, and creativity.

Satisfying jobs in this area are usually on a highly competitive, professional level, with a college education almost a must. Some supporting work-specific skills that relate to the workplace will help SIAs get started. They should usually plan to get a four year liberal arts or specialized degree, take electives in such subjects as business, computer technology, or health, or obtain a two-year vocational certificate and/or degree along with transfer requirements at a community college before going to a four-year college.

The social and investigative person who is conventional enjoys working with people to solve problems by following established guidelines such as those in human resources, labor relations, probation and law enforcement, health care, and sales.

Individuals who represent the enterprising and social combination have both drive and good people skills. Those who have or can develop both traits will usually be successful with people in business and public service administration. Often, the SIA personality has enough enterprising skills to work happily in many of the social/enterprising areas. Teachers, for example, must organize and motivate people and must serve as key figures in a group, in addition to using their investigative and creative qualities. Be clear on the main function that your highest personality components enable you to perform with enjoyment. When you can state what it is you wish to *do*, finding a place to do it will be much easier.

Realistic: Do the practical, physical work required

Investigative: Gather information (research) and solve problems

Artistic: Create fine arts, but also create systems in many settings

Social: Help people resolve problems

Enterprising: Initiate the work/project to be done

Conventional: Follow the guidelines of others to get the work done

People are doing positive work in all the options, responding to the challenges that face the inhabitants of planet earth. They work in industry and business, city ghettos and upscale communities, schools, prisons, banks, hospitals, and on farms. In all these places, workers can be concerned for the well-being of the planet and its people.

Back to the Future: Job Market Outlook and Opportunities[184]

During your career search, you may often find yourself wondering, "Who needs me out there?" The truth is that there is no way to predict the future needs of the job market with absolute certainty. It is comforting to hear that there is a shortage of workers, especially in skilled jobs.[185] And fewer than 10 percent of the next generation of workers born on this planet will be born in an industrialized country.[186] So the pool of available workers in these countries seems to be shrinking—good news for young job seekers.

Discovering your personality type and interests, analyzing your transferable skills in depth and zeroing in on your personal strengths, identifying areas of the job market to explore and companies to consider are all important steps in ensuring your future. No one can guarantee you a job after you have invested many years and much money training for it. How much are you willing to risk? How motivated are you? Have you looked for ways to use your training in alternate choices?

If you need some help in being your own futurist, you will find that the *Occupational Outlook Handbook,* published by the United States Department of Labor and generally available in any library or on the Internet, is a good beginning reference in which to explore projected needs for over 80 percent or 250 of the most popular careers in the United States. It outlines the nature of the work, average earnings, training requirements, and places to write for further information, along with the projected employment outlook.[187]

Learning about projected job market trends for your areas of interest may be helpful. In some job classifications there are large numbers of people working, but turnover is also high, so there will be many openings even though the category is not necessarily growing. Examples are cashiers, file clerks, mail clerks, office clerks, record and bookkeeping clerks, retail sales clerks, and truck drivers.[188]

Although change is here to stay and predictions are hard to make, those who research and weigh trends honestly will not be very surprised by the future. The Department of Labor makes job market predictions regularly and generally is able to give us a handle on what to expect from these "guesstimates."

Listed below are some of the jobs predicted by the Department of Labor to have the fastest growth and the largest growth between 1996 and 2006. These are not always easy-to-get jobs. For example, fastest-growing job categories may employ very small numbers of workers overall and they are not always the jobs with the largest growth—that is, the largest number of jobs overall (and which tend to be lower skilled and less well paid). The *Occupational Outlook Handbook* will provide more information on the education recommended and the number and percentage of jobs available.

Fastest-Growing Jobs 1996–2006[189]

Cashiers

Systems analysts

General managers and top executives

Registered nurses

Salespersons, retail

Truck drivers, light and heavy

Home health aides

Teacher aides and educational assistants

Nursing aides, orderlies, attendants

Receptionists and information clerks

The Ten Occupations with the Largest Projected Job Growth: 1996–2006[190]

√Database administrators, computer support specialists, and all other computer scientists

Computer engineers

Systems analysts

Personal and home care aides

Physical/corrective therapy assistants/aides

Home health aides

Medical assistants

Desktop publishing specialists

Occupational therapy assistants/aides

Every prediction of job availability carries with it a "yes, but" set of possible exceptions. The very best way to research job availability is to talk to people in your own area. A successful dentist who relocated from a busy city to a semirural place says that if he had chosen a site just five or ten miles away, he wouldn't have had enough business to sustain him.

So the availability of jobs is affected by geographical limitations, educational requirements, experience, the state of the national and even international economy, and the personal decisions of many individuals. Jobs that have a high salary potential and few openings will always have stiff competition even though their numbers may be growing. Your state employment office can supply information on the dynamics of your local job market. Remember that even career categories that are expected to decline dramatically will no doubt still need some workers somewhere, and you could be one of those. All *you* need is that one opportunity—yours!

We are confronted by
insurmountable opportunities!
—*Pogo*[191]

The world we live in depends on the input of all personality types, on all the talent that we can bring to the challenges that face us as we move along in the twenty-first century. The realistic personality can show us how to deal with the physical world capably. The investigative person will carefully explore, analyze, and critique various options. Artistic or creative individuals will keep us from staying with options that no longer work. They will be out there way ahead of the rest of us, trying new ones. The social person will be concerned with the effects of new systems on people and will urge us to consider ways to care for the planet and its creatures. The enterprising person will take the risks necessary to begin and move enterprises that will take us into a new century. The conventional person will keep us going in the right direction and will keep track of the data, urging us not to advance too quickly lest we lose artifacts and ideas of value.

Not only do we need each personality type to contribute that group's special talents to the workplace, but we also need the diversity of gender, race, ethnic background, and age. In the next chapter, we look beyond stereotypes to see the benefit of working with a diverse mix of people in the global marketplace. You, with your special qualities, will contribute to the future.

There are still other activities to help your decision along. One of the best ways to decide is to get some "inside information" through work experience, group tours of workplaces, and interviews of people who work in your area of interest. The following two chapters will deal with the inner workings of workplaces and workstyles. In these you'll begin to see that the career you choose will fit in many jobs and many workplaces, both old and new. You'll also begin to understand that many of the nontraditional/creative careers and lifestyles of today will be commonplace tomorrow.

Learning how to prepare for the job hunt as well as a structured decision-making process can also help you focus on where you wish to go and lead you to work that matches your values. The rest of this book deals with these concerns.

New Paradigms

Jean Houston's exciting brain/mind research asks, "What is the possible human?" and shows that we are on the verge of a giant step toward new forms of consciousness and fulfillment. She affirms that our human systems are vastly superior to anything technology could invent; we have only begun to plumb the depths of our inner selves. We may be reaching a "golden age of body/mind control that challenges us to a new humanity."[192] It's a time, then, for all of us to make thoughtful decisions about what we wish to be and what roles we want to play and what challenges we hope to meet. Growing as a person means changing, adjusting to both inner and outer reality. It means expanding into new and exciting areas of life.

Irish priest and poet John O'Donohue urges job seekers to make sure their workplaces are actually expressive of identity, dignity, and giftedness. He adds that if you sell your soul, you ultimately buy a life of misery.[193]

> When the imagination, the force of illumination
> in the soul, is allowed to stir,
> it opens up the workplace in a completely new way.
> —*John O'Donohue in* Anam Cara[194]

Although they are a part of high-tech systems, people are feeling and relating to each other in much the same way they did in ancient times and feeling a need to be part of a human community. Many people seem to be evolving into beings who are more aware of the world around them and their interaction with it, people who have the courage to act in harmony with that world.

Stereotypes about how we *should* be hold us back from becoming fully what we *could be*. That doesn't imply that change is simple and easy but rather that it is possible for people who are open-minded and open-hearted to be caring individuals and to prosper. To paraphrase Elizabeth Cady Stanton, "the true person is as yet a dream of the future."[195] Let's hope that that future is not too distant.

 Self-Assessment Exercises

1. Areas of Challenge

Circle the following areas of challenge that capture your attention. Tell which specific aspect of the challenge interests you and why.

Air and water

√Earth/trees/animal species

√Food/land

Planet people

Energy

√Shelter/created environment

Transportation

Safety: Health education, military/security

Science and technology

Industry and business

Ethics

_____

_____

2. Possible Responses

Which options might you use to respond to this challenge?

_____

_____

3. Possible Job Openings

Look up your first job choice in the *Occupational Outlook Handbook* and summarize what it says under "Job Outlook" about the possibility of future job openings.

_____

_____

4. Your Beliefs about the Future[196]

Circle all the items you agree with.

1. I have no control over my own future, much less the future of the world.
2. We can keep world conflicts within reasonable bounds.
3. We will be able to keep conflicts from becoming nuclear wars.
4. Conservation will become an acceptable way of life almost everywhere.
5. Luck or chance, rather than our choices, causes the outcome of events.
6. We can learn to live peacefully on earth. No – Human Nature to have conflict
7. Enough people will learn to be careful of resources to save us from destruction.
8. The future is created, more so than not, by choices that people make.
9. We can do little about overconsumption and the waste that causes excess pollution.
10. It is possible for me to influence the direction of my future.
11. I believe that the future will be shaped by forces outside my control.

12. Soon we will not have enough of anything.

13. There are enough people making good choices to keep the world from destruction.

14. Researching and planning ahead can make my future turn out well.

15. There may be shortages, but generally we will get through the coming years well enough.

16. The world is consuming, polluting, and populating itself to death.

17. The world's resources are abundant enough to provide food, raw materials, and energy for everyone.

18. Most of our energy sources will be renewable and nonpolluting in the not-too-distant future.

19. It is largely up to people to determine the options to be taken.

20. The future will happen no matter what a person does.

21. We can rely on most people to make wise choices.

22. I look forward to the future with hope and enthusiasm.

23. People are swept along by forces over which they have little control.

24. In a few years we will begin to see declining population, rising levels of affluence, and a world of plenty.

Scoring: Circle the same numbers here that you circled above to get an idea about how optimistic or pessimistic you feel about your future and how much control you feel you have. Where do you stand on the Pessimistic/Optimistic Spectrum?

Doomsday/Pessimistic–Little Control: 1, 5, 9, 11, 12, 16, 20, 23
Muddle Through–Some Control: 2, 3, 7, 8, 10, 13, 15, 19
Bright Future/Optimistic–Much Control: 4, 6, 14, 17, 18, 21, 22, 24

Pessimistic   Midpoint   Optimistic

 Group Discussion Questions

1. What does John Peers mean when he says, "We live three days in one compared to the 1950s. We do in one day what couldn't be done in a week in 1900, in a lifetime in the 1600s"? Give examples. Do you feel busy? Why or why not?

2. How do you feel about keeping up with the tech world? Explain. Do you believe everyone needs to keep up to be employable?

3. Describe your classroom, your community, your home, and your lifestyle as if you lived in 1900. What changes since then seem most dramatic to you? Explain.

4. How were these basic workplace functions carried out in early human societies: business, industry, education, entertainment/communication, health, government, and military? What are the major differences in the way work was carried out in those early societies and now?

5. Define economics, environment, and ethics. What would be the best ways for the needs of the economy and the environment to be met in an ethical way? What are the chief obstacles?

6. Community checkup: Note a challenge in your locality that relates to a career in your personality type and find an innovative option. Identify someone in your community who is working to meet that challenge. Report to the class.

7. What does it mean "to vote at the checkstand of the supermarket"? Do you choose socially responsible products? Do you live simply? Do you buy more than you need or can use? Do you ever really throw anything away completely? Explain.

8. Describe a practice that is legal but that you consider unethical. How many ethical principles can the group collect and agree on?

9. How can meeting the needs of all the earth's people increase our personal security?

10. Fantasize a world in 2050 in which all robot-made products are durable and beautiful. People purchase only goods and services that enrich their lives. Many people provide some basic needs for themselves. They work only one or two days a week. Many work at home via microchip devices. How would the world be different? Would there be more unemployment or could everyone find work? What kind of work? How could people use their leisure time? What resources would be conserved? How would you feel about that world?

5/

Workplaces/ Workstyles

Companies That Work

FOCUS

- Connect personality types
  with the seven categories of workplaces.

- Consider workplace rewards
  and their effects on workplace people.

- Explore and evaluate workplace
  values and diversity.

You have looked at the ways in which your qualities can find satisfiers in the workplace. You have reviewed the societal issues and trends that are facing all of us and are likely to continue as we work in the new millennium. All of this will provide good background as you decide on the type of workplace and possible workstyle that you would enjoy and that will suit you best. Workplaces and workstyles are often the subject of a person's daydreams. Do you see yourself playing a role in engineering at a huge corporation or promoting your own company with your laptop from a houseboat on the bay? Here we will look at more traditional workplaces and the benefits associated with them. In the next chapter we will consider alternative workplaces and workstyles.

You may be surprised to learn that workplaces can be divided into just seven categories: business, industry, education, communication/entertainment, health, government, and military. Each of these categories has hundreds and some even thousands of jobs, many of which have similar characteristics. If you're unable to choose a job title, just being able to pick one of these seven categories is a huge step in narrowing down your career choices.

Seven Categories of Workplaces

Business

The category of business includes many settings, from an executive suite to a deli down the street, and includes workers from retail clerks to shipping tycoons. Business occurs when two or more people get together to trade goods and services. Labor relations, human resources, contract negotiations, accounting, marketing, consulting in all areas, and hundreds of other functions make up the work of the business world and its many support systems.

The enterprising and conventional types are most at home in business, but all types can find expression there: the social person in dealing with people and their problems, the artistic person in creating or advertising new designs, the realistic person in managing products and production, and the investigative person in research and problem solving. Choosing business, then, will narrow down your choices and still leave the door open to a variety of careers.

To facilitate the flow of goods and services in business involves both paper data and mind data. The classification *paper data* includes reading, writing, and using computers; *mind data* encompasses researching, organizing, analyzing, and teaching. General clerical skills enable you to enter the field of business as a data-entry or shipping clerk. When you feel the need for more training, you can attend workshops and seminars or take college courses at the associate in arts (AA) or bachelor of arts (BA) level in fields such as accounting or marketing. Even with a BA or an MBA degree (Master of Business Administration), most people must start near the bottom of the ladder and work up—unless a serious shortage of personnel exists or you have special expertise or experience.

Industry

Industry can be defined loosely as a concern with products and with services that involve physical objects, not with people or paper (if you exclude the business end of industry). Repairing cars, flying planes, pouring concrete, and raising wheat are industries in this sense, along with manufacturing, testing, quality control, and quality assurance of products and services. Even the artist making clay pots at home is involved in industry. Working with machines and tools and tangible materials attracts the realistic person to industries of all kinds. Those realistic individuals with an investigative bent will enjoy scientific and engineering research directed toward practical problems. The ones with a conventional side will appreciate seeing that the jobs are done correctly and with care, following all the rules; realistic people with an artistic slant will enjoy inventing and creating; those with an enterprising side will find satisfaction in demonstrating products for sale; social realistic people will do well in technical supervision.

To enter jobs in this area, take high school, community college, or adult education courses that are related to industry. And look into on-the-job training (OJT) in industry as well as apprenticeship programs through trades such as carpentry or cement working.

Education

Many careers are available in the field of education besides teaching in schools and colleges. Corporations hire specialists to develop basic learning programs, and business and industry carry on employee training programs. People who teach various skills or crafts at home or at community centers also participate in the field of education.

The enterprising and social personalities enjoy the task- or people-oriented interactions of teaching, leading, and motivating others. Those with a realistic bent enjoy teaching such subjects as physical education, military arts, and shop, whereas the artistic types drift toward humanities and fine arts, crafts, and design. Investigative interests are needed for scholarship and research and for teaching the liberal arts and sciences; conventional personalities do well in teaching the basics. In fact, all personality types can be found in education. It helps to be a jack of all trades in many areas of education.

Communication/Entertainment

The communication/entertainment arena attracts the artistic personality. Workplaces range from circus tents to TV studios. Opportunities tend to be more limited than those in any other area because these "glamour" fields are generally highly competitive. To succeed here, you need exceptional ability, great quantities of luck, lots of courage and perseverance, and either some enterprising qualities or a good agent! The electronic media continue to grow erratically, and sometimes positions for creative people with enterprising, conventional, realistic, or investigative sides can be found in the marketing, business administration, clerical, engineering, and research areas of media. Because creative people usually like to work alone or in unstructured settings, many find it difficult to do routine work even though the workplace may deal with a creative product.

Realistic types who are creative may enjoy careers such as industrial design whereas conventional/artistic types may do well in such areas as computer-assisted drafting. Enterprising/artistic people may open their own galleries or become book publicists. With the incredible rise of the information society, opportunities will continue to open up for the creative person who is technically talented, word-wise, or number-nimble.

Health

When they think of the health care field, many people see jobs in a hospital or doctor's office, but in fact, health care workers also find employment in business, industry, education, and military settings. Specialization and technological advances have expanded the health profession rapidly, but growth slows when recession and unemployment pinch health care budgets.

So-called alternative health care is a rapidly growing area as people choose such practitioners as chiropractors, acupuncturists, and homeopathists. Over half the nation's health care dollars go to these health providers.

The investigative person with a good social orientation will enjoy the challenge of helping people solve their health care problems, whereas conventional/social persons will like the established systems found in some health care facilities. The enterprising person will enjoy managing health care. There may be a great deal of physical work, which may be attractive to the realistic person who likes to work with people. Several hundred job titles are associated with health care delivery.

Government

People of all types find employment with government in every setting—from agricultural stations to hospitals, from prisons to the great outdoors. You must usually pass a "test" to become employed at the federal level (and often at state and county levels, too). The test may combine an oral interview and possibly a written examination. Job applicants frequently receive additional credit for years of education, military service, and past work experience that can give them preference in the hiring process. Any type of personality can find satisfiers as one of the great variety of government workers that includes narcotics agents, food program specialists, museum curators, and public health workers. Your state and other employment offices have information about these and other civil service jobs.

Traditionally, a government job has implied security but low pay. In past years, the pay increased along with the number of jobs, but growing taxpayers' concern about government spending has brought lower pay and insecurity for many government employees. You need persistence to obtain these jobs, but many are still there for the person who is willing to try for them.

Military

Realistic and conventional personalities are attracted most readily to military operations and procedures, but here people of all types can also find opportunities from cooking to hospital laboratory work to sophisticated industrial research and design, along with frontline fighting. Like other government workplaces, the military is downsizing in certain areas for budgetary reasons, so many in military jobs are moving to other employment fields. Even so, new recruits may still apply and be accepted. For those so inclined, the military provides a very structured working and living situation, training in a variety of skills, and good benefits, offset by the chances of being assigned to undesirable duties or locations, or having to participate in wars or "peace actions."

You will find that workplaces have personalities just as people do. Some are austere, rigid, demanding, challenging, stressful; others are lavish, casual, supportive, easygoing. They reflect various combinations of the six personality types and tend to attract similar types who will be comfortable being together.

Choosing a category of workplace focuses your career exploration and can even get you started on a basic college curriculum or training program. Keep in mind the main functions your personality combination enjoys and imagine the sort of place where you would feel at home:

R: working with things	S: helping people
I: solving problems	E: initiating projects
A: creating new systems	C: following guidelines

Career Ladders Large and Small

You may find it helpful to match your satisfiers with one of the levels in the Career Ladder Chart and to be aware of other closely related factors such as size, complexity, and setting, both indoor and outdoor. There are four major levels on any career ladder: entry, supervisory/technical, mid-management, and top management. These are often divided into sublevels. Each level includes some support services such as human resources, purchasing, secretarial/clerical, and maintenance. Some companies are trying to group employees into a few broad job categories ("broadbanding" them) rather than naming them with the dozens of titles found in traditional systems. And others are flattening or shortening the ladder so that there are fewer managers. Moving up is still as difficult a climb with the short ladder! In some of these cases, moving over instead of up can be a good career strategy if the lateral move will help you gain new skills and confidence.[1]

Generally, the higher you climb on the career ladder, the higher your salary will be. Some people begin at the bottom and, with additional training, degrees, and experience, rise to the top. One young woman started as a nurse's aide, moved up to registered nurse (RN) with a bachelor of science degree (BS) in nursing, and then went on to earn a master of science (MS) in nursing so she could teach. She could also have gotten a master's degree in hospital administration.

Your place on the career ladder may be in a large and therefore complex structure, or it may be in one that is small and simple. It may have a rigid system like the military. It may have blurred lines of authority. No matter what size they are, all workplaces—lawyers' offices, large catering services, hospitals, or international manufacturing corporations—have similar structures and functions, sometimes repeated over and over in various divisions. A small staff might consist of the boss, who has many management functions, and one assistant, who does the rest.

Julie Martin-Pitts was a medical assistant in a doctor's office. She enjoyed the variety of doing billing, data entry, public relations, tax work, and research; she also supervised personnel, did a little family counseling, designed management systems—and on occasion enjoyed doing some interior decorating. Now a consultant, Julie helps people deal with the complexities and traumas involved in using the health care system.

In a larger workplace, entry-level workers can expect to do more limited and specialized jobs, such as putting lettuce leaves on a thousand sandwiches, soldering links in a thousand electronic circuits, or data processing a thousand letters. Possibilities for change, however, including moving both up and over, are greater in a larger than a smaller work environment. On the other hand,

THE CAREER LADDER

Position	Responsibility	Education	Support Staff
TOP LEVEL			
Top management and professionals, such as Presidents Board members Doctors Lawyers	The decision makers: responsible for nearly everything. There is more independence at this level.	PhD, DD, MD, MBA, etc. Technical and professional expertise	
MIDDLE LEVEL			
Middle management and professionals, such as Department heads Engineers Nurses Teachers Product managers	Share responsibility with the top level and enjoy some independence.	MA, MBA, MS, BS, BA, etc. Middle-level expertise	Operate at all levels to provide auxiliary services such as Human Resources Finance Communications/ Graphics Legal counsel Research Purchasing Marketing Data processing Secretarial/Cleri- cal Maintenance
LOWER LEVEL			
Lower management and technicians, such as Supervisors Lead persons Legal assistants LVNs	Are responsible for a small part of decision making. May supervise others.	AA, AS, vocational, or on-the-job training	
THE WORKERS			
Basic production and service work, such as Trades, crafts Assemblers Machinists Waiters/Waitresses	Are responsible for a particular function. Entry-level jobs; often repetitive work.	High school, apprenticeship. Usually *some* training or experience is needed.	

research shows that small and mid-size companies create many more jobs than large companies; are usually more productive, flexible, and creative; and may grow dramatically to become huge corporations, which tend to lose productivity, flexibility, and creativity! Small businesses employing fewer than twenty people make up 89 percent of U.S. firms.[2]

Visualize the size of workplace you might enjoy within one of the seven categories to help focus your choice even more. Is a multinational corporation for you, or a tiny business at home? A modest-sized company in a nearby city, or a cooperative venture in your neighborhood? Gather job titles that would work in these workplaces.

In the past decade or two, many corporations have grown dramatically, merged with or taken over others, and gone multinational. Smaller businesses have been able to fill much of the resulting employment gap in creative ways. They are able to respond more quickly, often at lower cost and with better customer services. Not necessarily high tech, small and family-owned companies may use technology to do tasks impossible without computers. Direct advertising, selling, and providing services on the Internet can take place even from home.

Erving Goffman wrote in *Asylums* that simply by reason of sheer numbers, institutions tend to become dehumanizing.[3] But large size doesn't always mean depersonalization. Within many large organizations, you can discover companies within companies and/or small, cohesive, caring groups of people looking out for each other's interests. This kind of support would be missing in a small business run by a tyrant.

Barbara Garson studied three workplaces in New York. She reported that two well-known companies had extremely restrictive policies for workers: no talking to other employees during work time, no personal phone calls about family emergencies, and other rigid rules. In contrast, the report described the accounting office of a community college where five older women worked very hard, often staying late to complete their tasks. They also managed to fit in noon parties, trips to the hospital to visit sick family members, and other personal ventures.[4] Want ads and job descriptions don't tell about these kinds of fringe benefits or perks.

Setting is another related factor. Some people like their career ladder outdoors where the structure is usually simpler; others like to be more on their own inside or on the road; others like a mix in which an office is their base but they move around inside the same plant, on the road, or outdoors; and still others like to be indoors in one spot on the spot. Such choices may move a person either farther away from or closer to the center of decision-making power in a company. This in turn may enhance or delay progress up the career ladder.

Then, before you discard some job titles, be sure you aren't stereotyping them in a way that distorts their possibilities. Food services might seem to mean frying hamburgers, but if you stop there, you miss management at local, regional, and corporate levels, finance, accounting, marketing, planning, and all the functions of any corporation. The possible work settings include industry, schools, hospitals, airlines, and even executive dining rooms, where highly professional food service personnel work a five-day week serving upper management and their guests.[5]

And consider food engineering. Engineering students at the Massachusetts Institute of Technology (MIT) found a great project by working out a faster, more economical system to put the hard candy coating on M&Ms. The

Reprinted with permission from Mal Hancock.

company sent them 1,500 pounds of M&Ms, not all of which went into the experiment! The students and professors grew in wisdom and weight and found that the food industry has "tremendous engineering prospects."[6]

Where do you want to fit in this scheme of things? How far up the ladder do you want to be? (It may be lonely at the top, but it's also exciting and challenging—but not everyone can get there. It may seem more comfortable at the bottom but often not so lucrative or so interesting!) You may want to move up the ladder within a career area but not to a higher level that requires more education and career commitment.

Determining the size and complexity as well as the type of workplace and the rung on the career ladder that feels right to you can be important factors in career choice. If you know where you want to be in a few years, you will make use of present opportunities and not choose dead-end jobs.

Wanted: Rewards on All Levels

Workplaces provide an income, which ideally satisfies basic physical/survival needs such as food, clothing, and shelter and some of the enriching wants on your agenda. Statistics diligently chart the rise and fall of average wages. In general, in the last three decades of this century, we have seen the buying power of low-skill worker wages decline and their jobs disappear. New but lower-paying jobs have come on line, often without benefits. At this same time, a new, well-paid, upper-middle class of "knowledge workers" has developed.

But also consider the areas of reward that go beyond a paycheck and that may in the long run bring more important satisfaction to your work: opportunities for fringe benefits and advancement; and subtle emotional satisfiers, such as a supportive atmosphere for you, your family, and your lifestyle; autonomy; and compatible values. Although for most people reasonable income is sufficient, others, even multibillionaires, keep working hard to earn more.

While your career choice puts you on a path to certain rewards, the workplace you choose can enhance or subtract from them. Robert Levering and Milton Moskowitz say—and the cartoon "Dilbert" confirms—that "most companies offer dreadful work environments."[7] We must ask, "What is happening to the individual in the workplace?"

First, in relatively recent times, changes in work have removed people from the natural world where our ancestors worked *for centuries*. Many drive along concreted wastelands; *like miners,* they often work in buildings without windows, having little awareness of the changing seasons. They work in cyberspace—a not-always-amusing theme park of virtual unreality. They have little say about what happens to their souls and bodies during the workday and on what schedule. Some companies—Disney, for example—provide so many amenities such as meals, spas, exercise rooms, and sports for some of its creative workers that they hardly ever have to go home! What are some of the rewards to look for in workplaces of the twenty-first century?

Don't Overlook Benefits

Fringe benefits are not just a minor attraction. These perquisites or "perks" represent a considerable, if hidden, part of your pay; if carefully considered, they can result in larger income and long-term savings as well as enriching activities off the job.

Health Care   Health care, for example, can include dental and vision care in addition to medical/hospital care. Many companies, especially smaller ones, find it a struggle to offer health benefits. As the cost of health care climbs, medical expenses can put someone without insurance deep into debt.

Stock Options   Stock options are the way companies may share control while sharing some profits—often a significant benefit. Though originally designed to reward worker productivity, some plans have lost sight of that. Nor are all such plans designed to give workers autonomy, though they may; rather, some may give the company advantages, such as reducing worker turnover. Before depending on these generous-looking benefits, research them carefully as to their short- and long-term effects.

Career Development   Consider too a company's record in career "pathing" or career development and the quality of their employee training programs, for these can lead to better-paying jobs. Some companies make a concerted effort to help their employees improve and grow on the job. They provide training on or off site, educational opportunities, and encouragement to employees to set goals and objectives—and help in meeting these goals. In the long run this type of benefit may be vastly beneficial.

Retirement   Although retirement can seem eons away, it's never too early to look at various options and plan for a financially worry-free retirement. As women tend to live longer, they need to plan ahead carefully since about 90 percent of them will be responsible for their own finances at some point.[8] Three times as many women as men over 65 live in poverty.[9] With the prospect of increasing longevity, some people welcome the opportunity to work after age sixty-five. To others, retirement (as early as possible) means liberation. Some retirement plans can lead to considerable income. Several, like individual retirement accounts, or IRAs, involve reduced or deferred income taxes. Some people manage to save and invest wisely enough to make their retirement free from financial worry. Many are taking better care of their health and finding enriching involvements or even new career areas. A T-shirt reads, "Retirement is a full-time job," as many who have retired will agree. With some creative planning, retirement could be on your career agenda sooner than you think.

Other Perks   Paid holidays and vacations; child/elder care subsidies; on-site recreation/health maintenance; personal, investment, and financial counseling; educational planning; courses for personal enrichment; use of a company car; expense accounts; dry-cleaning pick up; and even the use of vacation resorts are just a few of the benefits offered by some companies. Some give raises when workers acquire and broaden their skills; some provide sabbaticals that allow an employee, after some years on the job, to take several months off with pay for enrichment. Some offer "cafeteria style" benefits and allow employees to choose whichever combination suits them. Some may give you a vested interest in the company through a variety of employee–owner plans.

Companies are becoming more aware that when employees are frustrated and concerned about problems such as child/elder care, health care costs, and retirement, their energy and productivity are drained. As a job hunter, you benefit by knowing which benefits would help you solve important problems and which would simply enhance your work.

Rewards of a Different Sort: The Emotional Contract

For some, work itself is rewarding. Some people say they would almost be glad to pay someone to let them do their jobs! However, salary and fringe benefits are the usual prime motivators. Work also has intangible rewards on many levels that relate to the values of a company.

A company's "corporate culture or climate" is a common and shared set of beliefs and values that shape attitudes and behavior, and make for reduced conflict and greater efficiency. It includes the company's attitudes toward employees; its sense of respect, fairness, trust; its supportiveness toward people who work there, especially during tough times. It is something you depend on as if you had signed a contract with your employer.

For example, when you see others laid off abruptly and you live under the threat of your own "downsizing," you will find it hard to feel trusting of your workplace. The morale of everyone drops as salaries, benefits, and jobs are cut back. "There is [also] no good evidence of positive financial benefits" to companies that downsize, according to William McKinley, professor at the College of Business and Administration of Southern Illinois University at Carbondale. "Some 63 percent of firms eliminating jobs in 1996 were also hiring, according to a 1996 survey of l,441 companies by the American Management Association, making net job loss only 0.7 percent, but leaving behind a considerable drop in morale among employees left."[10]

Most workers want to feel they are valued not only for the work they do but also for themselves. James Kouzes and Santa Clara University professor Barry Posner, made the following observation in the book *Credibility*: "Generally we will work harder and more effectively for people we like and we will like them in direct proportion to how they help make us feel." In their research they found that people felt *valued, motivated, enthusiastic, challenged, inspired, capable, supported, powerful, respected, and proud* when they had leaders they valued. Yet they also found that less than half the employees surveyed by the Opinion Research Corporation could say that their companies treated them with dignity and respect.[11]

Even so, a 1997 INC/Gallup survey showed that over two-thirds of Americans said they were satisfied with their places of employment. The smaller the workplace, the more satisfied they were, with people owning their own business the most satisfied. Eighty-two percent said that they did every day what they do best. Less educated workers said they receive less praise, less opportunity to grow, and are less satisfied with their jobs.[12]

As time goes by, the intangible characteristics of a job may change. One newly divorced woman enjoyed her work in a small savings and loan office where the boss and coworkers were supportive. But the boss, who had decided to work harder at moving up, began to be more restrictive. The work atmosphere became unpleasant—but changed again for the better when the boss left and the then experienced woman became the manager!

No matter how carefully you plan your career, at some time you are likely to have a job that does not satisfy all your needs and wants. Some people have exaggerated expectations about the role the workplace and coworkers should play in their lives. For example, some people hope for more emotional support from coworkers and supervisors than these individuals are prepared to supply. Cultivating a reasonable amount of independence and a moderately strong skin can protect you against the ups and downs of the work world.

Some companies make a conscious effort to hire and keep only those employees who espouse their ideals, which can improve the emotional climate. Granite Rock, a rock-and-asphalt business in Watsonville, California, since the early 1900s and recipient of the 1992 Malcolm Baldrige National Quality Award, expects "their people" to value quality, service, and fairness.[13]

When you are hired, you agree to a company's beliefs and values, as though to an unwritten emotional contract. Your work life will be more satisfying if you choose an environment with just the right values and enough support for you. Other workplace motivators include enhanced self-esteem, prestige, rewarding relationships, and opportunities to actualize your unique potential. As you search out information about workplaces, try to find those ingredients—beyond money and benefits—that would inspire your loyalty to a job and the company.

Workplace Values: Ethics 101

What would you do if you found your employer involved in some illegal, unethical, or immoral actions, and you were expected to participate or at least keep quiet? What if your workplace exploits workers: uses underage employees illegally at home or overseas; allows unsafe working conditions and the use of dangerous equipment by untrained personnel; pays below the legal wage requirement. In addition, what is legal is not always what is moral and ethical. Companies may fire someone legally, for example, who takes time off for a family emergency, or pressure workers to put in excessive overtime—but are such actions ethical?

Work is value laden and the ethics of a company is a major part of the corporate culture. However, not everyone agrees on what ethical/moral behavior is in practice. We can say, however, that people are ethical when they are honestly and consistently trying to behave according to their values without shirking their responsibilities to society or harming others. Today, responsible workplaces, to avoid allegations of wrongdoing, are paying serious attention to their values and ethics.

To avoid serious ethical dilemmas in the workplace, do a little research ahead of time about the principles of companies you are considering. More and more companies are being evaluated for their level of ethics and social responsibility, a concern not only to workers but also to investors. The magazine *BusinessEthics* rates what its editors consider the 100 best corporate citizens.[14] A social screen was developed by U.S. Trust Company of Boston to advise concerned investors.[15] An expanded version of the social screen is presented below. You can use it to help you determine a given firm's level of social responsibility:

- Do they sell products and services that affordably fulfill basic needs or enriching wants of their target markets?

- Do they produce and market safe, high-quality products that are as beautiful as possible?

- Are they honest, fair, and trustworthy, following ethical principles in their business dealings on both national and international levels, without exploiting others, especially children?

- Do they provide a safe, healthy, humane work environment?

- Do they provide equal employment opportunities for women, men, and minorities?

- Do they have fair labor practices?

- Do they elicit worker loyalty through concern for their employees' welfare, not just that of their stockholders?

- Do they provide workers with information, tools, and an environment that encourages high performance?

- Do they support workplace democracy, encouraging and teaching worker participation, and rewarding creative suggestions using cooperation instead of confrontation?

- Do they respect and preserve the natural environment wherever they operate, including humane treatment of animals?

- Do they practice energy conservation, recycling, and use of renewable energy where possible?

- Do they contribute to, and invest in, the community where they operate without overwhelming its political, economic, and social life, while understanding the problems their workers face in meeting their needs there?

- Do they grow and compete in a balanced way?

- Do they make an effort to learn the history, language, and culture of international business partners, trying to understand their needs and worldviews?

- Do they operate under and depend on repressive governments?

- Do they depend on military weapons contracts?

- Are they willing to disclose information that gives answers to all these questions?

Companies who strive to be socially responsible win in many ways. They win the admiration and support of their stakeholders. For example, when Malden Mills—maker of Polartec fleece fabric—burned down, its president, Aaron Feurstein, continued to pay his employees while the plant was being rebuilt, a decision he said was a moral one. It definitely made good business sense for the company.[16] "Surveys show that up to 70 percent of American consumers say they won't buy products made under unsafe or unfair working conditions."[17]

Do we want businesses to be socially *irresponsible*? Socially responsible investors have already diverted over $610 *billion* away from corporations whose policies they didn't support and 80 percent of American consumers say that environmental concerns have led them to switch brands of the products they buy.[18] San Francisco–based Working Assets Funding Service, a $104-million company, has managed to combine twelve years of hypergrowth with a socially responsible business mission.[19]

Some companies struggle valiantly to get high marks on all of the above, but few are perfect. They do have to meet expenses; they do have mountains of governmental regulations to follow that sometimes hinder rather than help them; they may be in a period of difficult transition. Being socially responsible doesn't mean being impractical—for example, giving such lavish benefits that the company fails. But the bottom line is always a business's efforts to consider the needs of all its stakeholders, which include not only the stockholders but everyone with a stake in the company, such as clients, workers, the wider community, and the company's surrounding environment.

Workers also have ethical responsibilities to do their jobs well, to be honest, and to respect others. The personal responsibility skills you assessed in Chapter 2 will help you make yours a "high-performance" workplace where everyone profits. No amount of legislation or rules can take the place of the ethical behavior of individuals in a society. For both individuals and companies, "Free market competition works not because it is unfettered, but because of the moral dimension we each bring to it. Without these internalized social bonds, efficient competition becomes destructive chaos."[20]

Carefully research and ask questions about what a company really stands for. Sometimes advertising can be misleading. Do library research, including a review of the business section of newspapers and magazines. Ask around. You can be amazed at how much employees know about the ethics of their own company. The question, Can a company do well when doing good? (can it be both ethical *and* profitable) is being answered with a resounding Yes! It's important to find a company whose values match yours.

A group called Student Citizens for Social Responsibility at California's Humboldt State University initiated a pledge for graduates whereby they promised "to investigate thoroughly and take into account the social and environmental consequences of any job opportunity I consider." Now headquartered at Manchester College in Indiana, this pledge is spreading to other campuses.[21]

Autonomy Dimensions: Who's Boss?

Old industrial-style management techniques gave bosses complete authority over employees with whom they shared little about the business. In 1994, workers at a chicken plant in Mississippi complained that they needed a doctor's note to use the bathroom more than three times a week. Workers also needed to pay ten cents per cup for clean drinking water.[22] But authors Levering and Moskowitz assert, "The authoritarian work style . . . has failed."[23] Because the number of workers with college degrees is increasing, and because these workers are often underemployed, they are likely to challenge old-style management techniques with creative new ideas.

The information age is bringing marked changes. Many workers are taking responsibility for their own decisions based on access to computer data formerly reserved for management and now made available to people at all levels. The career ladder shortens as people become "more equal."

Commenting on leadership, authors of *Credibility,* Kouzes and Posner, add: "Leaders we admire do not place themselves at the center; they place others there. They do not seek the attention of people; they give it to others."[24]

Some businesses are experimenting with "open book" management based on the principle that making money should be the work of all the workers in an organization. Financial as well as other information is shared openly with workers, giving them insider status. Ken Eberhard, owner of the Eberhard Equipment Company, has been training his workers with painstaking care toward a day when they can take over the company. Promoting from within gives people a feeling that their work is valued. Companies that clearly connect performance with earnings usually find that employees will work harder.

However, as the workplace automates routine jobs, "doing one's job" is not always enough. The jobs that are left require that workers act like owners and create the job as they go. As people begin to look around their workplaces, if they can stay flexible, they begin to see new possibilities to do what fits them best and to benefit the company in the long run. William Bridges writes of a nation of owners working for "You & Co."[25]

Autonomy options also include democratic decision making, skills sharing through job rotation, and education in job and cooperative skills, profit-and-loss sharing, and shared ownership by workers. Autonomy requires workers to assume greater individual responsibility.

Management is learning that the more workers take responsibility in their jobs to make suggestions, solve their own problems, and learn new skills,

"INSPECTORS, ROBINSON, DO NOT
EXPRESS OPINIONS."

the more energy they will bring to their work, the more self-esteem and enjoyment they will derive from it, and the greater the profits will be for all.

Not everyone likes to take more responsibility for their work! Years ago
autoworker Joe Rodriguez was sent to Sweden to learn teamwork techniques
for his auto assembly line. He concluded, "If I've got to bust my ass to be
meaningful, forget it. I'd rather be monotonous."[26]

Even in companies that try to include everyone in decisions, there are
struggles with communication, over equitable working conditions, and over
salary and benefits for all levels of workers. You might consider what it would
be like to work in a company that tries to empower workers.

Doing everything better as a continuous process may be exhausting—
working for the latest, the best, *always* striving, trying to get ahead of the

competition. For others, it is exhilarating. If autonomy is important for you, zero in on workplaces that encourage it.

Workplace Diversity

Up until the last quarter of the twentieth century, U.S. workers in all but the least skilled jobs were generally white males. The civil rights movement of the 1960s and the women's movement of the 1970s changed the complexion of the workplace dramatically. Not only did women and minorities enter in increasingly greater numbers, but the media and the global economy brought us into closer contact with diverse groups of people from all over the world. People in these groups, including you, are looking for satisfiers in the workplace.

Everyone is learning new ways of doing business with and working with all these people, both inside and outside their organizations. At one of the Fortune 500's fastest-growing companies, Harry Pforzheimer, director of corporate communications, says, "The population here reflects the world population. That makes for an exciting melting pot of ideas. And I think it adds dramatically to our success."[27]

The tendency for those in the mainstream, however, has been to stereotype and exclude others as a group before getting to know them as individuals. Those left out often feel like foreigners in their own land. Elie Wiesel, Nobel Peace Prize winner and Andrew Mellon Professor of Humanities at Boston University, said:

> It is enough for someone to treat me like a foreigner for me to be one. If I am excluded, it is because some one has pushed me out. Therefore, it is my fault, too, if the other person is excluded, that is to say, deprived of a feeling of security and of belonging, of a sense of identity. For it is up to me whether someone feels at home or not in our common world, and whether he feels tranquil or anxious when he looks around him.[28]

Gender in the Workplace

It's hard to believe that only a few short years ago it would have been considered extraordinary for a woman to become an astronaut or a zookeeper, to head a Fortune 500 company, to venture into the world of venture capital—or, as was true in some states, to write a check, buy stock or property, or open a business without her husband's permission.[29] And it would have seemed just as extraordinary for a man to do a significant share of housework and child care. Still, gender is possibly the most powerful and pervasive influence in our lives, and traditional stereotypes live on. Sometimes before a baby takes its first breath, people ask, "Is it a boy or a girl?"

Gender Bender: Women

Worldwide, women are scarcely counted in the statistics and barely have any rights at all. In the United States, women have come a long way since the early 1970s, when they could expect to earn just 57 percent of the salary paid a man for doing the same job.

Globally

- Of the estimated 1.3 billion people worldwide living in poverty, more than 70 percent are women and girls.[30]

- Women's work represents half the total global economic input, equaling about $11 trillion—but is not included in the standard economic accounting systems.[31]

- Women receive only 26 percent of total earned income and constitute 70 percent of the poor.[32]

- Women are almost universally excluded from all but minimal education, and from political and economic decision making.[33]

In the United States

- Two out of three poor adults are women.[34]

- Forty-five percent of female-headed households live on incomes below the poverty line.[35]

- The median income of female-maintained families in nonmetropolitan areas is $12,742, compared to $21,997 for male-maintained families and $37,080 for married-couple families.[36]

- Half of those living below the poverty line in the United States are children, representing 8 percent of all American children.[37]

- Women earn 75 percent the salary of a male working in an equivalent job with the same experience. Even in traditionally female occupations where women outnumber males, they still earn less than men.[38]

- Women have almost achieved parity in educational attainment:
  - In 1996, 88 percent of women in the work force had completed high school compared with 84.4 percent of men.[39]
  - Still, without a high school diploma, women earn a median $15,133; men, $22,048.
  - With a high school diploma, women earn $20,373; men, $28,037.
  - With an associate degree, women earn $25,940; men $35,794.
  - With a bachelor's degree, women earn $35,378; men, $49,228.[40]
- With advanced degrees the gap narrows.[41]
- In 1996, women were 98.6 percent of secretaries; 97.1 percent of child care workers; 93.3 percent of registered nurses; 90.5 percent of telephone

operators. On average, however, they represented only 13.6 percent of such nontraditional female occupations as mechanic, dentist, engineer, or data processing equipment repairer.[42]

- Women in unions earned over 40 percent more than nonunion women.[43]

- In 1996, Hispanic women earned only 58 percent of the amount white men earned.[44]

- In 1996, African Americans earned 66.8 percent the salary of white men.

- Women appear in only 15 percent of front-page newspaper stories, according to a survey sponsored by Women, Men, and Media.[45]

- Sixty-two percent of mothers with children under six now work, up from 47 percent in 1980.[46]

- The tax code still favors the working man and the stay-at-home wife.[47]

Although the world's women have experienced improved health and educational opportunities, they still have few options for using their abilities.[48] In some countries, women have virtually no rights at all.[49]

In the United States, a large proportion of women continue to cluster in traditional clerical and personal services jobs, which are often low-paying, part-time, and dead-end, instead of the more lucrative, nontraditional jobs (of which 75 percent or more are filled with men).[50] There is still considerable sexual harassment for many women in educational institutions, the military, and other civilian workplaces. However, new laws and policies are sending the message that *sexual harassment* is not to be tolerated.[51]

Women have advanced significantly in the last half of the twentieth century. There are many more female CEOs, more women-owned businesses, more successful female politicians, doctors, and lawyers, often earning the same income as men at these higher levels. Still, they have a long way to go in many areas to achieve equality with men, not only in the workplace but also at home. Many women who earn more than their spouses (22 percent do) still find themselves doing more than two-thirds of the household chores.[52]

Gender Bender: Men

Over the past centuries, the male role has not evolved very much, though some men now help with housework and child care. Most men see their career as their main focus and a major element in their dreams and aspirations. They may experience crises as their careers and lives evolve, especially in their forties (mid-life) and sixties (retirement). Though career is still important, other areas undergo sometimes painful evaluation as well. Marriage and family are usually integral components of their self-image as are friendships/peer relationships, ethnicity/religion, and leisure.

Career decisions men make at these transition times are linked to their values. Workplace satisfaction, salary, prestige, commuting time, overtime,

"It seems like only yesterday I was on the verge of getting it all together."

pressure, travel, and colleagues all have an impact, positive or negative, on personal and family life for men as well as for women.

The results of the changes that many women have been making in their careers and personal lives have generally been positive for them. But these changes have forced men to change, not always in ways they find comfortable. For example, men now more frequently work with and are supervised by competent women, with fewer promotions coming their way. Trying to fit into new expectations about what they should do and how they should be is adding new layers of frustration and bewilderment to some men's lives. It is especially difficult when they feel they had their lives all figured out and are not sure what the new expectations really are or where these expectations will lead. Often men come to a dead-end where no more promotions are possible. Like many women, many men feel trapped in low-paying, monotonous, demanding, or demeaning jobs.

Still, a study from the University of California, Los Angeles, noted that white males hold 95 percent of the positions of power in the United States, and minorities including black, Asian, and Hispanic men and women occupy

FOR BETTER OR FOR WORSE © Lynn Johnston Productions, Inc./Dist. by United Feature Syndicate, Inc.

only 1 percent of top corporate jobs.[53] Despite that, the successful man as well as the unsuccessful one may be leading a life of quiet desperation. Many have buried themselves in their work and cut themselves off from nurturing by family and friends and from taking the needed leisure time that can be critical, especially at times of crisis. As the late Paul Tsongas, former U.S. senator from Massachusetts, said, "No man ever said on his deathbed, 'I wish I had spent more time with my business.'"[54]

Many men are willing to attend workshops provided by such companies as Merrill Lynch, American Express, IBM, and Time-Warner to help them resolve issues dealing with conflicts over family and careers. Companies are finding that when both men and women are certain that family responsibilities are being covered, they work more efficiently, turnover is lower, and profits increase.[55]

Family, Career, or Both? Minding the Family

As it has become more common for both parents to work, career choices have had to be integrated more fully into family life. Even the definition of family, a highly important life component, has been changing. Today the adults who manage a household may both be working and married with fewer children than preceding generations, or without children, or remarried with part-time children, or not married; they may be two single mothers trying to make ends meet; they may be gay or lesbian partners.

Only about half of American children live in the so-called traditional families consisting of a mother, father, and full brothers and sisters.[56] Whereas people may be slower to marry, fewer are getting divorced, and out-of-wedlock births are declining as people settle into more traditional family life, albeit in a style different from their 1950s counterparts.[57] Families headed by single men are the fastest-growing type of family in America, representing

15 percent of single-parent families.[58] Each year sees a drop in the number of traditional households. Today, 24.9 percent of households consist of one person compared to 6.8 percent in 1970.[59]

At last count, women are entering the workplace in greater numbers than men. They will account for 63 percent of the growth in the labor force, according to the U.S. Department of Labor and at least 55 percent of them will provide half the household income. At least 85 percent of new mothers return to work within six months after childbirth. Finding day care is a major concern for them.[60]

Most developed countries guarantee between 75 and 100 percent of a woman's pay for maternity leave that can range from eight to sixteen weeks, according to a study, "Maternity Protection at Work," by the International Labor Organization. The exceptions are the United States, Australia, and New Zealand.[61] And in the case of workers who work odd hours, "night care" has become a need as well. Companies who meet these needs find little absenteeism and greater worker productivity.

Fitting a career into the family equation presents singular problems, especially for women who still take major responsibility for home and children. Women in demanding positions wish they had a wife at home, while men still count on their wives for career support. Women who do divorce find that raising children alone can be difficult, with finances often a serious problem.

Dazzled by two incomes, many trend-setting, successful working couples find themselves on the "trend-mill" toward a frenetic and hard-edged kind of success. Anne-Marie Foisy-Grusonik says, "Frequently, after telling others about my family and my career, they would respond, 'It sounds like you have the best of both worlds.' But in my heart I felt I had the worst of both worlds, and they were constantly at odds." Someone once gave her a coffee mug that said, "'I am a working woman, I take care of a house. I hold down a job. I am nuts." And she responded, "I was!" She opted out of the work world after struggling with career and family concerns for some years.[62]

In her consulting work with women beginning businesses, Nancy K. Austin tells them, "The chances of 'having it all' are about as thin as a pinstripe." She adds, "I've learned that a love of work and a love of family, balanced so that one never injures the other, is only an illusion."[63]

As women move up in the workplace they are facing the dilemma that men have often faced—the prospect of being asked to relocate. If the decision involves a spouse and children, accommodations need to be made for the concerns of these significant others in the family: the spouse's career, the children's education, and perhaps care for elderly parents. Companies who wish to hold onto a valued employee will assist the family in the process, often helping the spouse with his or her job change, too.

Family fulfills some of our deepest needs and wants on many levels for physical, emotional, intellectual, and altruistic/spiritual support and growth. Families are those people who, theoretically, are enduringly present in a special way to see a person through the ups and downs of life and career. Trying to nurture both *is* a balancing act!

Child/Elder Care

For working parents, finding someone to care for their children—with care—while they work is a difficult, crucial, and often emotional task. The family-leave law provides up to twelve weeks of unpaid leave for specific family and medical needs.[64] If a person has elderly parents, perhaps living at a distance, eldercare may also present challenges. Many men still are reluctant to stay home with children or elders, but that attitude is slowly changing.[65] In 1997, the U.S. Census Bureau estimated that 1.9 million fathers were their children's primary caregiver.[66]

An increasing number of companies provide child care, flexible or part-time work schedules, and some form of family leave that their employees can use to care for children and elders. Whatever arrangements are made, dropping children off in the morning and picking them up from the child care center or sitter adds yet another chore in the work race for working parents. The challenges and needs of diverse households are beginning to be acknowledged in the workplace.

Teenagers and Young Adults

Teenagers who have done well in high school are usually confident and college bound; numbers of their peers, however, have not yet learned necessary job skills or experienced many feelings of achievement. Approaching the first rung of the ladder is the most difficult step in the entire lifetime career process. Statistics show that the unemployment rate for young adults is much higher than the rate for the remainder of the population, with young black teens having the most difficulty becoming employed.

Geographical locations add special constraints for young people. In rural areas, the upward-bound teen may have problems finding adequate higher education and good jobs. Inner cities may provide little support or career and educational opportunities for the ghetto teen.

Some people feel that for students to work while they are in school can be a valuable as well as a profitable experience, as long as their grades don't suffer. Such opportunities can help inexperienced workers gain badly needed work experience while they explore various facets of workplaces. Too much work, however, can add to the stress of adolescence and adversely affect grades, the low pay not worth the sacrifice of time or the encouragement it may give to overspending. Young people also need some time for social life and relaxation, time to become involved in a variety of activities, if their financial situation will allow it.

Schools can make the transition to work easier in other ways. Recognizing students' need to begin work, some high schools and colleges collaborate with businesses to offer them work experience, career and exploration programs, and internships. People in business are getting actively involved with young people, acting as mentors, and in some cases promising them college scholarships if they stay in school.

Supervised community service can help young adults get started. Such work often helps the environment and the community while the young person earns money. Entry into the job market for this age group should be easier in future years as many fewer young people will be in the job-market pipeline as we move into the twenty-first century.

The Aging Worker in the Workplace

People born today may well be alive in 2100,
since many more people will live to 100 and over.

As the U.S. family shrinks in size, the overall population is growing older and life expectancy is lengthening. The fastest growing segment of the population between now and 2050 will be those over 85. As the baby boom generation ages and fewer couples opt for children, the number of elderly people could outnumber the young.

Opportunities for rewarding work become fewer for both men and women as they grow older, especially after age forty. Many workers stay at jobs they've outgrown rather than face possible rejection in applying for a more challenging position. It seems that our youth-oriented, throwaway culture sees little value in older people. In playwright Lillian Hellman's words, they have "the wisdom that comes with age that we can't make use of."[67]

Betty Friedan estimates that we are being given an extra thirty years of life compared to our grandparents. Zalman Schachter-Shalomi says in *From Age-ing to Sage-ing* that these years can be used profitably in "eldering" or guiding and mentoring young people using the accumulated wisdom gained over a lifetime.[68]

A national council reports that, although they remain unemployed longer when seeking work, older men and women hunt more diligently for jobs, hold a job longer with less absenteeism, perform as well as or better than younger people, and are more reliable and more willing to learn. One study showed that employee theft was much lower when companies hired retirees.[69]

Employers are hiring older people in entry-level service jobs as the teen population diminishes. With a declining employee pool, older people will continue to find opportunities for satisfying employment. Elders are returning to school not only for enrichment but to learn new skills. Many of them are using computers with great success.

For those who are younger, it is important to plan a career path and retirement so that those years will be financially secure and filled with satisfying involvements. Opportunities for moving in and up in a large company may shrink, but many "seasoned citizens" begin successful small businesses, volunteer in satisfying activities, and stay active beyond previous expectations.

Older people are providing positive role models as they plow new ground. Many are handling retirement, finances, leisure, health care, increased longevity, loneliness, loss of independence, inflation, and productive involvement quite well. Because of the increasing number of elderly, jobs providing for their needs such as those in leisure activities and health care should increase.

Minorities/Immigrants/Refugees: The "Other"

In today's world, we encounter people whose appearance, language, customs and culture, social and economic background, and just plain style can seem worlds apart from our own. When Jesse Jackson was running for president in 1988 he told supporters, "Most people in the world are yellow, black, brown—they're poor, female, non-Christian, and young—and they don't speak English!"[70] We will see more and more diversity in the workplace. The numbers of Asians and Hispanics is expected to surge by 2050,[71] with Hispanics leading as the largest ethnic group in the United States by the year 2005.[72] Overt prejudice involving blacks, Hispanics, Native Americans, immigrants and refugees, and women, and the gap it creates in everything from job opportunities to education, is still a major and dismal hurdle.[73] Still, minority women and men are slowly increasing their numbers in better-paying jobs and positions of prestige. The number of interracial marriages and multiethnic children in the United States has grown so dramatically that it is difficult to say just what race many people belong to. Golf pro, Tiger Woods, includes his Caucasian, black, Indian, and Thai blood when speaking of his heritage.[74]

Increasing numbers of Hispanics are entering the middle class. The number of Latino-owned businesses tripled and sales revenues surged in the 1980s and 1990s, growing nearly three times as fast as business overall.[75] These businesses increased from 862 owned in 1992 to more than one million in 1996; they are expected to grow to two million by the year 2000.[76] Hispanic buying power has become a factor in marketing with many companies.

The black middle class with its attendant affluence is growing, and more blacks than ever before are visible in positions of influence; however, there is still a great deal of improvement needed in the community of blacks left behind. Racism is still a factor in American life, as evidenced by the push to dismantle some elements of civil rights legislation. Many in the Native American population have been left far behind also, and rarely are they even noted in the statistics. Twenty-eight percent of blacks live below the poverty

MEDIAN EARNINGS/YEAR-ROUND, FULL-TIME WORKERS 1996

- White men $32,966
- African American men $26,404
- White women $24,160
- African American women $21,473
- Hispanic men $21,056
- Hispanic women $18,665

line, compared with 11 percent of whites, with blacks earning sixty-three cents for every dollar earned by whites.[77]

Immigrants and refugees face added burdens. Never before in history have so many people migrated in fear and suffering during such a short period of time as in these past decades. Not only do people migrate to other countries, but because of wars, environmental destruction, and economic inequities, increasing millions of people are displaced within their own countries. These migrations have been due in part, according to former president Jimmy Carter, "to the failure on the part of the world to live by principles of peace and human rights."[78] The struggle to compete in a strange land like the United States with its assertive brand of success can seem overwhelming to these newcomers.

The Disabled and Their Abilities

A humorous article by Adair Lara says that, like the movie hero Forrest Gump, most people know how to do some things very well, and in the rest of life "kind of fake it."[79] Although everyone has some limitations, people whose disabilities are more visible have been assumed to be incapable of doing anything. That attitude seems to be changing, and society is finally recognizing that among people with unusual limitations there is a vast pool of valuable and important skills.

The Americans with Disabilities Act of 1992 made it illegal to discriminate in employment against anyone who has the skills, experience, education, and other requirements to do the essential functions of the job with or *without* reasonable accommodations by the employer.[80] High tech in the workplace is bringing greater support to people with obvious limitations: talking/Braille computers for the visually impaired; robots to assist with physical tasks.

Changing views has been the greatest help as people become comfortable with others who have differences. It has led us to the realization that

FOR BETTER OR FOR WORSE © Lynn Johnston Productions, Inc./Dist. by United Feature Syndicate, Inc.

everyone, regardless of role or job title, can make a positive contribution. Not only will you work with a greater variety of people, you will be supplying goods or services to an increasingly diverse population with new and different methods of supplying their needs and wants. It can lead to interesting new ways of working.

Stressed for Success

Many of us work according to rigid schedules that don't match our natural rhythms or leave leeway for personal needs. We are continually caught in a time bind in an increasingly complex world of ever-longer commutes, more complicated personal business transactions, and more involved maintenance of homes and gadgets.

Work occupies prime time. For the past fifty years, the forty-hour week and the 2,000-hour, fifty-week year have been the center of life, virtually set in concrete. Corporate cutbacks now often force remaining workers to work more hours. The Families and Work Institute in New York tells us that 45 percent of Americans work more than forty hours a week and 10 percent work more than sixty hours.[81] And then there are those folks who are on call twenty-four hours a day by fax, e-mail, cell phones, beepers, and computer link-ups—even when they are driving down the freeway! Many people are working two or three jobs just to make ends meet though some are also stretching those "ends" beyond what is necessary or enriching. Work plus the demands of family and the business of living leave many people with little time for other enriched choices.

Workplace stress has become a concern as companies downsize, move away, and otherwise squeeze their employees to produce more, with the threat of unemployment often only a paycheck away. Many Americans are juggling seven things at a time not just to succeed but to survive. Stress in great enough quantities can cause exhaustion, illness, and even death.[82] Stress is magnified by the pace of innovation and the necessity to beat competitors to the market. A difficult boss can be a source of stress as well as a hindrance to productivity. Lack of time to relax with family and friends and simply have fun often causes a life to go out of balance. Stress results when the demands of life become too great.

In the early 1980s, studies of some Silicon Valley, California, firms disclosed a higher divorce rate among their employees than for the United States as a whole; high rates of sexual and physical abuse of children; frequent drug use by children of families employed in high-tech firms; high numbers of strokes at work; and families living beyond their means.[83] Our biology has yet to catch up and blend with our technology without causing us to lose our identities or our health.

Many workers fear taking the time off that is due them for fear of falling behind or looking like they are not busy. (The boss may give them more work!) Shorter vacations have become the norm. U.S. workers average ten days of vacation a year, ranking them twentieth in a list of industrialized countries, with Austrian workers topping the list with thirty vacation days.[84] Oddly, people brag that they haven't had a vacation in years.

Not all studies agree, however, with some researchers showing that people work fewer hours than they did thirty years ago but have many more involvements that make them feel a time crunch. For example, people spend many hours watching TV, drive their children to many more activities, play sports, and socialize more than their parents did, and then feel the time crunch in other aspects of their lives.[85]

Hard work doesn't necessarily lead to excess stress if it is enjoyable. Zest and energy for life come with doing things that challenge us and make us feel valued. Some people, though they may be in a job that is not their preference, have the ability to put their energy into it and find enjoyment.

Here is a checklist to help you decide whether you are overstressed, with some tips for changes you can make to reduce your stress level:

- Are you very unhappy with your life or your work? It's time to reevaluate each life component to pinpoint and resolve the problem. Learning to accept yourself and appreciate your good points can be an important first step. Sometimes the changes needed may be very small.

- Are you feeling excessively fatigued? Do you feel overworked? Find some enjoyable activity outside of work that will give you new energy. Exercise, for example, can actually be energizing. Get someone to take over for you at home or at work for a couple of days while you spend time sorting out your priorities. What can you eliminate? How can you get the help you need? Plan regular meetings with a good friend or colleague to talk over your progress in keeping a balanced schedule.

- Do you feel regularly stressed? Take a minivacation—for example, a weekend at home doing nothing but soaking up leisure, letting other people deal with distractions. Alternate with a friend by providing respite time for each other. Watch funny movies because humor is a great stress reliever and even tears can help. Meditate, do yoga, play soothing music, enjoy a romp with the dog, or brush your cat.

Stress-reduction and health maintenance workshops are available at many community centers, conferences, health care centers, and even many companies; these teach simple relaxation techniques that can become a habit. Some companies, like SC Johnson Wax, that provide exercise programs have found that their people are more relaxed and productive and have fewer health problems.[86]

Leisure, for many, is hard won. John Kenneth Galbraith says, "Only if an individual has a choice as to the length of his working week or year, along with the option of taking unpaid leave for longer periods, does he or she have an effective choice between income and leisure."[87] Some workers are striking for more time at home—doing away with forced overtime and better pensions—rather than higher pay, a plus for family values.[88] Humans have always dreamed of a world without work or at least with less work. In *BREAKTIME, Living without Work in a Nine to Five World,* Bernard Lefkowitz discusses some alternatives to "work."[89]

Many more workers could be employed if some people worked fewer than forty hours a week, fifty weeks a year. The loss of income might be offset in many ways (even financially): saving energy and resources, enjoying a more enriched life, having more time for the business of living. Many people with special needs such as parents, the elderly, and the handicapped are able to work when they are provided with a shorter schedule. Writer and philosopher Tony Shively felt that with a shorter work schedule people might be more efficient. He said, "Society often demands more of a person's nature than it can give."

In the next chapter we consider various workstyle options with a view to helping clarify your career decision.

 Self-Assessment Exercises

The following exercises will help you decide on a category of workplace and understand its important rewards and characteristics.

1. Where Do You Fit In?

a. Number the categories of workplace in order of importance to you:

<u>2</u> Business   <u>1</u> Education   ____ Government

____ Industry   ____ Health   ____ Military

____ Entertainment/communication

b. Check the workplace/location that most appeals to you:

____ Very small   <u>✓</u> Moderate   ____ Very large   ____ Multinational

____ Local   ____ Regional   ____ Global

Tell why it is important: _____

_____

c. Check all the settings and styles you prefer:

<u>✓</u> Indoors   ____ Outdoors

____ Traveling/fieldwork   ____ Varied work setting

____ Alone   ____ With a team

____ Close supervision   <u>✓</u> Independent

Tell why:

_____

_____

d. How far up the career ladder do you think you want to go? Explain.

_____

_____

2. Workplace Rewards

Rate these workplace rewards H, M, or L (meaning high, medium, or low) in importance to you as a potential employee. Put an E on any that are essential for you.

<u>H</u> Salary

<u>H</u> Paid holidays/vacation

_H_ Medical care benefits

_m_ Dental care benefits

_m_ Employer stock option plan

_m_ Career support and development

_H_ Compatible values

_M_ Supportive emotional climate

_L_ Help with child/elder care

_L_ Such personal care rewards as on-site recreation, financial counseling

_M_ Retirement benefits

_H_ Autonomy

3. Workplace Values

a. Rate this summary of corporate values H, M, or L (meaning high, medium, or low) in importance to you as a potential employee. Put an E on any that are essential for you in a company you might consider working for.

_M_ Makes safe, quality, attractive, affordable products that fulfill legitimate needs and wants

_M_ Is environmentally conscious

_H_ Is an equal opportunity employer; follows fair and safe labor practices

_h_ Supports workplace democracy and worker participation

_H_ Is honest and fair in business dealings

_H_ Respects people of all backgrounds

_H_ Does not depend on repressive governments or military weapons contracts

_M_ Is a good member of the community

4. Identifying Major Components of Your Life

a. Rank these components of your life in order of importance to you.

<u>_3_</u> Career   _____ Ethnic/national ties

<u>_1_</u> Marriage   <u>_6_</u> Religion/spiritual development

<u>_2_</u> Family   <u>_5_</u> Leisure

<u>_4_</u> Education   _____ What else? _____

b. What problems do you see in fitting each of these components into your life? Into the lives of those around you?

_____

_____

_____

5. Stress

a. Which elements of your life components cause you the most stress?

Time - too little ṇit / CAREER _____

b. How do you take care of stress in your life?

_____

6. Thinking about Your Roles

On a separate sheet of paper briefly describe yourself by means of ten roles such as your gender, race, ethnic background, nationality, religion, student status, major, job/career, and other features that define (or that you feel do not define) you. Describe strong feelings associated with any of these roles.

 Group Discussion Questions

1. Write about or describe your ideal workplace and schedule to your group. Include your ideal community/geographical location.

2. In what ways is your household a workplace? Consider goods and services, management, finances, maintenance, communications, human resources,

labor negotiations, your degree of commitment, emotional climate, skills you use, and functions you perform. Does your household respect the rights of its members? Care for the natural environment?

3. How "ad proof" are you? Go for a week without listening to or reading any ads or buying nonessentials. How much money did you/could you save? Do you consider the ethics of a company before you buy its products? How?

4. What changes in the workplace (for example, in schedules) and in society could help solve the unemployment problem?

5. Do you believe most companies could live up to socially responsible guidelines? Name some that do. Could they improve? How?

6. What factors prevent workplace environments from improving?

7. Describe a society in which gender distinctions are still quite clearly marked. How do the expectations for men and for women differ? Do some of these expectations still exist in the United States? Besides obvious anatomical differences, are there real gender differences between men and women?

8. As a male, do you find it difficult to believe that women have been/are discriminated against? Explain. Have you observed sexual harassment against any woman? Do you personally feel any dilemmas about your gender role as a male?

9. As a female, do you feel discriminated against? How? Do you feel that you have been the victim of sexual harassment? Do you personally feel any dilemmas about your role in society as female? How? Have you ever observed sexual harassment of a male?

10. Describe yourself as an aging person facing retirement. How would you like retirement to be for you?

11. Gather information from an older family member about your ethnic background. Find out when your ancestors came to the United States and what the experience was like for them. Share the information with your group.

12. Name two successful people that you admire. Tell why. Did the various roles they play influence your choices? How? Jennifer Dunn, Nicole Kidman - Successful working mothers

13. Do you feel that affirmative action programs have been successful enough that we no longer need them? Why? How might we bring gender and race equity into the workplace? Give reasons you think it is important (or not) to do so.

6/

Timestyles/ Workstyles

Alternatives That Work

 FOCUS

- *Explore and evaluate various workstyles and schedules.*

- *Consider a business of your own.*

- *Learn how to research workplaces behind the scene and on site.*

Years ago, many people went to work in companies that paid a salary, required forty hours per week of work for fifty weeks per year, and provided some benefits and a job that often lasted for life. But these days, there are many other ways you might connect to the workplace—from very close and traditional to distant and innovative. You might work different schedules with varying styles. You may work "long distance," combine work in a company with a business of your own, or simply start your own business.

Work takes up prime time. Some workers would still opt for the forty-hour week but would like more flexibility. Others would prefer to cut back. About 15 percent of the U.S. work force are using alternative work schedules.[1] Two-thirds of Americans, regardless of gender, marital status, occupation, industry, education, or geographic location, say they would be willing to sacrifice pay just to have one or two more days off each week. Between 1991 and 1996, 28 percent of Americans voluntarily made changes that led to less income but a more balanced life, opting for time over money.[2] Here we will explore some workstyle options that might shed more light on your career decision.

Full-Time Alternatives

Flextime/Choice Time   Flextime allows employees to work any eight hours between specified times, such as 7 A.M. to 6 P.M. Compressed work schedules, such as four ten-hour days per week, are a variation on flextime. Three twelve-hour shifts, another variation, enable college students to work three weekend nights and still attend classes, or let working parents share child care.

Some employers allow employees to choose which holidays they will take off; some allow them to accumulate and use sick leave as paid time off. Some allow full-time employees to reduce work hours for a period of time in exchange for reduced compensation. Some allow "comp" (compensatory) time which gives an employee the option of time off instead of pay for overtime work. Instead of laying off large numbers of people, companies sometimes ask all employees to work fewer hours at a reduced salary.

The Bechtel Group, a worldwide engineering company based in San Francisco, felt that they would have an edge in recruiting valuable workers if they offered their people a nine-hour day, four days a week, with every other Friday off and the alternate Friday an eight-hour day. Their employees now look forward to twenty-six three-day weekends a year![3]

Thirty for Forty   Some innovative employers advertise a thirty-hour week for forty hours' pay. Sam Morris, plant manager at Metro Plastics Technologies Inc. in Columbus, Indiana, decided to try that system to lure workers during a time of low unemployment. It was so successful in increasing productivity and keeping workers happy that other companies are trying it.[4]

Job Sharing   Sharing one job allows two qualified people to work at one full-time position, in any combination of time schedules they can work out with their employer. One person might work mornings, the other, afternoons. They work out a system for sharing needed information.

Part-Time Work   More than thirty million Americans, or 18 percent as of 1996, are part-time employees—that is, they work from one to thirty-four hours a week. Thirty-eight percent are men; 62 percent are women; 27 percent are between the ages of sixteen and twenty-four. Perhaps as many as 80 percent would like full-time jobs but aren't able to find them.[5] Often, people work several part-time jobs just to make enough to live on since part-time work pays less well than a similar full-time job.

Temporary Work   A growing number of people opt for full-time but time-limited jobs. Such work is available in many areas such as office, technical, professional, industrial, and medical. All these fields require a wide range of skills for trained or trainable workers. People in these jobs may learn new skills and find access to jobs that are often available to those inside a company. In a survey of temporary workers, 38 percent said they were offered full-time employment by a company they entered on a temporary assignment.[6]

Manpower, Inc., the largest temporary agency in the United States, is also the world's largest nongovernment staffing services company. In 1997, they placed 790,000 temporary workers in this country. Over one-third of their temporary workers found full-time jobs as a result of temporary placement. Manpower offers an array of free training modules, skills testing, and a welfare-to-work program.[7] Some temporary agencies are moving toward being a person's main employer and may even provide a variety of benefits. Called contingent work, the trend toward part-time and temporary work seems to be emerging as a major feature in employment.

Although some people find that working part time or full time at intervals is quite to their liking, others find there are disadvantages. Full-time work is more likely to include benefits including health care, and retirement benefits, better wages, and a chance for promotion.

The continual uprooting of workers due to the greater ease with which employers can hire and fire affects both the workplace and the community. The U.S. Office of Personnel Management has issued regulations to limit the amount of time federal agencies can keep employees in temporary jobs.[8] Part-time and temporary workers are often considered expendable as companies strive to make business more profitable.

Overall, time flexibility may add to the work and cost of management, and part-time and temporary workers may demonstrate less commitment to the job, but research shows that absenteeism drops and productivity rises when companies adopt less rigid work hours. Businesses find that they benefit from the flexibility and the ability to change workers' hours and utilize work stations more efficiently.

The Computer Commute

Only in the last half of the twentieth century did people begin to commute to work on a large scale. Most of the United States was rural, and a great percentage of people either had their own farms or home businesses or they worked very close to home. In time, the easy commute became overtime spent in giant traffic jams speeding along at an average of five miles per hour!

Today there is a trend back to the old workstead as technology can bring people within sight and sound of each other even though they are hundreds of miles apart. One production plant was kept running weekends, even though the human in charge was ten miles away. Equipment that is thousands of miles in outer space can be operated and repaired from the earth by remote control. The Japanese have an experimental farm run by computerized robots.

A judge in Alaska hears cases at a distance by closed circuit TV, and sometimes she hears defendants who are at home by using a speaker phone in court. Telecommuting—using computers to communicate with others—has enormous potential for unclogging roads and saving energy, too. Productivity often increases for those who work at home.

Single parents, the elderly, and the disabled can find new opportunities worksteading. Lack of safety guides, however, and possible exploitation by an employing firm—meaning low wages, no vacations or benefits, and long hours—are causes for some concern. Isolation is another issue to consider. Career development may be put on hold when a person works at home.

Cost can be an issue. In some cases, workers may have to buy or lease equipment or office furniture. People may find their utility bills (for example, telephone link-up) and energy costs rising. A good computer system can be costly. A person who wants to telecommute needs to work out the parameters with his or her boss, including costs of computer, printer, modem, fax machine, telephone, and copier along with time restrictions and how to keep in touch with the main workplace.

Not all telecommuters chose this method just because they wanted to be home with children. Most of these workers do not feel isolated from peers; they took only moderate time off for breaks; and they smoked, drank, and took drugs less than regular nine-to-five, office-bound workers. Combining child raising with work at home, however, can also prove to be a stressful alternative. This and other family issues must be resolved: who can interrupt when; how late to work; whether to read a fax coming in at midnight; whether to do the laundry in the middle of the day!

About 11 million or more Americans telecommute, according to estimates of the New York–based research group FIND/SVP in 1997, compared with 4 million in 1990. Not everyone agrees that telecommuting is a good idea nor that it will continue to increase. There are bosses who like to see their workers work in person and there are people who enjoy going out to work rather than working at home. Some telecommute part time; some only temporarily. Many people find it highly satisfying and successful; companies find in many cases that productivity and morale improve among telecommuters.[9]

A down side to the ability to work long distance is that some companies have moved their data processing as well as manufacturing work to developing countries where worker wages as well as worker protection are minimal. This action subtracts from the available pool of jobs in the United States,[10] sometimes decimates the economy of a town or region, and often results in the exploitation of workers abroad.

Work in the In-Between

Some people would like more work independence but aren't ready to go out completely on their own. For them, here are some possibilities.

The *intrapreneur* holds an intermediate position between the cold, cruel corporation and the cold, cruel world of being on one's own. It is a term coined by Gifford Pinchot, III, a consultant to such companies as Exxon, to describe the *intracorporate entrepreneur*.[11] Intrapreneurs remain company employees while contracting their services to their employer. Using company resources and support, they act as self-employed persons, often developing services or products that the company wants but to which it is unwilling to commit with large-scale expenditures.

For example, one artistically handy employee negotiated a contract with her electronics company to make a number of working engineering models at home. As another example, an engineer could gather a team to do creative research. A teacher could be given a special assignment to develop a curriculum for his or her school district. A company benefits because it does not lose either a valued employee who might move to a competitor or that person's good idea. Intrapreneurship may require some capital, but it involves less risk than entrepreneurship. Look around your workplace for a possible intrapreneurial opportunity.

Franchises are for people who would like to be independent business owners but would prefer less risk and more support than they would have if they were totally on their own. Franchises have moved beyond fast food into such growing areas as hairstyling, quick-stop shopping, weight-loss systems, home/garden maintenance and remodeling, computer sales, and a whole host of other types of business ventures. A new franchise opens every eight minutes of each business day; one out of twelve business establishments is a franchise. While Fortune 500 companies downsized by over a million jobs during the last ten years, franchises were adding nearly two million jobs to the economy. Franchises account for 40.9 percent of all retail sales, and total sales could reach $1 trillion by the year 2000,[12] with home health care one of the leaders.[13] Franchises fail far less often than other small businesses and generally need less start-up financing. Many franchise companies are targeting young, energetic, and organized new college graduates as potential owners.

Some people use the equity in their homes for the initial capital. Some states—Maryland, for example—are encouraging women, minorities, and handicapped individuals to buy franchises by providing these fledgling investors with investment help. The parent company may provide training, equipment, marketing, name, themes, logos, uniforms, and other tools and support. The advantage of franchising to the parent firm is the opportunity to expand more rapidly than would be possible if it had to raise all the money necessary for moving into new markets.

Cooperatives, group-owned and democratically run enterprises, are an option for people to improve their work environments without having to strike out on their own. When a group begins a cooperative business, the venture often creates a kind of community and autonomy that have been lost in this century's development and expansion into giant global corporations. Cooperative enterprises often display social responsibility along with profit making and community involvement. They range from grocery markets to print shops, from forestry trusts to sewing cooperatives.[14] For example, food co-ops sometimes sell memberships to individuals who agree to work a certain number of hours a week in exchange for lower-cost food. These joint undertakings often result in increased motivation, sense of control, and productivity.

In the 1960s, women in Japan began a milk-buying cooperative that gave them more say about price, quality, and environmental issues in food production. Now working directly with farmers, they have a membership of more than 218,000 households in over 100 branches, each member contributing about $9 a month. With its own line of sixty products, they employ a full-time staff of over 700. As the fourth-largest co-op in Japan, they have $120 million in investments and in 1993 did $650 million in business.[15] Susan Meeker-Lowry says, "Cooperative businesses and worker-ownership are two of the most promising tools we have to regain control over our work lives *and* to revive our communities."[16]

A *buyout*—buying the company you work for—is one way to achieve greater autonomy, ensure that the company's value system matches yours, and

Reprinted with permission from Harley Schwadron.

become an owner. We don't envision an untested recruit buying out a company single-handedly, but some individuals and groups of seasoned workers have done so successfully when their plants have closed or one of their divisions have been "spun off." United Zipper Company in Woodland, North Carolina, became an employee-owned reality after months of hard, persistent work following near panic when the factory closed. And in 1994, 54,000 United Airlines employees sported buttons that declared, "You are talking to the owner!"[17]

Work of One's Own—the Entrepreneur

In time, the work you look for may be your own. Although a life without work may be beyond the dreams or desires of most people, many often wish they could be their own bosses. As the new century opens, self-employment is growing at a faster rate than wage- and salary-paying jobs. Most new jobs in the United States are being created by small, service-oriented firms or suppliers of parts—many of them women-owned—and this trend is predicted to grow into the next century."[18]

While large corporations were cutting back, in the last decade, small businesses were providing 80 percent of the net new jobs in the economy and almost all the innovation; many were based on socially and environmentally responsible practices. A survey found a surprising 37 percent, or more than one in three American households involved in entrepreneurship.[19]

Women are starting businesses at nearly twice the national average. The largest share is in the service sector, but there is huge growth in such nontraditional areas as wholesale trade, transportation/communications, agriculture, and manufacturing.[20]

- In 1996, women-owned businesses employed one in four U.S. workers, contributing nearly $2.3 trillion in sales to the economy.[21]

- Women of color own one in eight women-owned firms, with the greatest growth in nontraditional fields such as construction, wholesale trade, and transportation and public utilities.[22]

- Women own more than half of all U.S. businesses.[23]

- Women-owned businesses (mostly small) employed more people in the United States in 1992 than Fortune 500 companies employed in the world.[24]

- The salary differential between men and women is getting smaller.[25]

And while small businesses seem to fail, a survey by Bruce Phillips (of the Small Business Administration) and Bruce Kirchoff (of the New Jersey Institute of Technology) found that in reality only about 18 percent of all new businesses end in real failure. Some owners sell out, close a company, and begin another—perhaps in a different industry or location. Nearly 70 percent of companies formed in 1985 were still viable nine years later, with smaller ones having a higher survival rate than the larger ones. Kirchoff found that only about 20 percent to 25 percent of failed businesses he studied ended up owing money.[26] "Small firms—those with fewer than twenty employees, and especially those with less than four employees—will continue to play a dominant role in job creation." Women and minorities will continue to gain prominence in small business ownership.[27] Although half of the private sector U.S. work force work in small businesses, new jobs are created in them at a greater proportion. This trend is expected to continue.

It may seem beyond possible that a small, local company can enter the global market. But tiny Trek Bicycle in Wisconsin, which made its first bike in a rented barn, is now the world's biggest specialty bicycle maker. Its move into international marketing began with a small sale to Canada. The governor noted that "every time you sell one billion dollars of goods and services, you create 22,000 good jobs here in the state of Wisconsin."[28]

With increasing globalization of economies and affordable technology, many people find that they can begin a worldwide business on a desk at home. Called the "new entrepreneurs," the people who begin businesses are knowledgeable, experienced, technology literate, and willing to work with others; they set reasonable goals and work hard to achieve them. They are open to both creative and tried-and-true ideas about how to acquire a company, how to organize it, and how to keep it running well. Many of them are young people.

Small grassroots financial institutions are springing up around the world. They are dedicated to developing their communities and to helping all the community members, including the poor, to participate in the local economy. Some development programs begun by these institutions work with "incubators" that provide support, information, office space, and equipment for fledgling businesses. The Pajaro Valley Community Development Corporation in Watsonville, California, has supported a restaurant, produce market, soccer shop, bookstore, children's clothing store, hair stylist, and gift shop.

Some advisers encourage the budding entrepreneur to start with a flourish; others counsel going slowly and in small steps. It's hard to disagree that having a creative edge and perseverance with a new idea are pluses. At 3M, an engineer tried inventing a super glue that did not stick things together very successfully. Someone else tried the product and found a way to keep bookmark slips removable yet secure on the page. After he spent years trying to convince management the product had promise, the "Post-it" was born.[29] Each case is unique, but the facts show that planning and experimenting as well as having capital are essential. Most successful entrepreneurs have degrees, experience, and money, but we still hear and read about people with little background who begin small businesses with very little and in no time are making a profit. "Find a need and fill it" says an old adage that still works.

Some people decide to quite their jobs and create a home-based business. Pessimists say the day of the "Mom and Pop" venture is long gone, but this may not be so. Even though the competition from large chains is fierce, if Mom and Pop go high tech in a specialized market niche, they may well be developing highly efficient and successful companies.[30] Luke Elliott says that "even today, in the era of corporate cannibalism, it's possible to start a business on a shoestring." He and his wife Cindy started Photo Vision, a retail outlet for solar electric systems and other energy-related products with "$1,500 and a kitchen table."[31]

Here's what George Hellyer, a worksteading attorney, advises for someone who intends to replace a job by worksteading:[32]

> If a person is going to leave a job to work at home, [he or she] needs a very clear attitude about how [he or she] is going to live. I set up a rather modest goal of the kind of security I wanted to have before I left the law firm. I don't buy expensive clothes, for instance. I enjoy cooking so I don't go to restaurants much. If you have a place to live, where you can also work,

you can get along on very little. The rest of life doesn't really take too much money if you have a place to be.

Who knows what goods and services will be produced from the electronic cottage of the future?

Home-based entrepreneurs must be sure to check local zoning, traffic, and licensing laws before business starts booming, especially if they intend to use dangerous materials or otherwise impact the environment negatively, take up parking spaces, or have other features that would invade their neighborhood. Many local colleges and adult education centers provide workshops and counseling to help the prospective entrepreneur begin a business.

Many famous companies, including Apple Computer and Microsoft, began on a shoestring and became very successful. Jerry Pitts, a "downsized" health care manager, remodeled his garage and began a small sales operation for a telephone company. Some college students have begun businesses from their dorm rooms that bring in sales in the six-figure range: Absolute Screening and Printing turned out T-shirts with sales of $300,000 in the first quarter of 1993.[33] Millard Fuller, founder of Habitat for Humanity, started on his path to millionaire status while he was in college. He provided a service delivering birthday cakes from bakeries to students, paid for by their parents with a cut for him.

Karen Scott tested the possibility of a mail-order baby-products business in a unique way. She contacted 250 new mothers listed over time in her local newspaper, asking them by phone what products they sought. She began to focus on travel items and now Chelsea & Scott's travel items are top sellers in the $28 million business.[34]

You can avoid investing a fortune; start small by having a simple, inexpensive business card made. You can design it by computer and have it fast copied on card stock at your local copy store. Your first card does not have to be fancy. Then begin handing your cards out to friends and relatives, perhaps offering to do your first work free or for a small fee.

Using appropriate technology can be a plus for any business. Through the Internet you can network with people all over the world to gather information, share and test ideas, make contacts, and develop markets. Small businesses find that they can have as much exposure as large ones. Setting up a page on the Web may seem like the way to go for some entrepreneurs. If you are inexperienced, check with a good consultant and bone up before spending a mint on a combination that may not be right for you. A suitable system can save money and time and reach the people you are seeking as well as get you in touch with supportive colleagues.

Media messages to the contrary, the best advertisement is word-of-mouth by satisfied customers. You can use evenings and weekends to test the waters while keeping your paying job as a backup. Because of the expenses of setting up an office if you are a beginner, therapist Richard Patocchi advises you to rent office space part time; only after you have enough clients to justify expansion should you agree to rent the space for more time per week. If you need to hire some employees, providing the equipment for computer-at-home work can be a highly cost-effective way to expand your own business.

Contracting is a way many people begin a business. Companies both large and small may find that contracting with another entity can provide them with resources and skilled people they lack or can relieve them of burdens at a small cost. Contracting also enables them to focus their resources more closely on fewer tasks at the home company and to do what they do best. Also called outsourcing, this way of doing business lets companies hire out such jobs as specialized parts manufacture, data processing, warehouse storage, accounting, human relations/development, and health care provision. Such contracting entities may form a group with other companies and procure cheaper health insurance. Owners of small businesses as well as contingent workers often do not have access to health care or legal services as well as volume purchasing of such items as office supplies. One woman began her own business by contracting to do newsletters for a number of companies that didn't wish to produce their own.

Community enhancement offers another entrepreneurial opportunity. Some businesses are set up to help solve community social problems such as homelessness or drug addiction. "The social sector is the fastest growing of the country's sectors and the largest employer. There are nearly one million nonprofit organizations in the United States. Well over ninety million people are involved in nonprofit activities, including both volunteers and employed staff.[35] They often work with their municipalities and other government and nonprofit entities to obtain funding.

Some entrepreneurs are beginning nonprofit organizations that are supported by for-profit components, making fund-raising less of a chore. Delancey Street in San Francisco, a self-help, non-nonsense program, with *no* government funding, is a beautiful home and business complex built by its residents with donations of money and material from the business community. Their elegant restaurant with a view of San Francisco Bay nets $1 million each year; their moving company earns $3 million. Other businesses they've developed and run, such as printing and catering, add more. The five hundred, well-dressed and well-mannered men and women who live and work there were all headed for prison terms, some having committed violent crimes! With lots of hard work, they are able to turn their lives around, help those coming after them, and move on to a respectable life.[36] The Roberts Foundation book, *The New Social Entrepreneurs,* contains numerous case studies of recent such nonprofits which have an income-generating entity and are set up to help the disadvantaged.[37]

The person with a product or service to offer, the energy to do it all, and the personality to make customers feel valued by giving them excellent service

MOST POPULAR START-UP BUSINESSES[38]

Arts and crafts	Investment broker
Audiovisual production services	Landscape/lawn maintenance
Automotive services/repair	Marketing programs/services
Beauty shop	Painting
Building contractor (remodel/paint)	Real estate
Communications consultant	Residential/commercial cleaning
Computer services/repair	Restaurant
Construction	Retail store
Consulting/business management	Trucking
Designing	Wholesale trade: nonperishable goods

can find great satisfaction in being an entrepreneur. There is no question that beginning a business may be hazardous to your health on many levels, but you get to be your own boss—twenty-four hours a day! From the five-year-old selling lemonade to the weekend do-it-yourselfer remodeling the kitchen, self-interest is a powerful motivator for getting work done. Generally, business owners are happier with their independent work than people who are employees.

Jobs with a better than average success rate include educational services to private education, health services, legal services, insurance agents and brokers, and personal services. Amusement and recreation services had a very high failure rate as did oil and gas extraction and lumber and wood manufacturing; general building contractors and furniture and home-furnishings stores also ranked high in rate of failure.[39]

Beware of putting too much faith in statistics. In California during one month, two different sets of statistics showed that either 17,000 positions had been lost or 229,000 positions had been gained. A closer look found that many new industries were being created from old ones. For example, despite the popular perception, "an RLA survey of Los Angeles neglected areas—typically those with the highest ethnic population—revealed a concentration of more than 15,000 companies employing 357,000 people with annual sales of $54 billion in manufacturing sectors alone." Asians and Latinos accounted for most of the region's population growth in the 1980s and 70 percent of all businesses in greater Los Angeles, and they showed household income increases that were four to five times the statewide averages, some of the highest in the country.[40] The businesses involved included fashion, computer and computer parts manufacturing, and the world's largest maker of tortilla chips.[41]

Creative careers are simply unusual ways to work that can be successful in a company or on your own. As you interview people and observe them on their jobs, look for those who have taken an ordinary job and brought it to life in a creative way, sometimes within a very structured bureaucracy. The position of "store manager" with its attendant duties may sound formidable or dull. But Monique Benoit of San Francisco gave it new life. Well known for her community involvement, she loved to shop in expensive antique stores and boutiques. She also cherished her independence and loved to travel, so she created her own job to satisfy these qualities. She sent a carefully composed letter to managers of her favorite stores, offering to "shop sit" if they had to be away from the store for business or personal reasons. She received a good response and subsequent offers of part-time, temporary, and permanent full-time employment.

In Santa Monica, California, two women began a vehicle-repair referral service to put people in touch with affordable, honest, and reliable mechanics. They generated $750,000 in sales in 1992.[42] "Susie Skates" indulges in her favorite sport while delivering messages. "Flying Fur" delivers pampered pets around the country, and "Sherlock Bones" searches for missing pets. After being laid off, Geoffrey Macon decided to begin a business that designs and produces upscale ethnic dinnerware with African American motifs.[43] From Clutter Cutter, Rent-a-Yenta or Rent-a-Goat, Eco-Tourism or Eco-Weddings, to Mama's Llamas and Rent-a-Thief, people create careers with imagination instead of capital.

Here are a few ideas for small-scale, more traditional although not always lucrative careers: house sitting, pet sitting, matching housemates or travel companions; child care that includes instruction in a craft or hobby; shopping, transportation, or exercise classes for the elderly and disabled; photography at special events; house calls for sick plants; servant-in-costume at parties—for example, at parties for children's birthdays; teaching do-it-yourself house or auto repair. Add producing and marketing very special gourmet home-grown/homemade food and herbs, sometimes by prearranged purchase, and pick-your-own flowers; combining photography with a host of activities both recreational and professional; combining art with science; designing/evaluating children's toys for companies; designing play space, books, or furniture; making treasures from trash—for example, rag rugs and quilts; conducting estate sales. The homeless in one community market their own home-grown vegetables raised on a city lot; they also sell used clothing and other treasures gleaned from donations. The possibilities are endless. One major mark of a fulfilling job is the invigorating and energy-giving feelings it provides.

Note that, like the founder of Togo's restaurant chain, some entrepreneurs break all the rules and end up as resounding successes!

The U.S. Small Business Administration has lists of information as well as local groups that give assistance to budding entrepreneurs. Local chambers

TIPS ON STARTING YOUR OWN BUSINESS

IS SMALL BUSINESS FOR YOU? YOUR QUALIFICATIONS SUMMARY

- Are you enterprising: confident, enthusiastic, optimistic, persistent, good with people?
- Are you trustworthy, energetic, healthy, hardworking, flexible, independent, balanced, organized, good at record-keeping?
- Are you a responsible leader, good decision maker, self-starter?
- Are you willing to learn, take advice, observe, and study other options, new trends?
- Can you face your mistakes, learn from them, and change your behaviors and attitudes?
- Do you have/can you develop a good support network: family, friends, associates?
- When you get an idea, can you get it off the ground?
- Do you know when to move on, not stay in one place forever?
- Do you have experience/education in the business you are considering?

INFORMATION GATHERING

- List ideas that you might turn into a business.
- If you are taking over an already existing business, list its resources (including people), its strengths, and its weaknesses; then work out ways to deal with each, setting priorities.
- Describe each one in a paragraph.
- Put each one through the decision-making process described in Chapter 8.
- Rank your ideas in order of desirability and likelihood of success.
- Evaluate each product or service: Is it innovative, of good quality, desirable, without heavy competition, something you would enjoy working with?
- Contact people listed in the Internet, telephone directory Yellow Pages, and newspaper financial pages who run similar or related businesses or franchises. Use the information interviewing techniques discussed later in this chapter to discuss your idea with them.
- Explore the possibilities of working with a partner.
- Attend workshops for small businesses offered by local colleges, the Small Business Administration, or other centers. Go to meetings of business people in your areas of interest. Read related books and magazines.
- Prepare a résumé, just as if you were job hunting, to clarify your qualifications to yourself and to your clients. List qualifications of any staff needed.
- Do market research; sometimes just asking around can give you an idea of the market before you hire someone to do it professionally.

(continued)

TIPS ON STARTING YOUR OWN BUSINESS *(continued)*

- Explore locations/types of spaces available and their cost. Consider sharing space, providing a service to a company in exchange for space; remodel a home space and telecommunicate with employees.

- Consider asking for help of people who later could become your advisory board.

FINANCIAL/LEGAL PLANNING

- Begin with a clear statement of purpose.

- Develop a sample product or prototype and find out whether people would buy it. Have people test it.

- Cost out possible expenditures: goods, services, equipment, insurance, real estate, advertising; develop a good accounting system.

- Find out about permits, licenses, and other documents you may need to get started. Taxes vary widely from state to state.

- Work out a financial plan as carefully as you would a résumé or term paper. Do a complete description of the business, estimate of cash flow, one-, two-, and five-year projections, your own financial assets and liabilities, the amount of money you need to "tide you over" until the business gets going.

- Talk to a knowledgeable financial planner about various funding options.

- Get to know your banker. Getting credit is one of the largest hurdles, especially for women!

- Develop a credit rating by repaying a small personal loan promptly.

- Look into loans from banks and private foundations; taxes, partnerships, stocks.

- Negotiate the terms of loans and other contracts and expenses; don't just accept the first suggestion.

- See a knowledgeable lawyer about various legal aspects of the business.

- Now software is available that will "walk you through" the process of developing a business plan including those financial projections so loved by lenders.

of commerce can be of great assistance. The Department of Transportation, Office of Small and Disadvantaged Business Utilization will also send information. See Resources later in this chapter for specific information. Your library can refer you to organizations and publications that can guide you. Community colleges, chambers of commerce, and other local groups often run workshops for prospective and current small business owners. These free resources have been enough to get many businesses off the ground.

RESOURCES

The following are resources you may want to use for follow-up. This listing does not imply an endorsement. It is up to you to evaluate the data you find. For further information you might check this text and endnotes.

HOW-TO-USE THE INTERNET SITES:

Easy Internet: http/www.futurenet.co.uk/netmag/Issuel/Easy/index.html

The Complete Internet Beginner's Guide

Glossary of Internet Terms offers understandable definitions:
  www.matisse.net/files/glossary.html

Internet Beginners Directory gives a tour of the Internet:
  www.globalcenter.net/gcweb/tour.html

Not all Websites listed will be equally useful. They change frequently and often contain giant amounts of information that can take considerable time to sift. You will probably find sufficient free information. Be cautious about giving out personal data, including your credit card number, on the Internet. And *beware:* you can spend hours of valuable time surfing the Net when perhaps making one phone call would get you the information you need or will put you in the loop for a job.

RESEARCH WORKPLACES AND SMALL BUSINESS OPPORTUNITIES

Association of Enterprising Moms
  www.momwork.com

Bibliography of Small Businesses
  http://www.inreach.com/sbdc/book

Business Ethics
  P.O. Box 8439
  Minneapolis, MN 55408

Small Business Administration (SBA)
  http://www.sba/govSBA

Small Business Development Centers Information (SBA)
  (800)8ASK-SBA

College of Buisness and Economics publishes *The Journal of Small Business Management*
  West Virginia University
  Morgantown, WV 26506

CO-OP America
  Screens companies for social responsibility
  Publishes *National Green Pages, 1999,* which lists socially responsible companies
  1612 K Street N.W. #600
  Washington, DC 20006
  www.coopamerica.org; www.greenpages.org; www.socialinvest.org

(continued)

As a business starts growing, an owner has to decide whether to brave the world of venture capital. Experience, competence at what you had already accomplished, and a good adviser are usually essential before you go into the deep water of big business. A good beginning might include a micro-loan from a microlending organization as described in Chapter 4. But we can count on small businesses to continue creating more jobs than large corporations into the next century, and much of that work is happening at home.

Third-Wave Prosumers

When a truck driver with a college degree was asked what he intended to do with his education, he replied, "I will practice living, I will develop my

---

RESOURCES *(continued)*

OMB Watch
   1731 Connecticut Ave. N.W.
   Washington, DC 20009

Union Label & Services Trades Department of the AFL-CIO for union-friendly
   companies: www-unionlabel.org

U.S. Department of the Census
   http://www.census.gov

U.S. Department of Labor Bureau of Labor Statistics
   Occupational Outlook Handbook Online
   http://stats.bls.gov
   Or using GOPHER or Anonymous FTP: stats.bls.gov

U.S. Department of Transportation
   The Office of Small and Disadvantaged Business Utilization
   400 Seventh Street, S.W., Room 9414
   Washington, DC 20590
   Website: http://osdbuweb.dot.gov

Women's Bureau
   Bureau of Labor Statistics
   http://www.dol.gov.dol.wb.welcome.htm
   Clearinghouse: 1-800-347-5335
   Fair Pay Clearinghouse: 1-800-347-3743

Request a *Directory of Business Development Publications* and a list of videos
(including *The Business Plan* and *Marketing: Winning Customers with a
Workable Plan*) from U.S. Small Buisness Publications, P.O. Box 30, Denver,
CO 80201 or P.O. Box 15434, Fort Worth, TX 76119, or pick up copies at
any local field office. 800-827-5722 or Website at www.sba.gov

---

intellect, which may incidentally contribute to the elevation of the esthetic
and cultural levels of society. I will try to develop the noble and creative elements within me. I will contribute very little to the *grossness* of the national
product."[44] Organic farmers Tom and Denisse Willey agree as they seek to
provide pure and wholesome food to people, free of pesticides and other
contaminants.

Some idealistic people prefer not to contribute to an economy they feel
encourages the mindless consumption of goods, wastes energy and resources,
and contributes to a poor quality of life. These nonconformists are carving
out unique lifestyles. Do-it-yourself and self-help tasks, bartering, and sharing
are all parts of their diverse lifestyle. The psychologist who helps people grow
at the office may come home to a small farm and grow vegetables for self and
sale. Veterinarian Richard Pitcairn's varied schedule at one time included

part-time spaying of dogs and cats at an animal shelter, along with research, writing, and private consulting. He and his artist wife grew many of their own vegetables and repaired their own car. Their book, *Dr. Pitcairn's Complete Guide to Natural Health for Dogs and Cats,* reflects their caring lifestyle.[45] Families garden and raise chickens for eggs, bees for honey, and fruit for jam for barter and table. One artist bartered a stained glass window for dental work.

Bill Cane lives a frugal, solar-powered lifestyle, gardening and bartering many of his goods and services for others. He gives workshops and publishes a quarterly journal called *Integrities* four times a year. His small nonprofit supports projects in Latin American countries for women and men in need of support and development help. Bill wrote in his book, *Through Crisis to Freedom,* "In crisis, you are somehow enabled to get in touch with sources of life deep inside yourself—sources you never knew were there. And then mysteriously, like the blades of grass, you begin to know how to grow."[46]

These new "old" lifestyles aren't for everyone, but they are options in a nine-to-five world for those willing to take the risk. Many people lived these simpler lifestyles years ago. In the technological future, we may be able to do less work and enjoy more of life's good things.

New Views

Most people, especially males, begin work after graduating from high school or college and keep at it until retirement. But even the most exciting of career fields can pall after many years, and workers must take steps to keep up their motivation. Going back to school, seeking a promotion, changing positions or companies, looking for a unique approach to your job, finding enriching hobbies, fostering personal growth on all levels are ways to keep up your work energy. Some industries such as Intel, Rolm, and Seagate have experimented with giving their employees leaves of absence for social action, educational projects, or pure recreation.

An engineer working in Silicon Valley found that his boss expected him to live a very upscale personal life. He was urged to trade in his ten-year-old Honda for a new BMW, and in general was criticized for many of his lifestyle choices. He decided to let his wife carry them financially for a few years while he went back to school to get a degree in spiritual theology. He is back with a new electronics company and a whole new perspective on life. By riding the train to work, he has time to read in his new field, and he does church work on weekends, to his great satisfaction.

As people explore alternatives, they create a variety of new workstyles. Many find they can make a living by working part time at several jobs. People who teach a course or two at community colleges may run their own businesses on the side, publish articles, or do graphics and some computer consulting. They may fish in the summer, teach skiing in the winter, and do a little farming and construction work in between. Some live very frugally, trading income for flexibility.

Leisure Styles

The suggestions offered earlier are aimed at helping you not only to find satisfying work but also to find time for satisfying leisure. Many people are opting for a less pressured, more serene life with less frantic activity. They start small home businesses that require only two or three days of work a week, retire early, take time off to be with children instead of trying to juggle work and child care. Busy people are asserting their need for daily meditation, exercise, or other forms of relaxation to help them get in touch with deeper values.

We are just beginning to consider the possibility of integrating work and leisure. Some husbands are taking time off while their wives work; some people are easing into retirement with reduced schedules. Total involvement in paid work, then, may not be essential in an affluent, information society, though many find it invigorating. Others may experience satisfaction in volunteering for community work.

But not everyone would be comfortable in a nontraditional workstyle or with less work time. Some find leisure frightening. Some workers end up spending their vacations or retirements down at the workplace watching others work. For some people, work is life and they enjoy it. At the extreme, some highly successful people could be leading lives that are impoverished on many levels. Instead of getting in touch with other facets of their personalities, the total technologist avoids social gatherings and the confirmed clerk avoids art.

But most of us need *some* structure in our lives, even though we might like to think of ourselves as free spirits. Work is the basic organizing principle for most people, so planning and learning how to balance work and leisure so that both are enriching is a never-ending process. Too much work can consume us; too much free time can bore us. Too much materialism suffocates us; too little frightens us. Many people are continually trying to find the balance, but they are further ahead than those who don't even *know* their lives are out of balance.

When we look at basic needs and wants and compare them with the work that is being done, we might be tempted to say that *much of the work we do is not the work that needs to be done.* Aware people are evaluating their own work to see whether it not only meets their own needs, wants, and values but is socially responsible as well. After a certain point, they may wonder if the *money* is worth the *time*. They are often people with ideals, education, and skills who have some money behind them to aid in a unique transition. They find themselves working hard, often at jobs they themselves have designed, and doing work they feel benefits society. Leisure can enrich not only individuals but the planet as well.

Community

A workplace is not just an isolated entity existing in a vacuum. No matter how aloof it tries to stand, it is enmeshed in its community in innumerable ways. From farm to city, from ocean to mountains, from prairies to wetlands, the geography of a locale affects a major part of a worker's life and workstyle. The predominant products and services provided by the area—logs or jam, silicon chips or potato chips—certainly influence a place.

A workplace, whether it be a huge corporation in a small town or a small business in a big city, affects and in turn is affected by its location. The style of dress, housing, and transportation, the kinds of leisure activities, schools, social life, and economic achievement will vary slightly or greatly from one place to another.

We expect a good community to include elements that are equally to everyone's advantage such as affordable health care, effective public safety, peace among various groups, a just legal system, and an unpolluted environment.[47] In a speech, Senator Bill Bradley said,

> Civil society . . . is the sphere of our most basic humanity—the personal, everyday realm that is governed by values such as responsibility, trust, fraternity, solidarity, and love. . . . What both Democrats and Republicans fail to see is that government and the market are not enough to make a civilization. There must also be a healthy, robust civic sector—a space in which the bonds of community can flourish.[48]

All over the country, communities are asserting their importance as unique places. Watsonville, California, claims its large Hispanic population with festivals of dance and music and celebrates both its agricultural heritage and its scenic beauty.

In North Carolina, Mayland Community College teams up with Penland School of Crafts (one of the most prestigious in the country) to highlight and develop job training in local crafts. A collaboration of nonprofits works with government and business to create the Cultural Diversity project in Fargo, North Dakota, and neighboring Moorhead, Minnesota.[49] Logging companies and environmentalists get together to create agreements beneficial to the local community.

Many job seekers will choose a place that encourages the type of lifestyle they would like to lead. A person seeking a more sophisticated style may choose a Manhattan apartment and wear the latest fashions whereas the Big Sur Coast of California is dotted with the tiny and isolated cabins of artists and writers in sweatshirts and jeans.

But beyond the physical level, people seek "community" that nourishes their emotional, intellectual, and spiritual levels. Just as in a company, a community has an unwritten psychological contract about how it treats its members and what it values. Many people would seek out a community for these qualities: it is a hospitable and human-scale place that does not force people to join in but provides opportunities for them to share experiences with like-minded people and to feel that each of them is valued and supported; it enables individuals to have a sense of belonging to a place and a say in what goes on there. It is, in short, a place where they can feel at home! Sometimes just the design of a place can make it easy for people to meet. The local post office or friendly coffee shop may draw people together, or an activity centered around religion, community service, sports, recreation, politics, theater, or music may provide opportunities to gather.

But some people value isolation whether they live in the forest or the busy streets of a large city. There is always a trade-off between privacy and community. Many new living styles are developing to give people the best of both worlds, shared housing and co-housing among them, where people have private spaces but may share some meals, child care, and recreational space with a community.

Former English professor and farmer-poet Wendell Barry sees the United States as Jefferson did—a collection of communities where people share more values than just economic ones. These include hard work, devotion, memory, and association. He questions what we mean by "progress" if it satisfies the loss of land and community.[50] Generally, the more a location is taken over by gigantic businesses and mammoth traffic systems, and the more people absorb themselves in technologies such as television and computers, the more difficult it is to find human-scale community.

Workplaces, too, are valued not only for the way they treat workers but also how they treat their local community. Giving away tax breaks and other advantages to lure large companies may be a poor trade-off. These businesses usually require increases of infrastructure and services; they often leave when conditions look better elsewhere. Municipalities are finding that encouraging a vigorous turnover of small businesses "as needed" creates a lively, lucrative, though tumultuous economy. Workplaces are good neighbors when they use local people and resources as much as possible; spend profits locally; and enhance community life by positive participation, not depleting it by adding to its problems. When businesses serve the community by satisfying the basic needs of its members and fulfilling wants that really enrich them, including employment, the lives of all the residents improve.

The Ins and Outs of Workplaces: Doing the Research

You have been surveying various and important aspects of both traditional and nontraditional workplaces and workstyles of interest to you. *Now* it is time to collect specific information about workplaces you might consider. First, get a view from the outside in by reading about workplaces and eliminating those that don't match your needs and wants. The next step is the information interview: getting the inside story about careers and companies by talking to people on site.

How can you find out what services your community needs that you might provide? Imagine how much archaeologists of the year A.D. 10,000 will learn about us if they get a look at some of our old telephone Yellow Pages. Scanning the Yellow Pages is one of the best ways to survey not only the businesses in an area but also the lifestyles. These listings reveal surprising ideas for both employment and beginning businesses. Looking at the Yellow Pages from other geographic areas can also tell you about businesses that might work in your community. You can determine whether a town is somewhat affluent by the number of upscale restaurant ads you find and the types of car dealers who advertise. Rural places will advertise a great deal of farm equipment; Silicon Valley will have pages of electronics firms. Comparing old phone books with new ones will tell you what businesses have failed; for example, solar energy companies took a beating when government subsidies were withdrawn in the 1980s and the message went out that energy conservation was not a priority.

Talking to people who have similar businesses or who might order from you, and showing your product to people who might buy it, are some ways to test your idea. Look for "niche" markets, those small areas where there is a possibility for a product or service. Think of new businesses in your area that attract people, such as coffee or frozen yogurt shops with a flair.

Information about companies is available from many sources, which may also help you learn whether the claims a business makes are true. Most libraries have a business reference section; most librarians love to help people and take pride in knowing where to find data. Company unions, labor groups, environmental organizations, and consumer groups are other sources of information. Ask for an annual report and other literature from a company; notice who is on the board of directors and what their affiliations are; ask what legislation the company supports or has helped to get passed; attend a meeting of the company if these are open to the public. Business and professional journals in your field will provide a wealth of information. For further information, check the Resources presented earlier in this chapter.

Professional organizations, a source of job leads, also hire personnel—for example, in public relations and finance. Look at chambers of commerce, Better Business Bureaus, real estate boards, and trade associations at the national, state, and local levels, not only for information but also for possible jobs.[51]

The U.S. Department of Labor has general and statistical information on all aspects of the labor market in the United States for those doing research for themselves or their businesses. This agency also has regional offices. The U.S. Bureau of Industrial Economics has information on trends in various fields. Your local chamber of commerce can inform you about the businesses in your town. College career center libraries, placement offices, and state employment offices are often stocked with material about companies. Some companies have public relations departments that send information if you write or call.

Don't forget to use the Yellow Pages of your phone book, a gold mine of ideas because just about every business in your area is listed there according to what it does. If you read the business section of your local newspaper regularly, you will know who is doing what and where in the work world in your community.

Your local college and public libraries are probably on the Internet. Of course, if you are becoming Net proficient, you can surf your way into a wealth of free information. Free business directories are also available on some networks. The Department of Labor's Office of Safety and Health Administration (OSHA) has computerized records of workplaces that have been cited for worker safety violations, listed by industry. Environmental impact statements and records of environmental violations are available from the federal Environmental Protection Agency. Information on local companies such as deeds and licenses are kept by city or county governments.

Reading about jobs can leave some pieces of the puzzle missing. Those descriptions are only the bare bones of the job. You can put flesh on those skeletons by visiting workplaces and interviewing people about what they do. From here on, it's important to be *out*—talking to everyone about his or her job, observing work environments, talking to people with inside information to share about places of interest to you.

Unless you are an experienced and sophisticated job seeker with a broad knowledge of jobs, you need to gather as much firsthand information as you can *before* you choose a career, and perhaps plan courses and get a degree. Some guides list "hot careers" with high salaries. On talking with people in the field, you may find there is more education and experience required than you care to take on or that openings are very scarce. Why not learn all you out to be different from your expectations? You can also eliminate misconceptions about the preparation you need to be hired.

Information Interviewing

You have probably already done a great deal of information interviewing. How often have working friends given you a blow-by-blow description of life at Picky Products, Inc.? (Or how often have you gotten good information from friends about a class, or an instructor for that matter!) If *you've* worked for a company (or taken a course), you have information about it that's not easily available to an outsider. You know the people who are likely to help beginners; you know how tough or easy the supervisors/teachers are, how interesting or boring the work is—what it's *really* like! Obtaining this inside information about a workplace answers two questions: Is this a job you would really like? Is this a place you would really like to work?

Don't be afraid to contact people who sound interesting. Ask them to tell you more about what they do or congratulate them on some accomplishment or promotion. People appreciate positive feedback. Let them know that you are sincerely interested in some aspect of their work or workplace.

If you feel timid about approaching a stranger, practice by interviewing people in your family, then a friend or neighbor about his or her job. Talk to all the people you meet about what they do and how they like it, and whom they can introduce you to in your career field. Ask people you know for names of willing interviewees. It's amazing how you can usually find someone who knows someone who knows someone. Your school alumni office is often in touch with graduates in different fields. An instructor in a field of interest may know a person who will talk to you. Seek someone close to the level at which you are applying. Don't ask to see the president of a company if you are searching out information about safety engineering. Rather, find a person who *is* a safety engineer or industrial technologist or technical supervisor.

If you want the interview to go smoothly, do not drop in unexpectedly on a busy person (unless you explain that you only wish to make an appointment for a later time when the person isn't busy). It's much better to make an appointment ahead of time at that person's convenience. Avoid calling during lunch hour, early mornings—especially Mondays, when everyone is getting organized—and late afternoons, especially Fridays, when people are getting ready to wrap up the day's or week's work. If you feel uncertain about going to an interview alone, ask a friend to introduce you, or ask someone with a mutual interest to go along. If it seems appropriate and you are comfortable with the idea, invite the person you will interview out for coffee or lunch after you visit the workplace.

PEANUTS reprinted by permission of United Feature Syndicate, Inc.

Use the information interview sparingly, not casually. Wait until you have some idea of your direction. Then have carefully prepared questions you haven't been able to find answers to through your research. You want to encourage people to talk easily about their work. Most people are sincerely interested in helping information seekers, but sometimes they cannot spare the time. Don't feel discouraged if you are refused an interview.

Following your skills and interests may lead you into work environments ranging from serene to frenetic. As a writer, for example, you could find yourself researching in a quiet library or risking your life gathering news in a civil insurrection. There are many things you thoroughly enjoy but might hate if you had to do them under pressure—a thousand times a day—in a hot, crowded, noisy, and otherwise unpleasant place—for an irritable boss with high blood pressure! You may enjoy cooking but are fairly certain you would not enjoy serving some of a billion hamburgers every day. You might not like cooking regularly for any large group, even in the most elegant setting. You can find out by visiting various kitchens, talking to the cooks, and observing what they do. Barbara Rosenbloom and Victoria Krayer, who owned a charcuterie in Berkeley, California, showed one visitor the huge pots of heavy paté that had to be mixed, emptied, and cleaned, demonstrating that cooking can be very physically demanding.

Find out whether the company you are interested in (or one like it) gives tours. In some cases, you can spend a whole day observing someone doing a job you might like. Remember, when you talk with people in your career field of interest, you are gathering all their biases. Each person likes and dislikes certain things about the job. Each one will give you a different view. Keep your antennae out to receive the emotional content of their messages. Then weigh all these messages against your good feelings and reasoned judgment.

There are other ways to meet people in your field of interest besides visiting their workplaces. Many professional groups welcome students to their meetings and have special rates for student/lay participation; the Society of Women Engineers, for example, is one of these. The *Occupational Outlook Handbook* you used for your research in Chapter 4 lists names and addresses of such organizations. Throughout the United States, the American Society for Training and Development has chapters that hold monthly meetings and annual conventions. At such times you can meet people who have access to local business information and contacts. Chambers of commerce and other community organizations hold regular luncheons with speakers. In social settings like these, it's possible to make contacts easily and explore possibilities for on-site visits. Many of these organizations are also putting up Websites faster than the click of a mouse. At workshops or classes in your career area of interest, speakers and participants can share information with you both formally and informally. Trade or business fairs can be a great way to see products and visit with people from a variety of companies in the same or related markets.

Much of your success will come from keeping your eyes and ears open. Begin to wonder what just about everyone you meet is doing. Almost every media news item is about what people are doing. Which activities attract you? How can you learn more about these activities? Keep on looking, listening, asking questions—it's your best source of information. Eventually you will be talking to people who are doing work you would like to do. Something will click as you begin to share experiences and enthusiasms. You will make a network of friends who may later wish to hire you.

One caution. Most people are happy to answer most questions about their jobs until you come to salary, but there are ways to get an idea of what you might expect. Here are some possible approaches: "What is the approximate salary *range* for a position like yours?" "How much might an entry-level person expect to earn in this area?" A call to a local/state employment office can also provide approximate salary levels.

At first, many people hesitate to call a stranger in a large company—or even an acquaintance in a small one. One student, whose talents were apparent to everyone but herself, was terrified at the prospect. She grimly made the first phone call. To her amazement, the interview was delightful—that is, until she was advised to explore a graduate program at a nearby university. She forced herself to see the department head that same day. Another warm reception! Elated, she rushed out to call her career counselor from the nearest phone booth. She was chuckling, "Here I am, thirty-five years old, and as excited as any kid over talking to two human beings!"

Another student given the same class assignment simply didn't do it. She had been a psychology major with a love for art; she changed to business because it seemed more "practical," although it didn't seem to fit her creative "people" needs. Then she discovered organizational development and talked about her interests to someone who knew a management consultant who used graphic arts in his work. Her reluctance to interview vanished as possibilities began to open up.

If you plan your information interviewing carefully, you may find a well-respected, experienced person who can listen to you, keep what you say confidential, and be a guide in finding other people to interview. This person may even become a mentor, someone who will give you tips not only on finding a job but also on advancing your career. Over time, your relationship may become so trustworthy that your mentor may give you constructive, perhaps painful, but helpful, critiques. You may have more than one such person; you may have someone in your company whom you feel comfortable with and can trust, a person who can help you develop a special skill; someone who can support you through tough times, even stand up for you if you are in the same company. With restructuring, companies have fewer managers, and employees have fewer opportunities to get help with their career development. A mentor can fill in and a fulfilling relationship may result. Some companies are even setting up mentor programs. Mentors find, too, that they learn from those coming up behind them: new ways of doing things, new problems that arise that they never had to face. It is not just a one-way street![52]

Perhaps not everyone you meet will be helpful. You may meet a "Queen Bee" or a "King Pin"—someone who has made it and is unwilling to help others. Sometimes people are absorbed in a complex problem, are truly too busy, or have yet to learn what all self-actualizing people know: the more you help others, the more successful you'll be. Many successful people enjoy sharing their expertise. So if you don't give up, you will find warmhearted people who understand your needs, your confusion, and you! Keep on searching for those who are sensitive to your concerns.

When people have spent time with you, follow up with thank-you notes. This courtesy will be appreciated and help employers to remember you when you begin the job hunt. The information interview process puts you in the hiring network. It can be an adventure—and it can be very profitable.

The applicants best prepared for a job interview are those who not only know the company they want to work for but also have a broad knowledge of the work world, its people and challenges, and the ways they can help with options. Knowing some of the basics about a company, an industry, and its competition gives you confidence during the job hunt.

Work Experience

Work experience—even if you have to volunteer—is one of the best ways to get information. Try your school or state employment placement office for positions at different workplaces. Or sign up at a temporary employment agency with a good reputation so you can survey businesses, make contacts,

WORKPLACE TAKE-CHARGE GROUPS

These groups—each with a different focus—provide job leads and ideas and support for workplace owners and workers to cooperate to effect positive change. They encourage businesses to show greater fairness toward employees and customers. They show companies ways to improve their relationships with their physical environment and with their host communities. Contact those that interest you.

The Alternatives Center
    Education Resources and Consultation for Democratic Organizations
    1740 Walnut
    Berkeley, CA 94704

Business Ethics
    P.O. Box 8439
    Minneapolis, MN 55408

Center for Economic Conversion
    222 C View Street
    Mountain View, CA 94041
    Website: www.conversion.org

Clearinghouse for Community Economic Development
    University of Missouri
    628 Clark Hall
    Columbia, MO 65211

Earth Work, magazine of conservation careers
    SCA National Headquarters
    689 River Road
    P.O. Box 550
    Charlestown, NH 03603

Environmental Research Foundation
    P.O. Box 5036
    Annapolis, MD 21403

Essential Information
    Publishes *Good Works: A Guide to Careers in Social Change*
    P.O. Box 19405
    Washington, DC 20036

Good Money, newsletter for socially concerned investors
    P.O. Box 502
    Dover, NH 03821

and earn money on your own schedule. Once inside a company, you can get acquainted with people—the cafeteria can be a great meeting place—and watch the bulletin boards for job announcements.

Internships are sometimes available for students to do course research and cooperative work experience, sometimes with pay. These positions can last a day or two, a whole semester, or even a year. While these sorts of activ-

---

WORKPLACE TAKE-CHARGE GROUPS *(continued)*

ICA Community Economic Development Program
    Suite 1127 Statler Building
    20 Park Plaza, Suite 1127
    Boston, MA 02116
    E-mail: icaica@aol.com
    Website: http://members.aol.com/icaica/ICAPAGE.htm

Job Seeker, a listing of national environmental jobs
    28672 Cty EW
    Warrens, WI 54666
    E-mail: jobseeker@tomah.com
    Website: http://www.tomah.com/jobseeker

Microcredit Summit on the Internet: http://www.microcreditsummit.org

National Center for Employee Ownership (information on shared ownership
    and paid and unpaid internships)
    1201 Martin Luther King Way
    Oakland, CA 94612
    E-mail: nceo@nceo.org
    Website: http://www.nceo.org/

New Road Map Foundation
    Publishes a newsletter that encourages a low-consumption/high-fulfillment
    lifestyle and *Your Money or Your Life*
    P.O. Box 15981
    Seattle, WA 98115
    Website: www.newroadmap.org
    www.simpleliving.net

New Ways to Work promotes equitable scheduling and staffing arrangements
    and publishes *The Job Sharing Handbook*
    785 Market Street Suite 950
    San Francisco, CA 94103
    Website: www.nww.org

North American Students of Cooperation
    Publishes *Guide to Cooperative Careers*
    P.O. Box 7715
    Ann Arbor, MI 48107
    313-663-0889

---

ities give you the opportunity to survey companies, they also give employers a chance to get to know you. Such contacts may be valuable resources for you in the future.

With some actual work experience, a young person who loves animals may find working at the veterinarian's office exciting or, with sick animals and worried owners, traumatic. On the other hand, every job will gradually (or quickly) demonstrate some unpleasant aspects. Basically, work is often hard work! You must function within the economic and time parameters of an organization or, if you are self-employed, meet clients' and society's demands. When both time and money are in short supply, deadlines and shortages create pressure.

As you become familiar with workplaces and as you make friends there, your confidence will grow. By the time you are ready for an interview, you will understand the job and some of its problems. You will know some of the latest techniques in your trade or profession. You will know people in the field who may recommend or even hire you. Many people find out about job openings not yet listed simply by asking everyone they know for information about future possibilities. And with your newfound self-confidence, that first job interview will be duck soup—not sitting duck! You will be ready to hire an employer.

 Self-Assessment Exercises

The following exercises will help you decide what kinds of workstyles you prefer and will then help you locate those that match your preferences.

1. Identifying Alternative Workstyles

Choose one (or several that go together) of these alternative workstyles that interest you most and tell how you would (or would not) like to live it out: entrepreneur, intrapreneur, contract work, telecommuter/worksteader, career creator, third-wave prosumer.

_____

_____

2. Finding Interesting Careers

Name three people you know who are in interesting careers in order of importance to you. Include the job title of each one.

_____   _____

_____   _____

_____   _____

Describe the characteristics you like of the most interesting of these careers.

_____

Describe the characteristics you dislike.

_____

3. Locating Contacts

List three businesses in your field of interest from the phone book Yellow Pages.

_____

_____

_____

4. Researching Workplaces

Using library/computer resources as much as possible, research one workplace in your career area. Use the information interview to ask for answers this research does not provide.

Name of workplace _____   Phone number _____

Address _____   City/State/Zip _____

Organization

Divisions and locations_____

_____

_____

Products/services _____

Number of employees _____   Job titles of interest to you _____

_____

Performance

Past and present market _____

_____

Company earnings as of past year _____

Future projections for growth and profit _____

Stability _____

Competitors _____

Other factors

Reputation/integrity _____

Environmental record _____

Social concern _____

5. Information Interview

Interview workers in a career field that interests you. Write the results of one such interview either here or on a separate sheet of paper.

Name of person	Company name

Job title	Address

Phone number	City/State/Zip

Here are some questions you might ask.

a. Why did you choose this field?

_____

_____

b. How did you get your job?

_____

_____

c. What do you really do all day?

_____

_____

d. If you could redesign your job, which parts would you keep? Which would you get rid of?

_____

_____

e. What were your most positive career decisions?

_____

_____

f. If you had it to do all over again, what would you do differently in your career? What decisions do you regret?

_____

_____

_____

g. What are the major issues in your career field? The important books, journals, organizations?

_____

_____

_____

h. What is the entry-level job title and its salary range?

_____

i. What steps would a typical career ladder have, about how long would it take to move through each step, and what would each one involve—for example, job duties, salary?

_____

_____

_____

j. How available are jobs in this field expected to be in the future?

_____

k. What are the requirements for the job: training, certificates, licenses, degrees, tools, union membership?

_____

l. Will your company have openings in this field soon? _____Yes   _____No

m. Could you recommend someone else I might interview?

_____   _____
Name of person   Company name

_____   _____
Job title   Address

_____   _____
Phone number   City/State/Zip

5. *Workplace Checklist*

Using both the library/Internet and the information interview for information, rate one workplace of interest to you on the following checklist.

Put a "+" in front of the ten qualities that are of most interest to you.

Company name _____   Phone number _____

Address _____   City/State/Zip _____

Management Characteristics

	Good	Fair	Poor	Doesn't Matter
_____ Honest/fair/ethical	___	___	___	___
_____ Respectful of you as a person	___	___	___	___
_____ Gives helpful performance feedback	___	___	___	___
_____ Shows appreciation for good work	___	___	___	___
_____ Open about the status of the company	___	___	___	___
_____ Willing to answer questions; listens	___	___	___	___
_____ Cooperative	___	___	___	___
_____ Clear goals	___	___	___	___
_____ Stable management style	___	___	___	___
_____ Makes positive contribution to locale	___	___	___	___
_____ Makes workers feel proud of its goals	___	___	___	___
_____ Is open to innovation	___	___	___	___
_____ Flexible	___	___	___	___
_____ Promote job security	___	___	___	___
_____ Adequate preparation for layoffs	___	___	___	___

Use of skills/interests

	Good	Fair	Poor	Doesn't Matter
_____ Respects/encourages autonomy/ideas	___	___	___	___
_____ Provides varied experience	___	___	___	___
_____ Acknowledges achievements	___	___	___	___
_____ Is open to transfers/promotions	___	___	___	___
_____ Offers education/growth opportunities	___	___	___	___
_____ Provides training/development	___	___	___	___

Work environment

	Good	Fair	Poor	Doesn't Matter
_____ Location/setting	___	___	___	___
_____ Appearance of buildings	___	___	___	___
_____ Work stations	___	___	___	___
_____ Cafeteria	___	___	___	___
_____ Restrooms	___	___	___	___
_____ Colors	___	___	___	___
_____ Light	___	___	___	___
_____ Furnishings/equipment	___	___	___	___
_____ Safe/environmentally conscious	___	___	___	___
_____ Compatible coworkers	___	___	___	___
_____ Friendliness	___	___	___	___
_____ Orderliness	___	___	___	___

Salary/benefits

	Good	Fair	Poor	Doesn't Matter
_____ Salary	___	___	___	___
_____ Medical/dental/vision care	___	___	___	___

_____ Life/disability insurance   ___   ___   ___   ___

_____ Profit sharing   ___   ___   ___   ___

_____ Retirement benefits   ___   ___   ___   ___

_____ Vacations/holidays   ___   ___   ___   ___

_____ Maternity/paternity leaves   ___   ___   ___   ___

_____ Child care   ___   ___   ___   ___

_____ "Business of living" personal time ___   ___   ___   ___

_____ Travel benefits   ___   ___   ___   ___

_____ Compensation in case of layoff   ___   ___   ___   ___

_____ Fitness facilities   ___   ___   ___   ___

_____ Flexible schedules   ___   ___   ___   ___

_____ Moving/travel expenses   ___   ___   ___   ___

Financial stability

	Good	Fair	Poor	Doesn't Matter
_____ Sales prospering	___	___	___	___
_____ No likely takeovers	___	___	___	___
_____ Manageable debt	___	___	___	___
_____ Positive cash flow	___	___	___	___
_____ Special product or service	___	___	___	___
_____ Little serious competition	___	___	___	___
_____ Shows foresight and plans ahead	___	___	___	___

The community

	Good	Fair	Poor	Doesn't Matter
_____ Recreational/cultural facilities	___	___	___	___
_____ Medical/dental facilities	___	___	___	___
_____ Acceptable schools	___	___	___	___
_____ Good transportation	___	___	___	___

_____ Reasonable cost of living   ___   ___   ___   ___

_____ Other amenities   ___   ___   ___   ___

_____ Benefits to the community   ___   ___   ___   ___

c. Complete this statement: I would (or would not) like to work there because

_____

_____

d. What other questions might you like to ask a person you interview?

_____

_____

Group Discussion Questions

1. Describe in detail an alternative workstyle you might enjoy.
2. Describe a business you might like to own.
3. Share any insights you gained from the information interviewing process.
4. Ask for career information from members of your study group. Trade resources and contacts for information interviewing.
5. Explain the following quote and give examples: "Much of the work we do is not the work that needs to be done."

7/

The Job Hunt

Tools for Breaking and Entering

FOCUS

- Learn about creative job hunting.

- Gather information about yourself into a good résumé.

- Prepare for an effective interview.

You have thoroughly assessed your needs, wants, shoulds, values, and interests. You have envisioned your ideal lifestyle. You have researched your skills so thoroughly that you now have a marvelous list of what you can do. You have collected many words to describe yourself. You have looked over the whole job market and found jobs that would suit you well. You have reflected on many societal issues that will affect your life and your work. You have interviewed people, researched companies, and explored workplaces. You have considered the job versus career issue, the career ladder, possibilities for future goals, creative careers, and owning your own business. You have zeroed in on a job title or two and some companies where you have contacts. In short, if you need no further training or education, you may be ready at last for the job hunt!

It is also highly possible that you have not yet completed some or many of these steps, much less made a career decision. And if the job hunt is several years down the road, you may be tempted to wait to learn the process. However, putting it off might find you unprepared if a great job opportunity should arise or your current position should disappear. Being prepared puts you steps ahead. And learning the process can sometimes facilitate decision making because it helps you focus on what a job requires of you. However you use this chapter, reviewing it just before you go out to job hunt can enhance your chances for success.

> I am rather
> like a mosquito in a nudist camp;
> I know what I ought to do,
> but I don't know where to begin.
> —*Stephen Bayne*

Job Hunting

Job hunting is often a full-time job. And like work, it is often hard work, whether you are hunting for full-time, part-time, or temporary work. All require the same care in preparation. Networking, résumés, letters, applications, phone calls, and interviews can make your head swim. The challenge and excitement of a career search may wear thin as you travel this long and sometimes weary road. A six-month search is not unusual. Keeping your wits about you and keeping up your courage are two essential skills.

A third skill is good manners. You will be meeting many people, asking for their time, and depending on their assistance. *Please, thank you,* and *you're welcome* are good words to have in your vocabulary, whether you say them or write them. A businesslike, polite phone style is a definite plus, and be sure the message that greets callers on your answering machine reflects this same politeness. Shaking hands firmly, making friendly eye contact, climbing in and out of a car smoothly—all the things you've been doing forever—can quickly come undone in a stress situation. So practice these behaviors consciously to be sure you perform them automatically, even at difficult times. Good table manners will definitely make the right impression if you find yourself invited to coffee or a meal. Waiting until others are seated before you sit down, and seeing that they are served before you begin gobbling the first course will put you on the right track, along with handling your knife and fork with confidence. Some colleges are offering courses on manners. If you feel shaky and need some review, look around your area for workshops teaching good manners or check your library for a basic book on etiquette.

Some people find it useful to join a support group or start one to help them during the job hunt. Friends can be a source of ideas and emotional support if and when the going gets tough. Ask for assistance and understanding. It also helps to keep several options open—developing possibilities on your present job, taking a course or two, inching toward starting your own business—while you interview in several different areas.

An unfortunate atmosphere of caution and distrust is evident in some job hunts, brought about by the behavior of a small number of job seekers. Under the pressure of the job hunt, these applicants may falsify information they give to a potential employer. They may also threaten a former employer with a lawsuit if he or she releases unfavorable information about them to anyone who might hire them later. As a result, former employers are sometimes unwilling to give out information that may be damaging to a job seeker, even though they know that person might cause severe problems for a future employer.

Some companies, driven by workplace theft and violence, costly lawsuits over damages caused by careless employees, and the cost involved in hiring unsuitable candidates, are resorting to the use of detective-style background checks. These checks may involve scrutiny of an applicant's criminal, employment, credit, driving, and educational records.[1] Honesty is still the best policy.

If you are already employed, you may want to consider your strategy for bridging the gap between your old job and your new one. Will your present employer be unhappy if he or she finds out you are job hunting? Will that make your current situation uncomfortable? If you have a good relationship with your employer, would it be better for you to share the news that you *are* looking for a new position and ask for a good recommendation, for support, and leads? If you wish to keep your job hunting to yourself, you must be sure that prospective employers do not leave messages for you at work. If you quit without having a new job lined up, will you have enough money to live on for the weeks or months it may take to land another position?

There is no one way to job hunt, but use all the help you can get. Employers often use want ads and employment agencies, and now the Internet, and many people find jobs through these sources. Be aware, however, that private employment agencies are like used car dealers. Some are reliable. Some will search for you, charging only the employer if you are hired. For some, the goal is only to put bodies in place and collect a fee. Some agencies are less than honest. They may put false ads in the newspaper to attract clients and then use excessive flattery to convince these job seekers to sign a contract. They may be able to collect their fee even if clients find a job on their own without the agencies' help. Check with people who have used the services. Read the fine print before you sign over a big chunk of your paycheck for a job that may not be right for you. Even reputable companies may put a poorly written ad in the paper. If you think it is necessary, call the company for clarification about the job requirements.

People who have done a complete career search process already have prepared well for a successful job hunt—the natural next step in the process. They rarely have to pay someone to find a job for them unless there seems to be no other way to snag that very special job. In general, the *least* effective strategy is sending out dozens of résumés to personnel departments, especially if you are looking for a job in a competitive field (or employment is tight). You may get a nibble or two, but not too many people are hired this way. Here is where your information interviewing will pay off to get you into the hiring network. Someone you've contacted in your information interviewing may even be waiting for your résumé and application.

Networking

Networking means using all of your contacts to get hired. It is often a crucial part of job hunting in a stubborn job market. People are networking when they shake hands and exchange business cards. People talk business everywhere, including the business of sharing job opportunities—in the hallways, over coffee, on the golf course. These casual conversations may sound trivial, but they strengthen the links in the network.

Networking is *not* the same as information interviewing, although the two use similar techniques. When you do information interviewing, you are simply asking for information about careers and companies. You are not asking for a job, although one might be offered and you might accept. But networking implies that you are using various contacts, including those acquired while information hunting, to find out about job openings. Networking requires patience. Job openings are often only in the minds of the people who might be thinking of retiring, or moving out or over. Delays are commonplace and for many reasons. The company could be reorganizing. Managers could be feuding or be new on the job or both. Consultant Martha Stoodley, author of *Interviewing: What It Is and How to Use It,* reminds us that "companies

JOB SOURCES AVAILABLE ON THE INTERNET

The Internet sources noted below provide such information as available job openings and salary potential. Not all the sites are easy to use. It is also the nature of Websites to change frequently. *Inclusion here does not imply an endorsement although all these sites were obtained from reliable sources. Caution is advised in giving out personal information over the Internet.*

- *Alianza:* www.alianza.org
- Career Builder: www.careerbuilder.com
- *Career Magazine* for teaching positions: www.careermag.com
- Career Mosaic: www.careermosaic.com
- CareerPath: www.careerpath.com
- CIA Recruitment: www.odci.gov/cia
- Corporation for National Service/Volunteer: www.cns.gov
- E-Span: www.espan.com
- EthniCity, a Minority Search Firm: www.ethnicity.com
- FedWorld (government job openings): www.fedworld.com
- JOBTRAK: www.jobtrak.com
- Monster Board: www.monster.com
- National Association of Hispanic Journalists: www.nahj.com
- New Woman Entrepreneur Center: http://members.aol.com/focus2nwec/nwec.htm
- On-line Career Center: www.occ.com
- Peace Corps Volunteer: www.peacecorps.gov
- Riley Guide: www.jobtrak.com/jobguide/
- Small Business Administration Women's Business Center: www.onlinewbc.org
- U.S. Army Recruitment: www.goarmy.com
- U.S. Army National Guard Recruitment: www.1800goguard.com
- U.S. Department of Labor and some states: www.ajb.dni.us
- U.S. Military Recruitment, all branches: www.militarycareers.com
- U.S. Navy Recruitment: www.navyjobs.com
- Yahoo!: classifieds.yahoo.com
- JobSmart gives salary data on many jobs in regions across the country including those in the *Occupational Outlook Handbook:* www.jobsmart.com
- www.townonline.com/working will give you salaries for various jobs

are run by human beings who are trying to juggle their professional challenges and personal lives."[2]

Where do you stand in the networking game? If you are new at creative job hunting, the inner circle may look like a closed circle that doesn't include you! But think again. How often have you or people you know heard about a job opening from a friend? And bring it close to home. Suppose you want to hire someone to take care of a child or ailing parent, fix your car, clean your house. No doubt you would feel safer asking for a referral from a friend. Employers feel better, too, when they hire someone they know or someone recommended by a trusted friend or colleague.

If you have already done information interviewing, you have a good start on networking. Use the same process and the same contacts to find out about job openings and how to approach a given workplace. These insiders can offer you the inside story as well as moral support. And one contact can lead to another. Successful job hunter Mel Fuller says, "Believe the statistic that 70 percent of people are hired by word-of-mouth." He urged people to talk to their relatives, neighbors, friends, clergy, business contacts such as bankers, stockbrokers, insurance agents, doctors and dentists—in short, anyone who knows you. Go to association meetings, job fairs, and trade shows. But then target a few people who can and will help you specifically. Prepare for meeting them by knowing key points about them, even their leisure activities, as an icebreaker. And schedule follow-up meetings.

Even if you haven't developed a network of personal contacts, call on as many companies (or clients) as you can and apply for possible openings. Now is the time to keep your energy up. Plan a schedule: exercise, eat well, get plenty of rest, and talk to as many positive people as you can. In a tight job market it's important to keep up your courage. Remember that rejections are part of the game; they do not mean you are unacceptable. Chances are you are just one of many good candidates. Later, the company you are interested in may offer you a different job from the one you had in mind. If the business is a good one, you may be smart to take the alternate job; this will get you inside the company, where changes in position are more easily arranged.

Networking is not meant to give less-qualified people an unfair advantage over others, although it sometimes does. It can help you access the job market, but be aware that employers are required to follow legal hiring practices. They must advertise widely and screen an adequate number of applicants. This procedure gives as many people as possible a fair chance at the job and helps employers hire the best-qualified person. Some companies and government agencies have helpful material available about their hiring processes. Some will try to ensure that the help they give is available to all prospective employees. And some employers will simply be equally "unavailable" to all!

Networking has become easier for people using the Net—the Internet, that is. Companies are using it to post a wide variety of job announcements, for example. The Net can also connect you with a wide array of people in many companies who have the inside story and can help you weed out more quickly those that won't work for you. You can post your résumé and then set up a face-to-face meeting with likely leads. You can even look at résumés of competitors (and they can look at yours), which may make you rethink exposing yours for everyone to see! Although more and more transactions are moving onto the Net, not all are happening there! No one ever said the job hunt would be easy! Work on your résumé, schedule your time, set goals, and keep moving.

The Résumé

A résumé is a summary of personal information about you that is relevant to the job you seek. A good one marks you as a serious job seeker. Much has been written about the résumé. Some regard it as a sacred cow, *the* most important item to use in presenting yourself; others believe preparing a résumé is a worthless exercise. Still, many employers require them, so job hunters, an obliging lot, will continue to oblige, even though they realize that often they are one among hundreds of applicants.

There are two kinds of basic résumés: chronological and functional. If your work experience was fairly continuous and in related areas, use a *chronological* résumé, which lists your work experience in reverse order. A *functional* résumé, developed on the basis of three or four skill areas, can be used if you were in and out of the job market at various times or if your work experience does not appear directly related to the job for which you are applying. Writing both kinds of résumés may benefit you because this exercise gives you two different perspectives on yourself. It forces you to state clearly how your education and experience relate directly to the job you are seeking. Some people bypass both types and simply list achievements in skill areas that apply directly to the job they are seeking. Sample résumés are shown in Figures 7-1 through 7-9 and in the Appendix.

There is no one and only way to write a résumé, but some good basic guidelines to follow are these: (1) be brief, (2) be clear, (3) be neat, (4) be honest. The best résumé succinctly states *on one page* your education and work experience that specifically relate to the job for which you are applying. Employers want you to save all the exciting details for the interview. A résumé is easiest to read when it is in outline form with plenty of "white space"; has good spelling, punctuation, and grammar; and is well reproduced.

Those who hire say they can spot phony résumés very quickly, especially those that are done commercially. Although it is important that you be truthful, a résumé isn't the place for true confessions. Emphasize your good points! Ask experienced friends to read and criticize your rough draft, but have confidence in your own judgment about what is right for you.

If you have access to a computer, use it to do your résumé or have it done. The advantages are many: you can tailor each version to a particular job and/or company; corrections and updating are a breeze; and you can use some subtle touches like **bold print** or *italics* that will add to a sharp look if you don't overdo them. If you must type your résumé, you can erase, use correction fluid, and even cut and paste sections in with tape; a copy shop can still produce a copy that will look perfect. Use a high-quality off-white, gray, or beige-tinted paper. If you plan to mail it, prepare a carefully typed, matching envelope addressed to the correct person. For a final touch, add a handsome commemorative stamp. You want your résumé to get a second look rather than the usual thirty-second glance.

Some companies may request that you send your résumé by fax or e-mail. Then all your attempts to stand out from the crowd may fade into cyberspace or come forth on flimsy fax paper. To the dismay of the creator of the perfect, unique résumé, many companies now use computerized scanning systems to screen applicants. An optical scanner can store the images of a résumé in a computer database in less than three seconds. One such system, developed by Resumix, can look over each résumé; assess education, skills and proficiencies, and employment history; use a sophisticated logic process to decide which job category the applicant fits; and print out an appropriate reply. Evaluation shows it to be at least as effective as a human personnel director and much quicker at processing applications and résumés.[3] A personal contact can save you from getting lost in this world of virtual unreality.

You might send your résumé with an individual letter addressed to a specific person in a company. Sometimes the résumé is attached to an application or requested after an application has been received. The general idea is to give the employer a preview of you before an interview takes place. Always have your résumé handy and bring several copies to the interview because more than one person may want to talk with you.

Plan to spend at least twelve to fifteen hours writing a good résumé; then leave it and come back to it later for a fresh look. Because you can describe yourself in an infinite number of ways, doing a résumé means picking a winning combination that exactly fits the job you are seeking. The position objective you indicate must state that job title clearly and briefly and match the job for which you are applying. Employers do not have time to dig around in your résumé to find out what you want to do, nor do they have to, nor do you necessarily want to trust in the chance that a company (or computer) will do the job for you if you can't. Employers want to know what you are bringing to a specific job. Such clarity is especially important if you have not made previous contact with the employer.

FOR BETTER OR FOR WORSE © Lynn Johnston Productions, Inc./Dist. by United Feature Syndicate, Inc.

And of course, almost everyone wants an exciting, challenging job with opportunity for advancement (and a huge salary) in a dynamic and growing company with stimulating and forward-thinking managers and marvelous colleagues—that's understood; so don't mention the obvious. *You* decide if the workplace will work for you. And yes, you *do* need a separate résumé for each job title and sometimes even for each company!

As your career advances, you will not simply add new jobs to the list on your résumé; you will probably change the entire format. You may summarize early jobs, stress your newer high-level qualifications, and recast earlier entries to point toward your new job goal. The résumé will emphasize your achievements more, and each job entry will show increasingly greater connections to the next job goal. A top executive résumé may be more than one well-organized page, but it will include only those entries that are relevant to the desired goal.[4]

If you have been developing a list of file cards for each job, a résumé will not only be easier to do but will also be easier to adapt. Start with the lists you made of all your favorite activities and skills in Chapters l, 2, and 3. The ten basic skills empower you to *do* many different tasks in many different settings with data, people, and things because the skills are transferable. When you go job hunting, the key question a company wants you to answer is this: "What can you *do* for us?" The most important words to use on your résumé, then, are action verbs that tell what you've done, what you've accomplished, and therefore what you *can* do, and would *like* to do, and that relate to the job in question. Action verbs have an impact when they are relevant to the job you want. Collect businesslike nouns, adjectives, and adverbs to use with these verbs. Use words that clearly and specifically *express* what you can bring to the job; not words that only *impress*. A woman who worked for a sanitation district said she "gave messages to the guys in their trucks." On her

RÉSUMÉ FORMATS

Résumé formats are useful as guidelines for those who have never or only occasionally prepared a résumé. Examples of various letters and résumé styles are included in this chapter and in the Appendix at the end of the text. After you become experienced with them, you may wish to create your own format.

1. **Name, address, home, business/message phone, fax, or e-mail address:** List this information prominently at the top of the page. Be sure to give useful message/phone numbers and make sure that if you use an answering machine, the message sounds professional; a prospective employer should know where to reach you, day or evening. If you do not wish your present employer to know you are job hunting, ask someone to take messages for you, at your home number or another number you list, during your work hours. Don't tell coworkers you are looking if you wish to keep your job hunting to yourself.

2. **Position objective:** State as specific and brief a job title as possible.

3. **Qualifications in brief:** Provide a short summary highlighting your education, experience, and skills to capture the attention of the reader and assure him or her that you can do the job. Elaboration (but not repetition) is included in the body of the résumé.

4. **Experience summary:** Present experience in a form that is chronological, functional, or a combination of the two.

CHRONOLOGICAL

Begin with your most recent job and work backward.

> March 6, 2000–Present: COMPANY, City, State, Job Title. Add a brief, concise description of what you did. See Figures 7-1, 7-2, 7-7, and Appendix Figures A-2, A-3, A-5, and A-7.

You may include a section on community or military service.

As references are usually asked for on the application, it is not necessary to mention them on your résumé. Be careful whom you ask for references if you do not wish your job hunt made known.

(continued)

resumé, this phrase was translated to "communicated by radio with personnel in the field."

Many-faceted skills such as management can be divided into a variety of functions and subfunctions, which in turn relate back to the ten basic skills. Management involves only three of the basic skills: medium to high intelligence, verbal ability, and sometimes (but not always) medium to high numerical ability. Yet many action verbs would apply, such as advise, arrange,

RÉSUMÉ FORMATS *(continued)*

FUNCTIONAL

Arrange the information by areas of competence, expertise, effectiveness, or key functions that are related to your position objective such as **public relations, management, organization, program development, sales**. Follow each category with the businesslike action words you've collected, such as **planned** and **classified**; then summarize the type of things you accomplished. You may list employers and dates at the end or note them on the company's application form (see Figures 7-3 and 7-4).

COMBINATION OF CHRONOLOGICAL AND FUNCTIONAL

If you use this format, highlight special skills relevant to your position (see Figure 7-5).

5. **Educational background:** (Place before work experience if it is more closely related to the position objective.) List educational background to indicate general and specific training for a job. A person who has little or no educational training would omit this item.

   COLLEGE NAME, City, State, Degree, Major, Dates.
   If you received no degree or you are presently attending college, give the number of units completed (or say "degree candidate"), major, date, place.
   If you have not attended college, then include
   HIGH SCHOOL, City, State
   Add any areas of specialty, if applicable, but the date of high school graduation is not necessary as this indicates your age. It is illegal for employers to ask a person's age.
   Include also relevant workshops, adult education, vocational training, either in summary form or in chronological order.

6. **Personal paragraph:** If you wish, include a statement describing your personal attitudes toward work that make you a valuable and unique employee.

budget, communicate, control. Here is an example of increasing clarity and impact.

> Designed a marketing management program . . . ; 2. Designed an effective marketing program . . . ; 3. Designed an effective marketing management program that resulted in a 60 percent sales increase.

Even if no one ever reads your résumé, just doing one will clarify your background and make it easier for you to talk about the qualifications you have for the job you are seeking.

KEVIN DONOVAN
643 Eagle Drive
Dubuque, Iowa 52001
(319) 555-6789

JOB OBJECTIVE Customer Service Management Trainee

QUALIFICATIONS IN BRIEF

Learn job routine quickly. Possess ability to deal effectively with the public and flexible enough to work alone or in a team effort. Good driving record. Not afraid of hard routine work. Primarily interested in a swing shift to allow time to further my educational goals.

WORK EXPERIENCE

K-MART, Dubuque, IA   1998 to present
Customer Service/Bagger

Help customers with merchandise, stock shelves, maintain appearance of the store, bring carts from parking lot into building, and bag merchandise from checkstands.

DUBUQUE GYMNASTIC ASSOCIATION, Dubuque, IA   1996–1997
Gym Instructor

Sold memberships and equipment, outlined programs for participants, gave tours of the facilities to potential customers and guests, balanced monies and accounts daily, answered phones, and took responsibility for maintaining smooth operation of the gym facilities, adding a professional tone.

S & S WROUGHT IRON, East Dubuque, IA   Summer 1996

VAN'S FURNITURE AND MATTRESS CO.,
    Dubuque, IA   Summer 1995
Warehouse Worker

Moved furniture, paint, and equipment; helped with inventory control; assisted customers.

EDUCATION

LORAS COLLEGE, Dubuque, IA   1998 to present
Major: Business/Liberal Arts

Figure 7-1   Chronological résumé of a student attending a four-year college

JAMES N. RYAN
1801 Avenue Z
Sterling, IL 61081
(625) 555-1212

POSITION OBJECTIVE Route Manager

QUALIFICATIONS IN BRIEF AA in Electronics; three years' experience maintaining coin-operated amusement and music equipment; two years managing video arcade; course work in management; good human relations skills.

EDUCATION

SAUK VALLEY COMMUNITY COLLEGE, Dixon, IL   June 1998
Electronics Technology AS Degree; Certificate in Business Management

Courses in electronics, including "troubleshooting" and electronic applications. Certificate courses in business management including employee recruitment and selection, performance standards and evaluations, supervisory skills, accounting and legal principles, materials management, business computers, marketing strategies.

EXPERIENCE SUMMARY

BLACKHAWK MUSIC CO., Sterling, IL   September 1998 to Present
Service Technician

Service on site, pick up, repair, deliver coin-operated music and game machines; maintain equipment; collect revenue on two multi-town routes; supervise several workers; developed a more efficient equipment rotation plan.

BLACKHAWK FAMILY ARCADE, Blackhawk Mall, Sterling, IL
Arcade/Attendant Manager   September 1994 to August 1998

Supervised video arcade, made minor repairs on equipment, developed inventory system for redemption center; hired, supervised, and scheduled all part-time employees; developed sales promotions; handled day-to-day problems.

THE DAILY GAZETTE, Sterling, IL   October 1991 to August 1994
Delivery

Delivered papers, sold and collected subscriptions for 150 households. Increased route subscriptions by 20 percent.

COMMUNITY ORGANIZATIONS/SERVICE

SAUK VALLEY RECYCLING, Sterling, IL   August 1992 to Present

As center volunteer: sort materials, collect old newspapers, cans, and bottles from various locations. Manage yearly cleanup of riverfront.

Figure 7-2   Chronological résumé of a graduate of AS electronics program looking for position in video game distribution company

BETTY A. BUG
5403 W. Monroe Street
Chicago, Illinois 60644
(312) 555-9829

POSITION OBJECTIVE Industrial Employee Trainer

QUALIFICATIONS IN BRIEF

BA in English, Mundelein College of Loyola, Chicago, 1988. Four years' clerical experience in industry; eight years' elementary teaching. Fluent in Spanish; demonstrated skills in instruction, supervision, communications, human relations.

EXPERIENCE SUMMARY

INSTRUCTION: Planned, organized, presented language and mathematics instructional material to elementary students; developed teaching modules to solve specific learning problems; developed computer programs for instruction and instructional material; proficient on Macintosh computer; used computerized graphic presentations, audio and videocassettes, and a variety of educational software; did extensive research in various curricula; served on curriculum development committee; introduced new motivational techniques for students. Conducted staff in-service workshops, including installation of several teleconference downlinks.

SUPERVISION: Supervised student groups, teacher interns, and a classroom aide; evaluated students, peers, and programs; moderated student activities. Interviewed, trained, and evaluated support personnel, volunteers, and teacher interns.

HUMAN RELATIONS: Did effective problem solving/conflict resolution between individual students and between student groups; initiated program of student self-governance; acted as a liaison between families of diverse cultural, ethnic, and economic backgounds and school personnel services; conducted individual and group conferences to establish rapport with parents and to discuss student progress. Represented school to the community.

COMMUNICATIONS: Presented new curriculum plans to parent groups; sent periodic progress reports to parents; developed class newsletter.

CURRENTLY EMPLOYED Austin Elementary School, Chicago, Illinois

PREVIOUSLY EMPLOYED Brach Candy Company, Chicago, Illinois

Figure 7-3   Functional résumé of a teacher in transition to industry

LAURIE REAUME
361 Calle de Florencia
Santa Fe, New Mexico 87501
(505) 970-9120

POSITION OBJECTIVE Public Relations

ACHIEVEMENTS

WRITING/PUBLICITY

- Compiled and published public service directory.

- Coordinated and edited corporate newsletter.

- Designed publicity brochure and employee handbook.

- Wrote and placed employment advertising.

- Gave presentations on company's innovative policies.

- Contacted media regarding personnel changes and events of interest to the community.

ADMINISTRATION AND ORGANIZATION

- Hired, supervised, and trained contract employees.

- Established and maintained resource/reference library.

- Planned, organized, and promoted company picnic.

- Developed and conducted new hire orientation program.

- Coordinated and presented work effectiveness seminar.

EDUCATION

GOLDEN GATE UNIVERSITY, San Francisco, CA, MBA Candidate

UNIVERSITY OF WISCONSIN, Whitewater, WI, BA Cum Laude

QUALIFICATIONS SUMMARY

Self-starter, excellent organizer, resourceful, team player

Figure 7-4 Functional résumé targeted toward achievements of career woman moving into public relations from secretarial work

HELEN B. BELL
432 Spruce Street
Junction City, Kansas 66441
(913) 555-7035

POSITION OBJECTIVE Office Manager with Accounting Responsibilities

EXPERIENCE

Successful Accounting Work: Managed payroll, payroll taxes, accounts receivable, accounts payable, bank reconciliation, and executive credit card expense account; handled data entry. Acted as full-charge bookkeeper through monthly and annual profit and loss statements.

Supervision and Management Directed office functions such as secretarial, accounting, customer relations, sales, employee performance, and schedules.

PRESENT EMPLOYER

KINDERGARTEN SUPPLIER, USA, INC., Wichita, KS   10 years
Accountant

PREVIOUS EMPLOYERS

ELECTRA CORPORATION, Wichita, KS   1 year
Receptionist

RIDGEWAY COMPANY, Topeka, KS   1 year
Accountant/Secretary

ROD'S VAN AND STORAGE COMPANY, Topeka, KS   2 years
Accountant/Secretary

HUMPHREY MOTOR COMPANY, Junction City, KS   9 years
Accountant/Secretary

SCOTT STORES, Junction City, KS   1 year
Bookkeeper

PERSONAL PARAGRAPH

The accounting field with its attendant and complex problems is fascinating and thoroughly involving for me. I am interested in ensuring smooth flow, efficiency, and accuracy of accounts in a moderately sized, growing company. I am highly organized, have an excellent memory, and have facility with numbers.

Figure 7-5   Functional/chronological résumé of a senior citizen/housewife returning to the job market

Cover Letters

Many employment counselors and personnel managers say that a well-written cover letter (see samples following and in the Appendix) is an excellent door opener for an interview; it links you to the employer and acts as a lead for your résumé. After you have made personal contact with someone in the company who seems interested in hiring you, targeting your résumé to that company and addressing a cover letter to that person, both geared to a specific job, is usually an excellent strategy. In other cases, a cover letter may be superfluous and even undesirable. Some employers, such as school districts and government agencies, have step-by-step procedures that make cover letters unnecessary. These employers may want only an application with your résumé attached. It's wise to learn and follow the expected procedures when these are clearly stated. In companies with less formal application procedures, employers often appreciate a short and clear cover letter stating in a sentence or two what you are interested in. You can use it to amplify an important aspect of your résumé and to form a chain linking you directly to the employer (see Figures 7-6, 7-8, and Appendix Figures A-1 and A-4).

- *Connect:* State your reason for writing and your employment objective. Mention the person who referred you to this employer or the source of the reference, such as a classified ad.
- *Add more links:* Describe your experience in brief—one or two sentences should be ample.
- *Solder the links:* State what you can do for the company and tell how you will help this employer solve his or her problem.
- *Hold onto the chain:* Prepare the way for the next step by asking for an interview and indicating when you will call to set it up.

Sometimes you will get a negative response when you call for an interview. Rather than answering with a stunned silence, be ready with a positive answer to reinforce your possible contribution to the company. For example, to "We don't hire people without experience," your reply might be, "I do learn very quickly," or "I have had a great deal of experience as a student doing similar tasks such as . . ."

Letters of Reference

Be prepared to supply the names of people who have written or will write letters of reference for you or who will answer questions about you when called. *Do not* name someone until you have asked that person's permission to be listed as a reference and he or she has agreed. The people you ask should

5401 Monroe Street
Mobile, Alabama 36608
September 11, 1998

Ms. Jill Jones
Director of Marketing
PTT Corporation
Dogwood, AL 36309

Dear Ms. Jones:

As a word processor at Datatime Company last summer, I had occasion to meet with people from PTT. Your sales representative, Joan Carl, referred me to you. I was impressed with both your product and your personnel. I am a senior at Peachtree University. I would like to be considered for an internship position in marketing for the Spring Semester of 1999.

I am an energetic, enthusiastic person with a commitment to whatever I take on. My involvement in student affairs led me to plan and execute a successful campaign for student body vice-president. As vice-president, I met and negotiated with faculty representatives and members of the board of trustees and hosted visiting guests of the college. My junior project in marketing won departmental recognition, while my 3.2 GPA put me on the dean's honor list.

With these qualifications, I feel that I can make a positive contribution to PTT. I look forward to meeting your campus recruiter, A. J. Lupin, next month to explore a marketing internship position.

Sincerely yours,

Chris Cross

Figure 7-6   Cover letter of a college student applying for an internship

CHRIS CROSS
5401 Monroe Street, Mobile, Alabama 36608
(205) 555-1212

POSITION OBJECTIVE Internship in Marketing

QUALIFICATIONS IN BRIEF

BA Candidate in Marketing and Sales. Won departmental honors in Marketing. Word processor for two summers on PTT Systems. Good human relations skills, energetic, goal oriented.

EXPERIENCE SUMMARY

DATATIME COMPANY, Mobile, Alabama   Summers: 1996–1998
Data Entry
Did data entry for marketing and sales department; logged product sales, sales personnel progress, and regional growth; interacted with service representatives.

McDOUGAL'S HAMBURGER SHOP, Mobile, Alabama
Part-Time Waitress   October 1994–May 1995
Waited on customers, handled cash, oriented new employees. Suggested successful coupon marketing strategy that raised sales by 5 percent. Acted as hostess, manager.

COMMUNITY EXPERIENCE

PEACHTREE UNIVERSITY STUDENT BODY, Peachtree, Georgia
                                                            1996–1997

Vice-President
Planned and executed my election campaign, worked extensively with faculty, administration, and board of trustees; hosted visiting college guests; spearheaded senior projects such as the Homecoming Dance and Career Day. Participated in student activities all four years.

BLOSSOM HIGH SCHOOL, Mobile, Alabama
Senior Class Secretary
Junior Class Vice-President
Participated throughout high school in student body activities, science club, and intramural basketball and soccer.

EDUCATION

PEACHTREE UNIVERSITY, Peachtree, Georgia   June 1999
BA Candidate: Marketing and Sales

Figure 7-7   Résumé to accompany cover letter

5405 Monroe Street
Aurora, IL 60504
January 24, 2000

Dierk Van Symms, Manager of Technical Services
Effective Micro Systems, Inc.
130 Meridian Drive, Suite 411
Aurora, IL 60504

Dear Mr. Van Symms:

EMS Marketing Respresentative Kevin Skahan acquainted me with your company. Your services to your manufacturing companies are impressive. There is a great need for improvement of technical applications in manufacturing. Considering my almost five years of hands-on experience, both manual and computerized, in a manufacturing environment, I feel that I can offer special attention to detail that a manufacturing company or distributor deserves.

I have been with Watlow Electric Manufacturing Company since graduating from DeVry with a BS in Computer Information Systems for Business in 1994. My effective problem solving, communication, and planning experience with their office and factory applications has resulted in higher customer satisfaction and fewer complaints about scheduling and delivery.

I am now seeking a technical business position working approximately thirty hours per week. I would like to meet with you to further discuss the possibility of a work opportunity with Effective Micro Systems, Inc. I will call you in one week to set up a time convenient for both of us.

Sincerely yours,

Joanne M. Malatia

Figure 7-8   Cover letter to accompany résumé

JOANNE M. MALATIA
5405 Monroe Street, Aurora, IL 60504
(708) 555-1212

POSITION OBJECTIVE Programmer/Analyst

EXPERIENCE SUMMARY

WATLOW ELECTRIC MANUFACTURING COMPANY, Batavia, IL

Computer Programmer/Analyst/Mapper Run Designer   October 1994 to present

Major Contributions:
- Developed a cross-checking system to improve on-time deliveries for major customers.
- Designed and implemented a computerized raw materials purchasing system.
- Coordinated implementation of corporate-side order processing and sales analysis system.
- Performed sales forecasting and analysis that contributed to company strategy.

Responsibilities:
- Define data processing problems and objectives.
- Formulate logical procedures for problem solution.
- Perform general maintenance on all hardware at Batavia Plant.
- Instruct and train all positions on computer applications.
- Hardware: Unisys 220 Mainframe, IBM-compatible PC/DOS.
- Software: Mapper Database Language, BASIC, Microsoft Word.

LOVEJOY REHABILITATION CENTER, West Chicago, IL

Data Collector for Research/Education Department   January 1991 to October 1994

Major Contributions:
- Internship: Directed a system investigation of the Materials Management Department.
- Documented existing manual system; recommended purchase of computer system.

Responsibilities:
- Performed patient telephone interviews and evaluated data received.
- Implemented follow-up evaluation system and assisted with patient tracking system.
- Completed daily tallies of calls completed and maintained card file system.
- Entered follow-up collection of data, Hewlett-Packard PC/DOS.
- Assisted wth Statistical Analysis using SAS, SPSS, and BASIC.

MCDONALD'S OF STRATFORD, Bloomingdale, IL

Administrative Assistant to General Manager   June 1989 to February 1991

Responsibilities:
- Managed and balanced daily books and cash sheets while maintaining cash flow.
- Assisted managers with schedules and planning.
- Oriented and trained new employees.

EDUCATION

DeVry Institute of Technology, Lombard, IL: Bachelor of Science Degree, October 1994

Major: Computer Information Systems

COMPUTER EXPERIENCE: COBOL, BASIC, RPGII, Assembler, Pascal, JCL, IBM 3033, IBM PC/DOS.

Figure 7-9   Résumé of a technical person with a BS degree in computer science

generally be professionals who know you, such as teachers, school advisers, clergy, or doctors. The most valuable references come from individuals who can speak from personal experience about your work abilities. These may include supervisors, coworkers, and people who work for you. If possible, ask a person with the same background as your prospective employer to write a reference for you. Avoid asking people to write who may see you in an unfavorable light. Keep in mind that a potential employer may call anyone from any place you have worked, so keep your human relations with your co-workers as smooth as possible.

Ask the person writing the letter to mention your specific job and personal responsibility skills that relate to the position you are seeking. Some people who write many letters of reference may ask you to write the letter to revise and sign. And some may decline your request entirely.

Employers and their human resources personnel are less eager these days to give helpful references. If they tell the whole, unfavorable truth about a person unnecessarily and he or she is not hired, if what they say can be proven wrong, or if they note positive qualities and withhold information and later a serious problem occurs, they may be sued.[5]

When you apply for a job, the usual procedure with references is to provide names, if they are requested, or to bring copies of letters to the interview. Some college placement offices keep a file for each of their graduates with copies of letters of reference, a current résumé, and transcripts; the placement office will send these out to prospective employers for a nominal fee. If you have letters of reference on file at your college, have them sent to the prospective employer either right before or soon after your interview. If the competition is fierce and you are almost certain this is a job you want, it may be appropriate to ask a couple of key people to write or even make phone calls to the person who may hire you. Ask a teacher or counselor who knows your skills, an acquaintance in the company to which you are applying, or some other professional acquaintance known to the interviewer or to the person you will be working for to speak on your behalf. Understand, however, that this is not the usual procedure and should be used with discrimination.

The Application Form

The application form provided by the company may determine the employer's first impression of you. It must look sharp. *A form that is prepared carelessly or sloppily may cause you to be eliminated from consideration for the position. Be sure to fill out an application as clearly, completely, and neatly as possible.* Try to obtain two copies ahead of time. (Sometimes companies will mail them to you by phone request.) Use one copy for practice and keep it for your files.

Applications vary from one company to another, but each form requires an accurate record of your past work experience and education. To help you in preparing every application you will make, create your own file containing all the information you may need to include, using the format in the Data File exercise in Chapter 1. Check the records carefully for accuracy. You will need names, addresses, and dates for both education and work experience. Obtain this information now if you do not have it. Employers often verify these facts, and the information on your application must match what they learn from your former employers or educational institutions. The more careful you are, the better you look. Be clear if you are asked what you did. Know exact job titles, the types of equipment you've used, and your desired salary range. Some firms may accept—and even require—e-mail, fax, or Internet applications. Here are some helpful hints to remember.

- Read the *whole* application form *before* you begin to fill it in. Follow all directions, and note the fine print.
- Print with a blue or black pen, or better still, type answers carefully and completely, but succinctly.
- Fill in all blanks. Write in N/A (not applicable) if a question does not apply to you.
- Have your Social Security number available. Some companies ask to see a driver's license. (Revocation or denial of a driver's license can indicate a problem.)
- Your reason for interest in the position should state an advantage to the employer. Research the company and know what you can do for it.
- An arrest is not a conviction. Arrests need not be mentioned.
- Provide accurate names and addresses of those who have given you permission to use their names as references. Have original reference letters available, plus copies to leave if requested or agree to have them sent if they are on file or if the individual providing the reference wishes to send the letter personally.
- Reread the application carefully. Typos or other errors give a bad impression.
- Sign the application.

The Interview

Usually an employer interviews individuals whose applications, letters, or résumés have proven interesting, those who have made a personal contact, or those who have been referred. Many managers feel uncomfortable with the

"Hello, I'm Nesbit. I'm three, and I'm right on track."

interview and are not skilled at it, so be prepared to take control tactfully while letting the manager guide it. At least have some key points you would like to tell the interviewer. Some school districts and government agencies have a very formal interview procedure. Try to learn whether the employer uses a structured or an informal interview so as to be better prepared.

An interview is a purposeful conversation between an employer or delegated interviewer and a prospective employee. Its purpose is to exchange information. The interviewer needs to learn whether the interviewee has the qualifications necessary to do the job. The applicant needs to make sure that he or she understands the job, the company, and what is expected. In this chapter we cover the key points in the interview and review a set of practice questions and answers.

The interviewer may be a department head, project director, or even a series of people familiar with various aspects of the job. A group of staff members may act together as an interviewing committee. In a small business, you may be interviewed quite casually and briefly by the owner. Large corporations often employ professional interviewers. Reputable companies want their interviewers to present a positive image. Interviewers want to do a good job, too, by hiring the best people. Their jobs depend on it!

An interview is not a time for game playing or for one person to try to trap the other. It will be counterproductive for both parties if they deceive each other. *The interviewer will recommend an employee who doesn't fit. The worker will be dissatisfied.*

Like a good composition, the interview usually has a beginning, a middle, and an ending. Introductions and casual conversation are designed to help you feel at ease.

After a few minutes, most interviewers will guide you to the purpose of the meeting, which is to find out what you can *do* for the company and what your qualifications are for the job. A good interviewer will also give you information along the way to help you make your decision. The interviewer may discuss job duties, hours and overtime, salary and benefits, vacation and sick leave, opportunities for advancement, and company policies and procedures.

Interviews catch people when they are on their best behavior. Companies wish they could try an applicant. AlphaGraphics in San Francisco does. They hire likely applicants for one day for $100. Both employer and employee have been successful in making good matches.[6] Some companies even try tests of various sorts. Some may give an interviewee problems or situations to solve.

Some interviewers will give you a tour of the workplace. Depending on the level for which you are being considered, an interview might be over in fifteen minutes or last several hours or even extend over some days. Most information can be exchanged in thirty to forty-five minutes. Sometimes an interviewer doesn't seem to want to know anything and suddenly you're hired! Interviewers bring these meetings to an end and usually tell you when you will be notified about their selection of an applicant. They are generally seeing other people interested in the job, sometimes many others.

A successful interview might be one in which you *don't* get the job. In some cases, the interview reveals that hiring you would not be good for either you or the company, which only means that the interview has accomplished its purpose. *In any event, you want to appear at your best.*

Getting Prepared

When you are meeting someone you wish to impress, common sense and courtesy are your most reliable guides. If you are in doubt about dress and manner, it's best to lean slightly toward the conservative. Prepare what you will wear

---

INTERVIEW OVERVIEW

GET READY

Check: The company (from reference section
of library, public relations department of firm, contacts, friends)

Location
Products/services
Potential market
Earnings
Policies

Check: Important items you wish to cover:

How you fit in
Your strengths
Your experiences
Your interests

GET SET

Check: Items for your application:

Social Security number
References
Person to notify in case of accident
Details of past experience:
Name of company
Full address and phone number
of company
Dates worked
Salary
Job titles
Supervisors
Duties, projects, skills
Education (dates, majors, degrees)
Copies of résumé
Examples of work if relevant

Check: Exact time, date, location
(building and room)
Availability of parking
Name of interviewer
(and pronunciation)

GO

Check: Your appearance:

Neat, clean, conservative outfit
No gum, no smoking, no
fidgeting
No sunglasses or outdoor
clothing
Comfortable sitting posture,
straight but at ease

Check: Your attitude:

A serious job seeker
Definite goals
Willing to work and work up
Reasonable approach to salary,
hours, benefits, or other
aspects of the job
Uncritical of past employers,
teachers, coworkers
Evidence of good human
relations
Sense of humor
High personal values
Wide interests, openness,
flexibility

Check: Your manner:

Confident, not overbearing
Firm handshake
Enthusiastic but not desperate
or gushy
Courteous, attentive
Good voice, expression
On target answering questions
Prompt departure after the
interview

Go alone

---

ahead of time. Be sure that your outfit is clean, pressed, polished, and *comfortable*. When purchasing your "dress for success" outfit, try sitting in it,
moving in it. Then wear it a time or two, perhaps to an information interview.
And of course, be on time. Many companies are banning smoking because of

rising health care and maintenance costs and because many employers tend to look with disfavor on someone who does smoke. Seattle University professor of business William L. Weiss says that "in a race for a job between two equally qualified people, a nonsmoker will win 94 percent of the time."[7]

The very best preparation for an interview is practice—practice talking to people about their jobs; practice calling for appointments to see people in order to ask for career information. If you have done information interviewing and networking, you will be accustomed to sharing enthusiasm about the career of your choice, and this enthusiasm will come across naturally at the interview. Go to interviews even if you think you might not get a job, and then honestly assess your performance.

More immediately, do homework on the company you are approaching. Many have brochures; many are listed in standard library references. A call to the public relations department can sometimes result in a wealth of material. Find out if the company has a Website. Talk to people who may know the company. Ask questions at the interview about the job as well as the company's process and organization instead of self-serving questions that indicate you are interested only in what the company can give you, such as a long vacation or high pay! Try to see how you best fit in. Know the important facts about the job, including the salary range. Prepare to bring relevant examples of your work, such as sketches, designs, or writings.

In some career areas, salaries are nonnegotiable and not an issue—government, teaching, and union jobs are examples. In others, salaries are negotiable. In such cases, the interviewer may ask what salary you expect. If you have no idea of the range and were not able to find out ahead of time, ask. Unless you are a superstar, don't ask for the top of the range, but don't undervalue yourself, either. Know the minimum you'll accept—and know your worth. Place yourself somewhere in the middle and leave it open to negotiation. If you have been networking, going to business meetings, reading up-to-date material (for example, the February issue of *Working Woman* contains an annual salary review), and generally talking to people, you will have an idea of what a reasonable salary would be for someone in your situation. And check "Job Sources Available on the Internet" presented earlier in this chapter for other references. And again, don't forget to factor in other benefits such as the opportunity to own equity or stock in the company. Also, you might ask for a salary review in six months or so or make a proposal just after you have done a good job on a particular project.

It's better not to ask about salary and benefits at the initial interview, especially with a manager because sometimes he or she doesn't know the answers. It may sound as if that is your only interest in the company. A better way is to check out all this information beforehand. Ask the personnel or human resources office for brochures on company benefit plans. And definitely check them out before accepting a job offer.

Interview Behavior

As a job seeker, you should approach each interview by being yourself, being true to yourself, and trusting your own judgment about the style that suits you best. You can build self-confidence by practicing ways of talking and listening effectively and by learning to answer an interviewer's questions. Here are some key points to practice.

- *Good eye contact:* Get comfortable with and use this form of personal contact. If you like your interviewers, your eyes will communicate warmth and interest.

- *Appropriate body language:* Be relaxed and open, interested and attentive. Notice how bodies speak! Become aware of ways in which your body sends messages of boredom, fear, enthusiasm, cockiness, nervousness, or confidence. And become aware of others' body language. For example, your interviewer's body language may indicate that you need to paraphrase or restate a response or give a concrete example.

- *Appropriate voice melody:* Try to come across with vitality, enthusiasm, and confidence. Remember that low, relaxed tones convey confidence and competence; high, squeaky tones convey insecurity. Tape record your answers to expected questions so that you can hear yourself; at least practice them out loud, alone or with someone who will give you honest feedback.

- *Active listening:* Indicate that you have heard and understood what the interviewer has said. For example, if the interviewer mentions tardiness as a problem, say, "It must be difficult to have employees who are constantly late. I can assure you I'll make every effort to be on time."

- *Good choice of words:* Use language that is respectful but not overly formal. If you do your interview homework and practice, the right words should come easily. Much of what you "say" will of course be conveyed by your manner, not your words.[8] Some say as much as 95 percent of our communication is nonverbal.

Practice Questions

You will be asked questions about your previous work experience and education, your values, and your goals. You may possibly be asked questions about your family life and leisure activities, but very personal questions are not appropriate in an interview.

Questions dealing with factual information should not be a problem if you have prepared well. Have on hand your own card file of all education, previous jobs, and other experience, with correct dates, place names and addresses, job titles and duties, names of supervisors, and other relevant information in case these slip your mind. Usually this information is on the application. The interview centers on clarification of points on the application and résumé.

If you have been working regularly and successfully in your field for a period of years, the interview will be mainly a chance for you to tell what you have done. If you are a recent graduate, the discussion may focus on your education and casual jobs.

If you have been in and out of the job market or have had problems in the past, the interviewer will want to explore the reasons. Be relaxed and not defensive. Look on the interview as a chance to make a fresh start. Assure the interviewer that you will not be a problem but a solution. All the questions in the interview are different ways of asking "Can you do the job?" It's not fair to expect to be hired if you can't do the job well. If you keep that clearly in mind, you will be able to support your answer, "Yes, I can do the job," with all sorts of relevant data. Some companies will even say they don't care if the people they hire are smart. They're looking for people who are reliable and conscientious and who can get along with others. A poor entry-level hire can cost as much as $5,000 to $7,000, according to the Department of Labor.[9]

Practice answering interview questions until you feel comfortable. Prepare concise answers so you won't ramble. Omit personal information and especially any negative information about your past jobs and employers. Some people get carried away and start talking about their childhood, personal problems, and all sorts of irrelevant data that wear interviewers out and hardly charm them. And of course, when talking about your present workplace, be positive about managers, coworkers, and the company in general. No one wants to hire a complainer. And you definitely do not want to divulge any company secrets to potential employers who may assume you would do the same to them. Some companies even ask employees who are leaving to sign a statement that they will not do so, nor jeopardize the company's privacy in any way.

Here are some typical, commonly asked questions, along with answers for you to consider.

Tell me something about yourself. This request, one of the most frequently asked by interviewers, could be followed by a dismayed silence as you race your mental motor trying to find something to talk about. If you are prepared, you will jump in happily with the reasons you feel your skills, background, and personal attitudes are good for the job and how you see your future with the company. You will seldom have a better opportunity than this to talk about yourself.

Why are you leaving your present job? (Or *Why did you leave your last job?*) If the circumstances of your leaving were unpleasant or your present conditions are unbearable, these personal problems will be the first answers to pop into your mind—but they should be the last answers you give. Everyone leaves a job for more than one reason, and negative reasons can be made positive. If your boss was oppressive, your coworkers were disagreeable, or the job was too difficult, a move can provide you opportunity for growth in a variety of ways. It's difficult for anyone to improve on a job when his or her feelings are all negative. Here are some possible replies:

- "I seemed to have reached a point where there was little potential for growth."
- "I have learned my job well and would like to try new dimensions in a growing [or larger, or innovative] company."
- "I decided to change careers, and I just got my degree."
- "I left to raise a family, and now I am ready to return to work permanently."
- "I moved [or the company reorganized or merged or cut back or slowed down]."

Your application indicated that you have been in and out of the work force quite often (or haven't worked in some years). What were you involved with in those periods of unemployment? Here the interviewer has several concerns. Your skills might be rusty or you may have had some problems keeping a job. Another is that you might be likely to leave after being trained for this job, a cost to the company. Be prepared to give assurance that your qualifications are such that you can handle the job and that you plan to stay with the company. Knowing your abilities and what the job demands can clarify this subject for you.

What are your weaknesses and what are your strengths? Smile when they ask this one. Have a list you have memorized about what you do best, such as, "I work well with other people on a team basis." If the job you are applying for matches your personality type, your weaknesses will be in areas not important for the job. On a conventional job (C), for example, artistic strengths (A) would get in the way. So you might say, "I'm not very creative. I prefer to follow a set routine." Or if the job calls for machine work (R), you might say your communication skills (S) aren't the best. Investigative applicants (I) may say that they get absorbed in their research, whereas enterprising (E) ones may say that, rather than developing a product, they prefer making contact with people to influence them to buy the product. Whatever personality type the job calls for, weaknesses of the type opposite yours on the hexagon can be turned into strengths!

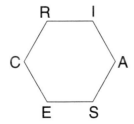

Do you have any reason to feel that you cannot perform the described job duties well? In some cases, physical or mental limitations can interfere with job performance, but it is illegal for an employer to discriminate against anyone only on the basis of a disability. The Americans with Disabilities Act says it has to be clear that disabled applicants cannot do the job even if reasonable accommodations are made for them.

Made-up situations that test a person's knowledge of the job may begin with questions like "What would you do if . . . ?" The quality of your solution is not nearly as important as your attitude and your creativity under fire. A calm approach is a best bet. It's better to cushion your statements with answers like, "One of the things I might consider would be . . ." If you commit yourself to a process of what you *would* do, and it isn't the solution the *interviewer* would like or consider, you are in an awkward position. Give your answer a cushion of several possible choices, and indicate that you would carefully assess the situation.

How did you get along with . . . ? This question can be asked about supervisors, coworkers, subordinates, even teachers. Few people get along with everyone. If you generally do, say so. If you had a problem with someone, there is usually no need to tell the whole tale here. The willingness to work out problems is a plus. Be positive, not blaming or complaining.

Would you accept part-time or temporary work? Employers are more inclined to hire for full-time work from a part-time or temporary employment pool than to take a person from the outside. If you plan to stay with the company, ask if a temporary or part-time job may result in a permanent hire before you say yes. If you want a temporary job and are offered a permanent position, however, consider their cost and time of training you. It takes most employees at least several months to begin to earn their pay. "No" is a better answer if you really want temporary or part-time work when you are offered a permanent, full-time position.

Why do you want to work for our company? Most people looking for a job are more interested in getting a good job than in being particular about where they work, and this attitude can make them appear not to care about the company. One of the most important things you should do before you go to an interview—or ask for one—is find out all you can about the company. Identify some positive aspects of policies, procedures, or products you can discuss with interest. Do your homework—so you will have work to come home from.

How long do you expect to work for us? The truth is that a company will not keep employees past its ability to use their skills. And you are not going to work for a company past the time that it is good for you. The best answer might be, "As long as it is good for both of us." Companies also do not appreciate people who do not plan to stay for a reasonable amount of time. It is very costly to recruit, enroll in benefits, and train a new employee only to have that person leave.

Do you have any questions about the company or the job? An interview doesn't have to be one-sided. Be ready for this question by preparing some questions of your own ahead of time to show your interest. Employers, down at the bottom of their company hearts, believe the myth that good people are hard to find. If they are asked to define a good person, that person is always someone who is really interested in the company and in the job that he or she does. So this is an ideal time to relate your interest, enthusiasm, and commitment to the company and the job.[10]

There are some questions you must resolve honestly ahead of time:

- Are you willing to or can you move or travel, work overtime, take a temporary or part-time job?
- Do you have plans for your next job, your next few years, starting your own business, changing fields, going back to school?

In every case, the real questions are these: *Can you do the job? Will you stay with the company?*

Sometimes you may be asked questions that startle you. If you feel unprepared, it's wise to say, "I need a few moments to think about that." Then take a few deep breaths, relax, and begin confidently. If you still draw a blank, be prepared to deal with the situation, perhaps saying, "Maybe we could come back to that later," or "I really should be prepared to answer that but I'm not." It's a learning experience and you learn that you can keep cool.

Be prepared for some difficult ("whew!") questions if you have a poor work record, have ever been fired for serious problems, or have been convicted of a crime. Take a deep breath, relax a minute, look at the interviewer, and say in your own words something like this: "Yes, I made a mistake [or have done poorly in the past], but I learned my lesson, and I'm determined that it won't happen again." Then stop. Do not keep on explaining. If you sound confident and not defensive, the interviewer will be more likely to accept your answer. Perhaps you can include some recent experience as evidence that you've made some changes in your life. Again, you need to reassure the interviewer that you are capable of doing the job.

You might be startled by inappropriate or personal questions that appear to have nothing to do with job qualifications but may indicate discrimination. Questions about age, race, religion, nationality, home ownership, credit report, physical characteristics, organizations, political views, or disabilities are improper unless the answers are job related. Also inappropriate are questions that discriminate between males and females—such as questions about family planning, child care, or pregnancy.

Decide in advance how you will answer such questions if they are asked. If the issue is not really important, you might prefer to answer the question rather than risk alienating the interviewer with a refusal. If you'd prefer not to answer, you might say, "I prefer not to answer that question." Or you may say, "I wasn't aware this was a requirement for the job" or "Can you explain how this question relates to the job?" You can appeal to the law in obvious cases of prejudice; in less serious instances, a good sense of humor and respect for others can be enormously helpful. Don't win the battle and lose the war!

Nelva Shore, a California employment specialist, says, "It really doesn't matter what questions are asked as long as you can talk!" Be ready to talk positively about yourself, your goals, and your reason for applying. Practice talking. There is no other way. One woman who stood out in an interview later told about how she had practiced sitting down in front of a mirror; she practiced talking out loud, answering questions, making eye contact, controlling voice melody—every phase of the interview—until she felt totally at ease. Her enthusiasm came through unspoiled by anxiety. You can learn these skills, too.

Follow-Up

If you aren't told the results at the end of the interview, feel free to ask when you will hear them. In the private sector (nongovernment), it is appropriate to send a thank-you letter right after the interview that encourages a reply (see Figure 7-10), perhaps asks for more information, or accepts an offer (see Figure 7-11). Then call after a week or so if you haven't heard. It is also important to give notice promptly if you decide to decline an offer.

Sometimes there is a delay in hiring someone after an interview. Several months may go by because of changes inside the company. A key employee may decide to quit or retire, for example; or an employer may decide to fill another position first; or a complex reorganization may take more time than planned. Tactfully keep in touch with your contact in the company or with the personnel department until you are certain there is no opening for you or you are hired. Job Shop participant Hal Thomas suggests returning after one to two weeks to learn whether the position has been filled; returning in one to two months, perhaps with work samples, to show continued interest; and then sending a letter and work samples (if applicable) in six months.

After you are hired, you may be asked to supply such items as a birth certificate, proof of citizenship, a green card if you are an immigrant, a photograph, and proof of age. Have these items ready if you feel they might be required.

Job Offers: Too Many or Too Few?

You probably will not get a job offer during your first interview. But suppose you do get a job offer—or two or three—in this early phase of your career search. Maybe you had planned to do work in marketing, but the welding

5405 Monroe Street
Aurora, IL 60504
February 26, 2000

Dierk Van Symms, Manager of Technical Services
Effective Micro Systems, Inc.
130 Meridian Drive, Suite 411
Aurora, IL 60504

Dear Mr. Van Symms:

Thank you for the chance to discuss a work opportunity with
Effective Micro Systems, Inc. I have completed the EMS
Interview Survey, and it is attached for your review.

I am pleased about the possibility of working for EMS. After
meeting you and your staff, I feel that I would fit in quite well on
your team. Each of you has confirmed what I already sus-
pected—that EMS is a quality organization.

I look forward to meeting with you again. Please feel free to call
me at home or at work.

Sincerely yours,

Joanne M. Malatia

Enclosures

Figure 7-10   Thank-you letter following an interview

"Night work! You mean when it's dark?"

© Jim Unger /distributed by United Media, 1998.

shop would welcome you! Beware quick decisions. You can easily get carried away with excitement and leap into the first job that comes along. When recruits are in short supply, companies may try to give a job seeker little time to weigh a decision. If you have researched the company and know you want to work there, your decision will be easier to make.

Some jobs sound rewarding in terms of personal growth opportunities, but the salary is so low you could not live on it without making sacrifices. Another job pays very well, but the work sounds dull and disagreeable. You might even be offered a temporary job; it would fulfill your immediate needs, but you'd be back on the job market in six months or so. Should you accept one of these less desirable jobs just to get hired or to get experience? Some companies and even employment offices have been know to advertise one job but place you in another, far less desirable position or increase your beginning work load to unmanageable proportions just to see if they can avoid hiring a second person. Called *bait and switch, corporate-style,* this unsavory practice can stall a career but make the victim much wiser in checking out a job ahead of time and also knowing when to quit an unreasonable situation.[11] When either employer or employee is less than honest in the hiring game, they both lose.

Now is the time to review your needs, wants, and values to become very clear about what you want the job to do. Perhaps your goal is just to get into a special company that you've chosen. Taking a job you don't particularly like could give you this chance. If you do your best in that job, you may be able to obtain the position of your choice—or one like it—should an opening occur. Some companies will hire on a temporary basis and then transfer and promote from within before they open jobs to outsiders.

When you do decide on a job offer, work out details such as schedule or benefits, before final acceptance. Then your acceptance letter can "confirm our conversation."

If you aren't hired for the job you really want right away, you may be only one of many well-qualified applicants. In a competitive field, you may spend six months or more of continuous hunting to find a job. Whether you should take a less desirable job depends on how long you can afford to wait and continue the search. If you job hunt for many months without a nibble, you may need to consider alternatives: other careers, new training, other opportunities in your present position, additional paid or volunteer experience that might be useful in a different kind of job.

Choosing may be difficult because you have in mind a portrait of the perfect workplace. But when you actually go job hunting, you will find that perfection doesn't exist. You need a job because the rent is due and you have car payments to make.

You may have to start at the bottom and work up to the job you want. Suppose you, a business major with a fresh degree from a good university, are offered a job as a mail clerk. Or you have a master's degree in computer programming, but you are offered a job as a computer operator. You may feel such offers are beneath your dignity. But before you ride away on your high horse, consider these facts: one major oil company makes a practice of hiring as mail clerks new graduates who are candidates for all management and public relations jobs. In so doing, they have a chance to look you over before entrusting a more important job to you. And you have a chance to network inside and explore possibilities before getting too entrenched. Be wary of turning down a job that fails to meet your expectations. Ask some company employees what the offer means. Ask the interviewer what the growth potential of the job is and whether you might be given a performance review in three to six months for a possible promotion.

Job hunting requires that you keep involved at all times in some part of the process. The more exacting your requirements, the longer you will job hunt and the more often you will be turned down. But if you can accept some

5401 Monroe Street
Mobile, Alabama 36608
October 30, 1998

Ms. Jill Jones
Director of Marketing
PTT Corporation
Dogwood, AL 36309

Dear Ms. Jones:

I am very pleased to accept an internship in marketing with PTT Corporation. It will be a pleasure to associate with the people I have met at PTT. The work you outlined in your letter sounds very challenging. I appreciate the chance to further my education in this way.

I look forward to starting on February 1. Please call if you wish to discuss any aspect of my internship further.

Sincerely yours,

Chris Cross

Figure 7-11   Acceptance letter

frustration as a normal part of the job-hunting process, you will not be discouraged. Keep in mind a clear picture of the place you would like to work so you will recognize it when you find it. Focus on the changes you can make to find more satisfaction in the workplace.

 Self-Assessment Exercises

1. The Job Hunt Begins

a. Begin a rough draft of your résumé. Then polish and type a good copy.

Name _____

Address _____

Home phone _____   Work phone _____

Fax _____   E-mail _____

Position objective _____

Qualifications in brief _____

_____

_____

Experience summary (optional: try *both* chronological and functional)

_____

_____

_____

_____

_____

Education _____

_____

_____

Personal paragraph _____

_____

_____

_____

Special notes (honors, works published, organizations, etc.) _____

_____

_____

b. Write a cover letter to accompany your résumé.

2. Practicing an Interview

Some interviewers use a rating scale to grade your performance on various points of importance to them. Figure 7-12 shows a scale used by recruiters who come from various workplaces to interview students on campus. Role-play an interview. Then, using the interview rating chart, rate yourself or ask someone to rate you on your interview skills. Here are some what/how/why practice questions.

Work Experience

What have you done to get to your present position?

What were your major responsibilities on your last job (or last military experience)?

What did you like most about that job?

What did you like least about that job?

What problems did you face? How did you overcome these problems?

What did you learn on your last job?

How do you feel your last job used your ability?

Why did you leave (or are you planning to leave) your last job?

What impressions do you think you left on your last job?

Why do you want to work for us?

What do you feel you can contribute?

Education

What were your favorite courses (workshops, seminars)?

Why did you choose your major?

How would you rate your instructors?

What activities and clubs were you in? How did you participate?

How did you finance your education?

What further education are you planning?

INTERVIEW RATING CHART—CONFIDENTIAL
Santa Clara University
Career Planning and Placement Office

Firm _____

Recruiter _____   Date _____

I. CHARACTERISTICS OF CANDIDATE

A = Interview preparation
B = Clarity of career objectives
C = Realistic career objectives
D = Appropriate academic preparation
E = Personal appearance
F = Communicative ability
G = Emotional maturity
H = Self-confidence
I = Motivation
J = Overall rating

II. EMPLOYER INTEREST

1 = Particularly high interest
2 = Interest with further consideration necessary
3 = Prefer not to make offer
4 = Needs placement counseling

III. ADDITIONAL COMMENTS

RATING SCALE   1) Outstanding   2) Above average   3) Average   4) Below average   5) Poor

NAME	I. CHARACTERISTICS OF CANDIDATE										II.	III. COMMENTS
	A	B	C	D	E	F	G	H	I	J		

Figure 7-12   Interview Scale

Skills and Values

How do you get along with people (supervisors, coworkers, instructors)?

What are your transferable (general) skills?

What are your work-specific skills?

What are your personality–responsibility skills?

What are your strengths?

What are your weaknesses?

How important is money to you?

How well do you work on your own?

How many days did you take off last year for sickness and personal business?

How do you feel about overtime? Flexible hours? Part-time or temporary work? Travel? Moving to a new location?

What do you do when a coworker is behind schedule?

What kind of decision maker are you?

Goals

What do you see yourself doing in five years?

How do you plan to get there?

What areas of growth and development do you plan to work on?

What salary would you like to earn?

Tell me about yourself!

3. More Interview Questions

Make up some questions you would like an interviewer to ask you.

4. The Application Form

Carefully fill out the application form in Figure 7-13 and sign it.

5. *The Job Hunt Checklist*

If you are job hunting now, establish a goal: for example, you will contact fifty people by information interviewing, networking, applying for jobs, writing letters, making telephone calls, and sending résumés on request. To check your progress, answer the following questions *yes* or *no*.

_____ Have you interviewed twenty-five people to obtain information about jobs and companies?

_____ Have you applied for work directly to twenty-five companies?

_____ Have you written an effective résumé for each job title?

_____ Have you contacted a network of at least twenty-five people who could help you?

_____ After each interview, do you critique yourself honestly?

_____ Have you written letters to thank the people who interviewed you?

EMPLOYMENT APPLICATION

Personal Data

Position Applied For   Application Date   /   /

Name (last, first, middle)

Social Security Number   Driver's License Number (if required by job)

Address

City   State   Zip Code

Home phone (   )   Message Phone (   )

Date available for work ____ / ____ / ____   Have you been employed here before? ❑ Yes ❑ No
Are you legally eligible for employment in this country? ❑ Yes ❑ No
(Proof of U.S. citizenship or immigration status will be required upon employment.)
If you are under 18, can you furnish a work permit? ❑ Yes ❑ No
Type of employment desired: ❑ Full Time ❑ Part Time ❑ Temporary ❑ Seasonal
Have you ever been convicted of a felony in the last 7 years? ❑ Yes ❑ No
(Such conviction may be relevant if job-related, but does not bar you from employment.) If yes, please explain.

Employment History

List your last four employers, assignments or volunteer activities, starting with most recent employer, including military experience.

| From | To | Employer | Phone (   ) |

Job Title   Address

Immediate Supervisor & Title   Summarize the nature of work performed and job responsibilities.

Reason for leaving.   Beginning rate/salary $ per   Ending rate/salary $ per

| From | To | Employer | Phone (   ) |

Job Title   Address

Immediate Supervisor & Title   Summarize the nature of work performed and job responsibilities.

Reason for leaving.   Beginning rate/salary $ per   Ending rate/salary $ per

| From | To | Employer | Phone (   ) |

Job Title   Address

Immediate Supervisor & Title   Summarize the nature of work performed and job responsibilities.

Reason for leaving.   Beginning rate/salary $ per   Ending rate/salary $ per

Figure 7-13   Application Form

Courtesy of Alida Stevens, President, Smith & Vandiver, Inc., Watsonville, CA

From	To	Employer	Phone (	)	

Job Title   Address

Immediate Supervisor & Title   Summarize the nature of work performed and job responsibilities.

Reason for leaving.   Beginning rate/salary $ per   Ending rate/salary $ per

Skills and Qualifications

Summarize special skills and qualifications acquired from employment or other experience that may qualify you for work with our Company.

Education Record

High school   Dates attended

Degrees or diplomas   Course of study

College/University   Dates attended

Degrees or diplomas   Course of study

Other   Dates attended

Degrees or diplomas   Course of study

References

Name   Phone number (   )   Years known

Name   Phone number (   )   Years known

Name   Phone number (   )   Years known

It is understood and agreed that any misrepresentation by me in this application will be sufficient cause for cancellation of this application and/or separation from the employer's service if I have been employed. Furthermore, I understand that just as I am free to resign at any time, the Employer reserves the right to terminate my employment at any time, with or without cause and without prior notice. I understand that no representative of the Employer has the authority to make any assurances to the contrary.

I give the Employer the right to investigate all references and to secure additional information about me, if job related. I hereby release from liability the Employer and its representatives for seeking such information and all other persons, corporations or organizations for furnishing such information.

Signature of Applicant   Date   /   /

8/

Decisions, Decisions

What's Your Next Move?

 FOCUS

- Survey the options.
- Learn a decision-making process.
- Set realistic goals.

*I*n the last half century, opportunities and choices have grown faster than at any other time in history, particularly in the affluent, technological segments of the world. Ordinary people can see other lifestyles around the globe through travel and television, talk to thousands of strangers over the Internet, become educated, control family structure, and enjoy a proliferation of consumer goods unimagined by emperors of old. These innovations bring forth a growing array of careers available in previous times to only a very small percentage of the population. As a result, decision making is more difficult than it was in times past, especially when you are trying to stay true to your values. Maintaining your own unique values is hard when you are awash in a very strong popular culture.

Throughout the career-search process you have been making many small decisions, often without even realizing it. And because of them, you have likely zeroed in on a general career area, if not a job title, and you have focused on the educational background that you would need for this type of career.

Author and educator H. B. Gelatt reminds us that most people make most decisions easily most of the time without thinking too much. Each personality type has its own decision-making style, ranging from the dynamic, energetic, and enterprising risk takers who are always ready to meet ever new and greater challenges, to the conventional, slower moving, and more careful people who are ready only for those challenges that look most manageable.

Although few people can be fully defined according to personality types, one may say that, generally, the following behavior patterns commonly occur among different personality types. The social person often acts out of caring for others but is not always practical. Both the realistic and the conventional types are practical folks who tend to stay within secure societal norms. The conventional type follows the lead of others; realistic types will decide independently, often disregarding people's feelings but generally staying on the conservative side. The creative/artistic person, on the other hand, will see so many possibilities—including some that follow no known guidelines—that he or she will have difficulty making choices. And, whereas the enterprising person leaps first and gets the facts later, the investigative type keeps researching, hoping that working on a decision long enough will make the results absolutely clear and certain. What kind of decision maker are you?

> I try to take one day at a time,
> but sometimes several days
> attack me at once.
> —*Ashleigh Brilliant*[1]

We can fantasize a perfectly self-actualized person bringing all these factors into balance: caring for others with just enough hard-headed realism to be practical, creating new systems while following guidelines when appropriate, searching out just enough facts before risking the decision.

In *Please Understand Me,* authors Keirsey and Bates note that people whom they call *judgers* want things in their lives settled, so they make decisions promptly and with satisfaction. The opposite personality type, called *perceivers,* like to keep all their options open, so they tend to delay decisions until the last possible minute.[2]

For anyone faced with tough decisions, for the person who tends to agonize over every decision, for those who delay decisions, organized steps can provide perspective. In this chapter we consider a *decision-making dozen:* four attitudes, four options, and a four-phase, decision-making process. Its purpose is not to nail you down to a decision but to show you a structured method for reaching one.

Attitudes

Four attitudes can help you make a good decision: stay calm; be persistent; keep your perspective; be confident.

Stay Calm

Although a certain amount of anxiety can motivate a person to make a decision, too much can interfere with it. If you are under severe pressure, you may try to escape through any of a million fantasies: quit work or school altogether and drop out; join the Marines; end your marriage; run off with your secretary; sell everything, hitch up the wagon, and head west! The uncertainties are as numerous as the fantasies: Am I OK? Is there anything at all in life for me, or is this all there is? Will my health hold up? Will my kids ever get settled? Will I? Will I ever have kids? Will I look like a fool if I go back to school? Can I keep on succeeding? Do I even want to? Sometimes turbulent thoughts can seem like part of the decision-making process. You can practice letting them go, however, just like leaves in the wind, by affirming that you have made good decisions in the past and you can do so now.

Be Persistent

Take one step at a time. You rarely have to put a major life decision into action in one immediate, straight-line leap! It often takes thought and some zigzag testing to sort out all the possibilities. If a decision to get a four-year degree seems overwhelming, a small decision to look at college catalogs in the library or talk to an educational counselor or teacher may be a manageable first step. But make up your mind to keep moving toward the goal you seek.

Keep Your Perspective

Stop and occasionally review your direction. If it is helpful, use the exercises in Chapter 9 to assemble information that is relevant to a career decision. Identify your strong and weak spots as well as areas you still need to explore. Keep focusing on what you want your life to be like.

Be Confident

If you are honest, you know that you have made some good decisions in the past—from what to wear to where to work! A lack of confidence can be a giant block on the road to good decision making. As Ken Keyes, Jr., says, "Beware what you tell yourself!"[3] Compare the person who says, "I don't deserve success, I'm just not good at much of anything," with the person who might say, "Everyone—including me—deserves success." Sometimes our bad feelings can send us in search of a problem: "Don't cheer me up because it will ruin my misery program." Affirmations, those positive and negative thoughts we think over and over again, are so powerful that the authors of the children's book *Make It So!* ask children to speculate, "So—I've been wondering—could most of my problems be caused by me?"[4]

You can't know the future. Some decisions will work out; some will not. In order to improve your life, you change what can be changed, accept what can't be changed and work with it, and hope you have the wisdom to know the difference.

> When you don't know which way to turn, son,
> try something. Don't jest do nothin'!
> —*Grandpa to grandson in* Cold Sassy Tree[5]

Four Options

At this time you have four options. Go back to or remain in school, seek a new job or involvement, keep the same job with a new approach, or keep the status quo by deciding not to decide.

Back to School

If you are already in school, committed to staying there, and clear on your program of studies, then you have already made a decision and do not need to look at this section.

More and more people are returning to school more often, staying there longer, and attending in nontraditional ways. According to researcher Arthur Levine, president of Teachers College at Columbia University, less than 16 percent of college students are eighteen- to twenty-two-year-olds attending full time and living on campus. Fifty-five percent work, 50 percent are over twenty-five years of age, and 42 percent attend part time. These students expect the college to serve them as adult consumers, not treat them as youngsters. Traditional dating patterns are a thing of the past as students resist making commitments to relationships.[6]

The school you choose will reflect the community in which it is located and may influence your career choice. Colleges in Silicon Valley relate to the computer industry; those in a rural, agricultural area will reflect careers that support agriculture.

Learning to learn, to be a generalist, to have a broad view of the world, to continue learning and developing abilities—these are essential skills for the future. The majority of jobs now require some postsecondary education and training; many unskilled jobs are either being automated or moving offshore. Industry is slowly realizing that trained people are more important than new hardware, but upgrading workers is more difficult than they realized.[7]

Past are the days when a high school graduate could expect to get a life-lasting and decent-paying job that would support the American Dream of a family, house, car, and yearly vacation. A high school dropout is eight times more likely than a college graduate and three times more likely than a high school graduate to be unemployed.[8] And women still need more education than men to achieve parity in salary, although they have almost achieved educational parity (91 percent of women to 88 percent of men have at least a high school diploma; 27 percent of women to 29 percent of men are college graduates).[9]

And these days, with the intensity of the global economy, most people with the slightest connection to the business world seem to be thinking of going for an MBA—master's in business administration—if they haven't done so already.

Literacy skills are of great importance in seeking employment. The U.S. Department of Education shows that, on average, the most competent readers, who have a low unemployment rate of 4.2 percent, can expect to earn $910 a week, and the poorest readers, 16 percent of whom are unemployed, earn an average of $355.[10]

Although college degrees have been declining in value lately because increased numbers of people are obtaining them, a degree will still have greater earning power than a high school diploma. Every year, a class of dropouts who leave school earn about $237 billion less than an equivalent class of high school graduates, and they pay significantly less in taxes.[11] In 1991, about 82 percent of all Americans in prison were high school dropouts, representing an average yearly cost each of $20,000 to taxpayers.[12]

On the educational scene, the picture for younger and college-educated women is improving. Though many continue to avoid pursuing degrees in the sciences, math, and engineering, even though these are pathways to lucrative professions, the numbers of women enrolled in these courses are increasing. Those who study these disciplines tend to drop out at higher rates than men because they find the classes subtly or not so subtly male oriented unless they study at women's colleges. Even so, enrollment in these schools increased 33 percent in the fall of 1994.[13]

More minorities are enrolling in minority colleges, especially since changes in affirmative action programs in some places have made them feel less welcome. The number of blacks earning college degrees has increased: for men by 20 percent, for women by 55 percent over the past twenty years, with Howard University preferred by many of these students over Ivy League campuses.[14]

The high school graduation rate for blacks reached about the same level as that for whites, increasing by 87 percent in 1995. Eighty-two percent of all Americans twenty-five and older have completed high school. Twenty-three percent of adults received bachelor's degrees in 1995, according to the Census Bureau.[15] Degrees will continue to make employment, upgrading, promotions, and raises more attainable.

And of course, there are always the notable exceptions: people with little education who make a dramatic contribution to their work. Commitment, opportunity, and sometimes hard times can spur people to achievements their circumstances would not predict. But generally, without knowledge and training, a worker's survival in the 2000s will be difficult.

If you simply cannot endure more education, face facts realistically and plan very carefully. Experience will teach you many of the skills you may need for your work. And realize that age and experience may change your motivation and ability to go back to school.

Do not let your age or your previous school record discourage you if you are older and returning to school. The average age of all adults going to school is over thirty, and there's no maximum in sight. One newspaper article described an eighty-two-year-old student who earned an associate degree in business in 1990, sixty years after graduating from high school. She now writes and works for the student newspaper.[16]

People returning to school after a long time away are often fearful: "Am I too old to learn, too old to compete with younger college students?" Some people feel that they are incompetent because they had difficulties with certain subjects in their early school years. The surprise comes (and this happens with few exceptions) when reentry students report a great growth in confidence along with newfound goals, even though they may have previous school records that qualify as disasters. Because they are mature and motivated (although they don't always *feel* that way), they can reach their goals. So can you.

"If I have to keep going to school, all the best
jobs are gonna be snapped up."

© Jim Unger/distributed by United Media, 1998.

A Mini-orientation to College   You may wonder what courses you would take
if you returned to school. If your high school education was incomplete or
deficient, or if you began college and picked up some poor grades, consider
basic skills courses in language and math at adult education centers or community colleges. You also may find courses for personal growth and enrichment in these schools. Many are noncredit courses that provide an easy way
to start back to school. Training in communications, for example, can be a
good way to gain confidence to face difficult situations both in the workplace
and at home.

   At the community college you can also sample various majors (areas of
specialty), explore and prepare for a career, or take courses to transfer to a
four-year college. Pick up a catalog at the college bookstore and look for
introductory courses. The titles of these courses frequently include words such

as "beginning," "orientation to," "introduction to," or "principles of." The catalog will tell you the required courses and general degree requirements for each major. Usually advisers or counselors will be available to help you through the maze of choices. Search for someone who understands where you are now and how you feel.

If you want a four-year degree, you can do your first two years at a community college and transfer, or you can go directly to a four-year college. In either case, your course of studies will be something like this:

First year: General education courses (GE), introduction to a major, and electives (free-choice courses)

Second year: Exploration of a major, GE, and electives

Third year: Major requirements, electives, and remaining GE

Fourth year: Major requirements and electives

You will probably need more math if you are interested in science, health, four-year business or technical fields, architecture, or engineering. Adult education programs offer math courses at the high school level and sometimes beyond. Community colleges offer not only high school level courses but also most of the college courses at the freshman and sophomore level. Both offer remedial arithmetic. The usual sequence is this:

High school: Arithmetic, introductory algebra, plane geometry, intermediate algebra, trigonometry, college (pre-calculus) algebra or "senior math"

College: College algebra, analytic geometry, calculus (two to three semesters or five quarters), and other advanced courses as needed and required

First, check to see how much math you need for various programs. (You may not need any at all.) Then try to start where you left off or where you feel most comfortable. Before you try to enroll in any course, however, find out whether you must complete any prerequisites first. (A *prerequisite* is a course that you need to take before enrolling in a more advanced course. Sometimes experience will take the place of a prerequisite.)

Because most people will be working in the global economy or at least in areas of the United States with a diverse population, they will have contact with people of other cultures and languages. Consider enrolling in a language, history, or anthropology course as part of your general education to give you some understanding of other cultures.

Educational Possibilities   If returning to school seems impossible—because of time or distance, for example—investigate "distance learning." More and more colleges are putting classes online—that is, on TV with communication by e-mail and library through the Internet. No doubt, more schools will do so, though it takes a great deal of discipline for students to use these at-home methods of study. Some colleges and universities administer tests such as those in the College Level Examination Program (CLEP), which enable you to earn credit by examination. Some schools give credit for work experience. You may be required to go to the campus to take exams or to attend certain classes, but overall such programs decrease the time you need to spend on campus. Some colleges offer courses in weekend sessions that can lead to a degree.

Despite the news that college tuition is rising rapidly, there are many ways to keep college costs within bounds without going into debt. If finances are a problem and you haven't planned ahead, apply for financial aid. Students of all ages can get grants and low-interest loans for education. But some graduates have found that paying back a loan is a struggle, especially if their first jobs do not pay well. Some graduates change their lifestyles; live at home; mortgage, sell, or rent their houses; sell their cars and ride their bikes; work part time and go to school part time.

Local community colleges can provide two years of your education at the lowest cost of any institution. A graduate of a four-year private college went back to a community college for courses relating to a newly found career goal. He was surprised to find excellent instructors and courses. He lamented the money his parents had spent based on mistaken stereotypes about "junior colleges," especially since his major had not resulted in satisfying employment.

Some call the two-year colleges the new graduate schools for returning students, one in four of whom has a bachelor's degree or higher.[17] Businesses in the community work closely with these institutions, advising them about the kinds of course work they would like their workers to pursue, and the colleges develop state-of-the-art programs as a result.

You may be in school wondering if you should be out. Most everyone will tell you that returning is difficult once you leave, as you know already if you have ever stayed out even a short time. And if you begin working, perhaps start a family or buy a house, returning to school can become a very remote possibility very fast. On the other hand, many people have found that being out of school for a time was a good experience for them. They have worked, traveled, joined the military, and found new energy to return to school. Talk to people who have gone either way: those who have managed to survive the struggles of college learning and those who have stopped out for a time. Talk to a counselor, get some help with your studies in the meantime, and then make your decision following the steps discussed later in this chapter.

You may be working and feel that going back to school is impossible for you. But remember, further education is not. Wise people set goals to learn as much on the job as possible and learn while earning. They take on new tasks, extra tasks, find a mentor. You may even set up a development program with your manager.

You can teach yourself many things, and you can find other people who will help you learn. You can enroll in college work experience courses or seek internships where you will work at your same job and earn credit. You can join in the work of a nonprofit community organization or even get on a working board of directors and learn much about business management, marketing, fund-raising, public presentation, and other skills. A lot depends on having a goal and working toward it—and being flexible enough to see alternatives.

As you know, most jobs by definition require only average to somewhat-above-average skills. Talking to people in the field can help you assess your motivation to go on with your education, especially if it looks as if your desired profession will require years of training. Remember, however, when

---

VARIOUS ROUTES TO EDUCATIONAL CREDIT/TRAINING

HIGH SCHOOL CREDIT

Adults can earn high school equivalency certificates through the General Educational Development (GED) program. Contact your local school district or

> GED Testing Service
> American Council on Education
> One Dupont Circle N.W., Suite 250
> Washington, DC 20036-1163
> Website: http://www.acenet.edu

COLLEGE SEARCH

ApplyToCollege will enable you to send your application to over 1,000 schools that accept the standardized form: www.applytocollege.com

CollegeEdge gives help sorting out various colleges: www.CollegeEdge.com

Free Application for Federal Student Aid at U.S. Dept. of Education: www.fafsa.ed.gov

FastWEB gives financial aid information: www.fastweb.com

Federal Student Aid Application: www. fafsa.ed.gov

Hispanic Financial Aid: www. hispanicscholarships.com

Information Page sponsored by aid administrators to link with scam alerts, scholarship databases, and cost calculators: www.finaid.org

Kaplan's College Selector: www.csearch.kaplan.com

Peterson's Guides and *Peterson's College Money Handbook* (with charts of costs and software to explore 1,700 campuses)

Department 1308
P.O. Box 2123
Princeton, NJ 08543

Peterson's Guide to Distance Learning Programs
800-225-0261
www.petersons.com

Sallie Mae is a government-sponsored corporation that services college loans and gives basic financial aid information: www.salliemae.com

Yahoo! includes a quick college search program under education: yahoo.com

(continued)

VARIOUS ROUTES TO EDUCATIONAL CREDIT/TRAINING *(continued)*

COLLEGE CREDIT: ALTERNATIVES

At various colleges, look for flexible alternatives, such as distance learning, weekend programs, credit by examination, and credit for work experience.

Credit by Examination

Earn college credit by examination. Contact the College Level Examination Program (CLEP) for a listing of the 2,900 participating colleges and universities:

CLEP
CN 6600
Princeton, NJ 08541-6600
Website: http://www.
   collegeboard.org
E-mail: CLEP@ets.org

Credit for Noncollege Learning

The Center for Adult Learning and Educational Credentials at the American Council on Education evaluates courses given by private employers, community organizations, labor unions, government agencies, and military education programs. Contact

American Council on Education
The Center for Adult Learning and
   Educational Credentials
One Dupont Circle N.W.,
   Suite 1B-20
Washington, DC 20036

Credit for Experience

You can apply to institutions for college credit for your work experience. See *Earn College Credit for What You Know,* Lois Lamdin from Kendall/Hunt Publishing at 1-800-228-0810 ($24.95) or for information about institutions, contact

Council for Adult and Experiential
   Learning (CAEL) National Head-
   quarters

243 South Wabash Avenue,
   Suite 800
Chicago, IL 60604
Website: www.cael.org

INC's October 1996 cover story on
   MBA programs: "Too Cool for
   School?"
   Available at www.inc.com

Intered's list of schools, degree programs, and questions to ask:
   www.intered.com

Credit for Correspondence and Independent Study

University Continuing Education Association (UCEA) sponsors a wide variety of correspondence and independent study courses that are available through its membership institutions. The Association publishes *The Independent Study Catalog, the UCEA Guide to Independent Study through Correspondence Instruction.*

UCEA
Suite 615
One Dupont Circle, N.W.
Washington, DC 20036
E-mail: postmaster@nucea.edu;
   Website: http://www.nucea.edu

A book entitled *Bears' Guide to
   Earning College Degrees Non-
   traditionally* (1990, $23.95 plus
   shipping) is available from

C&B Publishing
P.O. Box 826
Benicia, CA 94510

Distance Learning: DETC
   Publications
1601 18th Street N.W.
Washington, DC 20009
E-mail: detc@detc.org; Website:
   http://www.detc.org

For additional information on accredited distance learning, contact the following organizations:

VARIOUS ROUTES TO EDUCATIONAL CREDIT/TRAINING *(continued)*

Charter Oak State College
66 Cedar Street
Newington, CT 06111
E-mail: info@cosc.edu

The Ohio State University Clearinghouse on Adult, Career, and
Vocational Education (ERIC)
1900 Kenny Road
Columbus, Ohio 43210-1090

Regents College Degrees: A Virtual
University
ACT Test Administration
7 Columbia Circle
Albany, NY 12203
Website: http://www.regents.edu

Thomas A. Edison College
101 West State Street
Trenton, NJ 08608
E-mail: Admissions@call.tesc.edu
Website: http://www.tesc.edu

International University
Consortium
University of Maryland University
College
University Boulevard at Adelphi
Road
College Park, MD 20742-1612

*Specialized Programs: Degree,
Nondegree, Apprenticeships*
Conservation Directory (Lists
college degree programs related
to the environment)
National Wildlife Federation
8925 Leesburg Pike
Vienna, VA 22184

CO-OP America
Publishers: *Guide to Environmental
Education Programs at U.S.
Colleges and Universities,* $5, and
National Green Pages 1999.
1612 K Street N.W., #600
Washington, DC 20006
www.coopamerica.org

Ecology Action/Bountiful Gardens
19550 Walker Road
Willits, CA 95490

Food First/Institute for Food and
Development Policy
398 60th Street
Oakland, CA 94618
Publishes *Alternatives to the Peace
Corps* and *Education for Action*
Order from Subterranean Company,
Box 160, 265 South 5th Street,
Monroe, OR 97456; fax (503)
847-6018 or call (800) 274-7826

The Green Center
237 Hatchville Road
East Falmouth, MA 02536

International Honors Program in
Global Ecology +Cities in the
21st Century
19 Braddock Park
Boston, MA 02116
E-mail: info@ihp.edu
Website: http://www.ihp.edu

Institute for Social Ecology
P.O. Box 89
Plainfield, VT 05667
http://ise.rootmedia.org

University of Wisconsin
Clearinghouse of distance-learning
information
www.uwex.edu/disted

For the free publication *A Woman's
Guide to Apprenticeship,* send a
self-addressed label to
Women's Bureau
U.S. Department of Labor
Washington, DC 20210

For help with College Prep On-Line
Summer School: www.freeuniv.com
will give you help with writing,
vocabulary, grammar, study skills,
and test taking.

you meet competent professionals who are all trained, experienced, and "way up there," they didn't get there in one step. The most valuable asset you can have in acquiring a high-level ability is the patience to persevere until you learn it. Hard work is fun if you are doing what you enjoy. As you go along, new horizons will open up. You can also float to your level; that is, before the end of your training, you may choose to stop out at a point where you feel comfortable. Instead of going straight on to become a certified public accountant, you might try working as an accounting clerk, which might lead you in a direction that you hadn't seen before. Or you may find along the way that you'd like to float sideways to a different area with similar satisfiers. The more homework you've done on your interests, the more quickly you'll be able to make such changes.

If you want to get more detailed information about your skills, your aptitudes to develop skills, or areas in which your skills need sharpening, you can contact a counselor at a local college, in your state employment office, or in private practice. You can arrange to take such tests as the Career Ability Placement Survey (CAPS) or the General Aptitude Test Battery (GAT-B).

For special training programs, contact your local state employment office. For alternative routes to educational credit and training, for financial aid resources, and scholarship information refer to Various Routes to Educational Credit/Training earlier in this chapter.

Back to the Job Market

If you are not going directly into the job market or if you do not plan to change jobs at this time, you may wish to skip this section. For some people, seeking a job after some time out of the labor pool can seem difficult. One woman who from choice had not worked for years had this to say:

> Last fall, quaking and shaking, I had made up my mind I must not put off the job-hunting ordeal any longer. I told friends that I was going back to work and one responded that her husband needed an assistant. An interview was set up and I found myself two weeks later working with a fine man who has been very understanding of my initial lack of self-assurance. My 60-day performance report was a very satisfactory one (was delighted to have "initiative" get the best grading); and at six months received a 12 percent raise, but, best of all, the following remarks: "in recognition of outstanding contribution to the department." I love the work, and most of all, I love the self-assurance it's given me. Tell others as scared as I that it's not all that hard. Take that first plunge, and you've got it made. And on a second note, my family is delighted with the new and confident me!

> —Carol Shawhan

Same Job/New Approach

If you are not employed, you may wish to skip this section for now. Those who are already working and have looked over the job market may find that their present job isn't so bad after all. "Then why," they wonder, "do I feel dissatisfied?" One common explanation is, "I'm not comfortable with my co-workers." Would some fine tuning in human relations/communications improve your work life?

Human relations can absorb much of your energy as you seek to accommodate the various personalities from many backgrounds whom you meet at work. Sometimes a change in yourself can make a vast difference. You can learn to communicate more effectively, assert yourself in a tactful way, grow in self-confidence, and become more considerate and understanding of the problems of others. Usually you will find it necessary to strike a balance: not make a federal case out of every annoyance, yet be able to make changes in a situation that clashes sharply with your sensibilities. Review your personal responsibility skills from Chapter 2.

If your job is beginning to call for new duties, such as public presentations or writing, some of your basic skills may need improving. Put energy into your job and learn as much as you can in order to grow and develop. Your self-confidence will improve along with your skills.

Some people create a job within a job by assessing the tasks they like or dislike. Sometimes it's possible to trade tasks with others, ask for a reorganization, even hire someone to work along with you if your workload warrants it. Tackling a new project, changing departments, doing the same function in a new locale—each of these can be a creative way to get a fresh start.

Amazingly, some people are so successful they are promoted beyond the level of their own self-confidence, which has to catch up with their new position. Sometimes a step down—a career direction we rarely consider—can be a welcome change and may come closer to actualizing your values if the job pressures become really unbearable. One executive, laid off and then rehired into a lower position, says, "The money doesn't add up, but for the first time in my life I don't give a damn. I haven't felt this good in years!"[18] If you are dissatisfied with yourself, consider enrolling in some personal-growth classes—or at least do some reading in the area of personal growth. If a problem is weighing on you, discuss it with a trusted friend or a counselor. Many problems have obvious solutions that we may miss when searching alone.

There may be problems in the workplace, such as discrimination, sexual harassment, and poor management, that you have not caused. You may blame yourself or believe that you can solve them alone. You may press charges where there are violations of the law, but often it's wise to get some advice first from relevant government agencies or groups such as the National Labor Relations Board or, if you are a woman, the Commission on the Status of Women. Try to find a trusted guide who can help you if you decide to go that route. Even if one workplace doesn't work for you, the career itself may still be a good choice. Try to separate the job from the place and people. You may simply decide to move on to a different workplace while keeping the same career.

Deciding Not to Decide

If you already feel comfortable about your direction, you may decide to skip this section; others may not feel ready to make a commitment to a career/life decision. When you keep the status quo, you are deciding not to decide—which can be a good decision. Sometimes important decisions need time to percolate for insights to come. You might stay in the same job, take more classes, or continue to be at home with your children. But if you feel that your life needs change, try to set a time limit for your next move—say, six months to a year. If your present situation is uncomfortable for you, take some sort of action to work toward improvement—even if it is just reading helpful books or writing out a plan.

Decision Making: A Four-Phase Process

Those who find decision making difficult or who have not zeroed in on a career/life decision may find this four-phase process helpful: gather information, weigh and brainstorm alternatives and outcomes, check values, and design strategies.

Gather Information

Every decision calls for accurate information. In working through this volume you have been gathering all the information you need to make a career decision. You have learned how to pull information from a variety of sources and resources. You have already made many decisions about who you are and what you like. This is a process of using all the small decisions you have been making throughout this book to focus on a career. You may want to stop here and review this material.

Weigh and Brainstorm Alternatives and Outcomes

Examine Possibilities There are probably more possibilities out there for you than you can imagine; that is, there are many things that you *could* do; for example, you would like to change careers and you could become either a nurse or an engineer. Whichever alternative you act on will have several outcomes. Some outcomes may seem desirable, others undesirable. Before you make an important decision, try to imagine what the result will be, in both the immediate future and some years down the line. Without a workable crystal ball, it's hard to predict exactly how a decision is going to turn out. You make the best one you can and then see what adventures it leads to!

People are often able to picture only one type of outcome. Some, burdened by fears, see only disasters—major and minor. Other overly optimistic folks see nothing but grandiose positive effects. Most major decisions, however, produce a mixture of outcomes. You can take a job with a good salary, for example, but find that you will need training or have to work overtime. Even a dark outcome can have a light side. The extra training you get may feel like a waste of time, but later it turns out to be just the background you need for another situation. Working overtime may result in your making new friends. Hardly any decision has perfect results.

Even the most carefully reasoned, good decisions can bring disappointing results. Everyone at times makes decisions that don't bring the hoped-for outcome. In such cases, try to avoid blaming yourself; instead, give yourself credit for having taken the risk. Many alternatives seem risky only because they involve the risk of others' disapproval: What will people think? In fact, you may find yourself preserving the status quo solely out of fear of others' opinions, giving them power over your life. There is no way to change and grow without some risk. It is also important to avoid repeating the same mistakes.

Every change, however, even if it's only rearranging the garage, has an impact on others. Caring for those around you involves bringing them along with your decision making—that is, communicating your own needs honestly while listening to theirs, keeping them informed as you make changes. Hardly any change is perfect. There will be advantages and disadvantages to most moves. The idea is to *maximize the advantages.*

> It would be easier to play my part in life
> if I had a copy of the script.
> —*Ashleigh Brilliant*[19]

Brainstorm Alternatives   When you brainstorm, you write down every possibility without censoring it. Don't worry about whether an idea will work or what others will think. The important part is getting down as many alternatives as possible and then sorting them out. If you omit any, you may miss one that, on second look, might turn out to be possible and desirable for you.

You may have decided on a career for which there seem to be few opportunities. To find related alternatives, list all the functions of a person in that career. Then check the functions you think you'd enjoy most. If "history teacher" is on your list, do you like history, or appearing before an audience, or both? What can you do with history besides teach?

You could develop a unique lecture series on a topic of current interest—such as the architectural history of Victorian homes in Dubuque—to present to community groups. You could tutor, learn to be a docent (a person who conducts groups through such places as museums), work as a tour guide or as historian for a state park department, or get involved in history-in-the making in politics.

If you can get along without teaching, you could develop a tour series on tape or by map—for example, a walking tour of Atlanta or other historical places; you could write news articles about historical subjects, such as the Indians of the Upper Michigan Peninsula; you might work in a library, publishing company, heritage or historical center, or a bookstore where you might specialize in historical books.

Perhaps, after thinking it over again, you will decide that teaching is more important to you than history. Consider teaching other subjects (check school districts for local trends); volunteer in schools, recreation centers, and senior citizen centers; work as a teacher aide; teach small classes at home in areas such as woodworking, cooking, vegetable gardening, or auto repair; try teaching or giving lectures on these or other subjects to community groups such as the Parent–Teacher Association or Girl Scout and Boy Scout troops. Consider teaching recreation skills such as dancing, yoga, riding, swimming, tennis, music, bridge, exercise, skiing, golf, massage, boating. Some fitness "trainers" now visit people in their homes to show them how to use and plan a program for their exercise equipment and to monitor their progress.

With a little work, some of those activities can be parlayed into a lucrative business; others cannot. A job must fulfill the needs and wants of other people to such an extent that they will part with something, usually money, in exchange for goods or services produced in that job. For people who would like to teach and earn a more secure living, an often-overlooked area is industry. Larger industries have training programs and orientations for new employees and inservice training for continuing employees. Someone must be the teacher in these industrial settings.

Working in marketing and sales, public relations, or human resources, including such areas as job development or affirmative action, can involve you in many situations similar to teaching: training, giving site tours, helping people find employment, and working with other people problems that arise. Again, know what functions you would like to perform, and many more options may become visible.

Go back to the Key Qualities Indicator exercise in Chapter 2 and the Job Group Chart in Chapter 3 and look at the factors that are important to you. Consider related jobs again and *brainstorm* with friends, relatives, neighbors, acquaintances, strangers, or anyone who will give you five minutes of time and a dip into his or her experience pool. For just about any career you choose there are alternative jobs that can offer you most of what you would enjoy.

If you still want more than anything to follow a career that is highly competitive, don't be afraid to face that competition. Here are some other ideas to give you a start:

- Don't overlook entry-level or support-service job skills, such as word processing and cashiering, to gain access to careers of interest to you. Often you can then work into jobs closer to your interest field, in places from art galleries to auto shops, by beginning at the bottom.

- Use your main career interest as a hobby while you work at something else to support yourself. Who knows where it will lead? Walter Chandoha pursued a business degree while maintaining his interest in photographing cats. He has been a professional animal photographer for many years now and is doing better than he ever dreamed.[20] Maybe his business background has been a help! He also writes occasional articles for organic gardening magazines, another use of his creative talent.

- Investigate training programs in various industries, government agencies, and temporary agencies like Manpower.

- Consider earning extra money, perhaps at home, in one of these areas: catering; cake decorating; woodworking; picture framing; custom design of clothing or toys; recycling or redoing clothing, furniture, or household appliances, or other tools or gadgets; auto repair; house painting; yard cleanup; pet care; growing vegetables on consignment; translating; making telephone wake-up calls or operating an answering service; providing income tax service; computer work, perhaps in a medical, technical, scientific, or legal specialty, doing bookkeeping, newsletter layout and editing, or other graphics such as designing stationery or business cards. Your telephone Yellow Pages will give you additional ideas. More people than ever are finding work at home to their liking.

- Consider direct selling for companies of good reputation, for whom you can virtually be your own boss. Ask advice from friends who have sold such items as cosmetics or cleaning products. Consider franchises. They exist in a wide variety of fields from construction to specialty foods.

- Consider temporary employment, a growing area that provides flexible time, a sense of independence, and in some cases many employee benefits. Taking jobs through one of your local agencies can provide a way to survey businesses, make contacts, and make money on your own schedule in a wide array of jobs. Advertise your skills and classes through friends, supermarket bulletin boards, local community groups. Donate samples and do demonstrations. Be aware that finding a job in an area of your favorite hobbies may not be as satisfying as you might think. Mark Twain fulfilled his dream of becoming a full-fledged riverboat pilot, but said, "Now, the romance and the beauty were all gone out of the river. All the value any feature of it had for me now was the amount of usefulness it could furnish toward compassing the safe piloting of a steamboat." Author Lyle Crist concludes, "He [Twain] had gained the mastery . . . and lost the beauty."[21] Keep your options open. The wider your "satisfaction band," the more likely you are to achieve satisfaction. When you have done everything you can but you end up with a job you don't care for, you still have some choices.

- Volunteer experience can be extremely valuable in skill development. Some groups even pay volunteers a small stipend and provide them a place to live. Pinpoint the skills you would like to develop and ask for experience doing these things—for example, public relations, fund-raising, supervising people, organizing materials or activities. Be specific. Ask to be paired with a pro who will teach you some tricks of the trade. Be aware, however, that volunteer organizations are usually just as accountable for time and money as any business and cannot always accommodate your needs.

  The Commission on Voluntary Service and Action, Inc., publishes *Invest Yourself, the Catalog of Global Volunteer Opportunities,* a list of over two hundred independent organizations seeking change in the conditions of hunger, homelessness, injustice, and environmental destruction. Their address is P.O. Box 117, New York, NY 10091 and phone number is (800) 356-9315. Community Service, INC publishes *Community Service Newsletter,* P.O. Box 243, Yellow Springs, OH 45387. Many of the resources listed in Chapter 6, Workplace Take-Charge Groups, are non-profit organizations that could provide a source of employment.

Weigh Alternatives   There are many ways to weigh alternatives, all of them basically similar. We will use an exercise called Decision Point to organize and clarify these alternatives.

For example, if you were trying to decide whether to take a job in New York or one in Chicago, you would put the New York job in the balance first and write in such projected negative or undesirable results as longer work hours and hectic commuting conditions. On the positive side, you might list high pay, exciting work, status, closeness to family, and cultural opportunities. You then check whether the result is likely or unlikely to occur. You may find, for example, that high pay is not very likely. On the other side, hectic commuting may also be unlikely if the company allows telecommuting and flex-time, or if affordable living space is reasonably close to the job site. When you indicate that a possible outcome is unlikely, you're wise not to let that factor influence your decision very much if at all. Going further, you might want to rank your likely positives and negatives to see which are the most important.

Next, of course, you would weigh Chicago in the balance, for who knows what possible positives might turn up that would make the Windy City irresistible—a fabulous job and luxurious, affordable housing close to old college friends? Then compare the results to see which looks better to you, New York or Chicago. Overall, the positive results of one alternative may quite outweigh all the negatives. And you may choose to ignore the negatives. It's up to you! What decisions have you made in the past? How have they turned out for you? Review one of these decisions as if you were just about to make it now.

Decision-making exercises can help to organize and clarify your possibilities, but they cannot make the decision for you. They require you to use your rational, logical self. After such a process, give your intuition time to voice your sense of appropriateness and certainty about the decision. At some deeper level, you will usually know that your choice will work for you. You will feel finished and at peace after the struggle. You will be ready to let go the alternatives, perhaps with a twinge of regret, for there are good sides to everything. You will be ready to move on and take the steps you need to reach your goals.

Check Values

As you make choices, you express your value system—because values are revealed in what you do, not in what you say. Every step of this career search process has been related to your values. As a final check, consider your decision in terms of these values. If you want to live very simply, why seek a high-powered, energy-consuming job, the only reward for which is money? On the other hand, if money seems important to you, look at the bottom line. If you want both a family and a career, plan for it. You might wish to review Rating Values from Chapter 1 and any other values that might possibly be affected so that your choice reflects these priorities.

Design Strategies

This book outlines a great many steps you can use in making a good career decision. To carry out your next career/life decision, develop a good set of strategies—that is, a step-by-step procedure to make it a reality. Think of each step as a goal. Your goals need to be clearly stated. It won't do to say vaguely that you will "do better in school" or "start job hunting." Rather, set a specific goal: "I will read and outline history notes for two hours each evening and review them for half an hour every morning until the midterm," or "I will call five people tomorrow to ask for an information interview." Set time limits for reaching one successive step after the other. The time limit helps to discourage procrastination. And when you successfully accomplish your goals, you will find that your zest for continuing will increase.

> Goals are dreams that are measurable.
> —*Anonymous*

"I've done it again."

It is very important to be persistent, but it is also important to assess your strategies and to give up those that honestly don't seem to be working for you instead of repeating them. If time is a problem for you, learn to manage it. Some people pack their lives with so many activities that they experience failure, frustration, or frenzy instead of accomplishment. Others take on too little and end up feeling bored and uninvolved. Here are some techniques for managing time:

- List all the tasks on your agenda and rank them in order of importance.

- Keep a "very important" list, a "so-so" list, and a "nice if I can get around to it" list of tasks that need doing.

- For one week, keep track of all your activities on the weekly schedule at the end of the chapter to discover where you are spending your time.

For further help with time management, read Alan Lakein's *How to Get Control of Your Time and Your Life.*[22]

Some people want to rush ahead to that satisfying job. They may leave school without finishing a degree, leave a job too soon where they were getting valuable experience, or miss the job they really want by grabbing anything that comes along. As difficult as it seems at the time, waiting and finishing one phase of life before starting another is sometimes the best decision.

At age eighty, Giuseppe Verdi explained why he decided to write one more (and very difficult) opera. He said, "All my life as a musician I have striven for perfection. It has always eluded me. I surely had an obligation to make one more try!"[23]

Job Hunting . . . Again? Again!

Many people are rushed into a career decision these days without being the least bit prepared. The reason? They find themselves laid off. Whole towns are shocked to realize that they have depended for almost all of the employment in a community on one company that now decides to leave. Even a whole country can face hard times when it depends on one industry. The collapse of the Philippines' sugar industry due to falling prices worldwide in the 1980s put the whole country into a severe economic decline. A war, a political decision to fund or not to fund certain projects and programs, any number of happenings can lead to downsizing or restructuring as well as expansion in your workplace.

Challenges and options that seem so far away move right into Main Street. The farming community of Watsonville, California—during a year that included earthquake, drought, unexpected freezing weather, and the lure of cheaper labor—saw farms fail, food processing plants move to Mexico, and businesses close, affecting the whole community. As we approach the twenty-first century we will see more and more workers being dislocated, relocated, and retrained as the global economy shakes out into new forms. Many people will be repeating the career search process.

You may have earned a degree and learned new skills in preparation for your career. You may have found that dream job that embodies your most important values and interests and in which you are encouraged to develop your skills. You may have put a great deal of energy into your job and plan to stay with it. You may have a growing family and a hefty mortgage. But even if you planned to stay at the same place in the same job for a long time, some day, burnout or boredom may prompt you to wonder, "Is this all there is?"

Even with a job that seems secure and satisfying, it is always wise to have your résumé ready and a game plan in mind in case you (or your employer) decide to call it quits. Job hunting in a tight job market with your benefits running out, the mortgage payment due, and applications that generate only rejections can undermine the strongest ego. Here is what some people do all the time: they keep up the contacts they have made by networking; they continue the self- and career-assessment process; and they keep learning new skills. Preparing for change is an important part of career development.

Although you may not need to move on, you may find that having a network of people in your field can prove helpful in your job. Many people call on colleagues in other companies for advice on various sorts of problems both in their careers and in their work.

It helps to be moneywise and to have a plan for lean times. Consider what you really *need* to survive and look for sources to fund your needs. Some people try to have money saved that can pay their expenses for a few months. They keep bills paid and pay cash instead of using credit cards. In a time of under- or unemployment, some reduce expenses, move to a less expensive location, use cheaper transportation, have a garage sale and sell off excess baggage, plant a garden of basics to save on food bills, join or start a small co-op to buy food wholesale, find people who could share resources. Your expanded activity lists from Chapters 1 and 2 may indicate what you might do to earn needed cash. Psychological as well as financial preparation will greatly enhance your confidence when the time comes for a move.

Bartering creatively can bring surprising results. One young man with no money or place to stay bartered lawn care at a veterinary clinic to get shots for his dog, while a neighborhood soup kitchen and some friends saw him through his rough times. Connie Stapleton of Middletown, Maryland, asked a service station manager if he had any work she could do in exchange for repairs on her car. When that brought a negative response, she asked what he liked least about his job. He said, "Collecting bills!" She began making collections in exchange for free car care.[24] Artists barter their work for professional services.

If you have been fired or laid off, evaluate the causes so that you can avoid them in the future. Despite the very real trauma involved in being jobless, you can use the experience to advantage by preparing for your next job. Ask for help with job hunting from friends, relatives, and neighbors without hiding your job loss. As everyone knows, it can happen to anyone.

If you are unemployed and haven't had a chance to prepare for it, now is the time to work out a plan of action to avoid sitting at home reading the want ads and feeling terrible. Being a couch potato will rarely bring success! First, review both the data collected in this book and the job market information in the Job Group Chart (in Chapter 3) and related resources. Second, follow good job-hunting techniques: update your résumé, renew your contacts, and collect letters of recommendation. Third, join or start a support group. Fourth, work out a daily schedule of things to do that include not only job hunting but other important business-of-living activities like exercising and visiting friends. In the meantime, consider temporary work, part-time work, "just any job," negotiating to share a job, going back to school. Try to keep your life in balance on not only the physical but also the emotional, intellectual, and altruistic levels. Enjoy the "unemployment benefits" such as sleeping late some mornings, catching up on errands, or enjoying an occasional walk. The more you can relax with your new leisure, the better you'll be able to plan your next step.

Basic physical needs may seem so imperative at such times that concerns about emotional, intellectual, and altruistic needs and wants can fly out the window as you begin to believe that any job will do! But perhaps this is the time to gather some emotional support, to use every bit of your intelligence and knowledge to carve out more than a survival path. The insights you gather may be just what you need to boost your confidence and morale and open up unsuspected possibilities. Survey the skills you developed on your last job. Did that job put you in touch with new interests? What did you dislike about that job?

A layoff can be a liberating experience—if you don't get too hungry— and a good time to reevaluate a career and make changes. Unemployed people have started businesses, often on a shoestring, found rewarding partnerships, and created satisfying new careers. Many people have moved from the corporate complex to small-business ownership. They have gone from designing microchips to designing sandwiches in their own delicatessens, from making hardware to making beds in their guest cottages by the sea. Numbers of individuals who were forced to make a change as a result of unemployment have been delighted with the results.

Even if a risky venture isn't for you right now, get together with others to share such resources as physical necessities, ideas, job leads, and support. Call your local school career center for help. If you are unemployed, keep busy with courage.

In any case, you will find a more balanced and satisfying life by developing your potential as far as possible in all areas. There are those who have even found that volunteering to help people more needy than themselves gave them new insights into all the resources they *do* have. A number of them have even met individuals who offered them a job.

And on a consoling note, despite the negative press regarding enormous layoffs, the *New Yorker* says that "the job-creating capacity of the United States economy is the envy of the developed world," and that in the main, people are still finding equivalent jobs after layoffs.[25]

The Great Gap

Some people complete the entire career search process without making the big decision. If you are still unable to choose a career, you may need more time to gain confidence and clarify your values. You may need to give your creativity time to work. There is a point—we could call it the Great Gap—where you must cross over from process to action. No matter how much support you've had, how many inventories you do, and how many people you talk to, the decision is yours alone to make alone.

Perhaps you need to take a "dynamic rest" along the road to success. Read some books about the problem that's holding you back. Discuss it with a trusted friend or counselor. Paradoxically, sometimes we need to accept the status quo before we can change it.

And reassessment time will probably come around again and again because people change careers and jobs often in their lives. Some people take some time each year to evaluate their situation. They review the balance in their lives among its physical, emotional, intellectual, and altruistic/spiritual components. Which of these need levels motivates *you* most? The more you grow, the more your lower needs will be fulfilled, and the more you will become a self-actualizing person who acts out of concern not only for yourself but for other people and the planet. Everything you do will express what is finest in human nature. All your motivation will flow from the altruistic.

"In *Elegant Choices, Healing Choices,* psychologist Marsha Sinetar, Ph.D., says that elegant choices are those options in life 'tending toward truth, beauty, honor, courage.' They are choices that are life supporting, whereas choices that take one away from truth, morality, and self-respect are life-defeating."[26]

> Until one is committed, there is hesitancy, the chance to draw
> back, always ineffectiveness. Concerning all acts of initiative

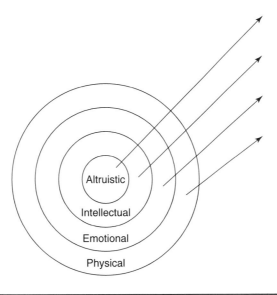

Sources of Motivation Courtesy of Mission College/IDS

(and creation), there is one elemental truth, the ignorance of which kills countless ideas and splendid plans: that the moment one definitely commits oneself, then Providence moves too. All sorts of things occur to help one that would never otherwise have occurred. A whole stream of events issues from the decision, raising in one's favor all manner of unforeseen incidents and meetings and material assistance which no man could have dreamed would have come his way. Whatever you can do or dream you can, begin it. Boldness has genius, power, and magic in it. Begin it now.

—*Goethe*[27]

Change Is Here to Stay

H. B. Gelatt says,

For those of you who are worried that I might change my mind again, let me assure you, I will. Fortunately, this is a trait whose time has come. Changing one's mind will be an essential decision-making skill in the future. Keeping the mind open will be another. Learning to be good at being uncertain is becoming a modern-day asset in decision-making. The hard part to learn is to be positive about the uncertainty.[28]

Thus does decision-making expert Gelatt laud a trait he calls "positive uncertainty." Some people might like to avoid it, but in this age, change is inevitable. Some understanding of your past, confidence in your future, flexibility, and the willingness to accept "ambiguity, inconsistency, and uncertainty" will make the process of decision making more manageable.

What causes people to make life changes, sometimes very far-reaching and dramatic ones? Often, consciously or unconsciously, people may be searching for something new, working out the details without expressing the process to anyone. And when they reach a decision, it may seem sudden to the observer.

Sometimes people have such a powerful experience that they begin to see their lives in a totally different way. They or someone close to them may have a serious accident or become quite ill; someone they care about may die; their marriage may break apart; they may travel to and live in a very different culture. Often experiencing a war or the extreme poverty of a developing country can cause people to question their lives. A retired military man and vice-president of a bank made such a change after working in Guatemala and seeing the activities of an older couple involved in helping the rural poor in that country. He felt so alive and energized by these experiences that he went back to Yale to get a master's degree in forestry that he could use to help the environment in developing countries.

People are more than squares on a page or checks in a box. They are pain and purpose, hopes and dreams, woundedness and wholeness. They are a compendium of cultural constraints and conditioning with the ever-present possibility of breaking loose into wondrous patterns with surprises at every turn.

> I have never begun any important venture
> for which I felt adequately prepared.[29]
> —*Anonymous*

Success: New Directions

We began this book by looking at success, and since then, you have been learning good things about yourself: your interests, values, and skills. You've learned how to find or make a place for yourself in the job market. You've learned to assess jobs and workplaces and how to network effectively. You've learned to change attitudes and feelings and "own" all the good things about yourself by positive affirmations. When you believe in yourself as a capable person, you are on your way to further growth, to self-actualization, to fulfillment. When you are true to yourself and all that is best in you, you will be a success!

You are unique. The person you are and could become, the success and happiness that you can achieve, can be done only when you listen to your own voice. Mythologist Joseph Campbell says, "If you follow your bliss, you put yourself on a kind of track that has been there all the while, waiting for you."[30] Some people just won't give up until they have found their bliss in satisfying work and a lifestyle that is uniquely their own. Experiencing and living your dreams can be both invigorating and frightening.

"A mark of the adult is the willingness to recognize material limitations, to recognize that no single life can embrace the multitude of experiences available to humankind: climb all the mountains, chart all the seas, master all the arts," wrote Ted Berkman. "Freed from the tyranny of 'want it all,' I find that I have all I need: books and friends, the beach at sunrise, the towering silhouette of the Santa Ynez mountains. . . . There is time to savor and to serve."[31]

Success has been popularly defined as achieving your goals. But in this day and age of the global village, with a new millennium underway, success is much more than that, much more than media and corporate images. Success must be seen in a larger context with a deeper vision. Success must ultimately include a balanced life, a life in which we have taken care of ourselves and those dependent on us, but in the context of global concerns. Success, then, means achieving realistic goals, using effective strategies based on our interests, skills, and true values, accounting for the basic needs and the legitimate, enriching wants of ourselves and others. The most far-reaching successes are those that transform us into better people and creators of a better world. Some people create so much joy within themselves—despite facts, trends, and predictions and often against significant odds—that they are happy anywhere. Perhaps that joy, after all, is the key to success. The steps you take will create your life. May your career choice make you a "true person." May your dreams be actualized.

> The richest person in the world is not the one who has the most
> friends, nor the one who knows the most, but the one who is wise
> enough to distinguish between the essentials of life
> and the nonessentials and go forth like an adventurer,
> with the wind and the rain and the sun in his face.
> —*R. L. Duffus*
> The Tower of Jewels:
> Memories of San Francisco

Self-Assessment Exercises

1. Decision-Making Style

How do you make decisions? Check (✓) the appropriate columns. Then mark plus (+) before items you'd like to improve.

	Usually	*Sometimes*	*Rarely*
■ I make decisions after considering alternatives.	_____	_____	_____
■ I make decisions easily, on time, without undue agonizing.	_____	_____	_____
■ I base decisions on reasoned judgment of the information available.	_____	_____	_____
■ I base my decisions on feelings and intuition.	_____	_____	_____
■ I tend to think my decisions will turn out to be disasters.	_____	_____	_____
■ I tend to imagine my decisions will have spectacular positive results.	_____	_____	_____
■ I consult with others, but my decisions are my own.	_____	_____	_____
■ I compromise when the needs of others are involved.	_____	_____	_____
■ I make some decisions to fulfill my own desires.	_____	_____	_____
■ I "test out" major decisions ahead of time if possible.	_____	_____	_____
■ I take responsibility for the results of my decisions.	_____	_____	_____
■ If a decision doesn't work, I try another plan, without great regret.	_____	_____	_____

2. Decision Point: Selecting Alternatives

If you are on the verge of a decision but are having trouble choosing the alternative that would work best for you, list those alternatives here (for example, if you are trying to decide which geographical location would suit you, list all the possibilities; if you are deciding on a career, list those possibilities):

Alternative a. _____

Alternative b. _____

Alternative c. _____

Alternative d. _____

3. Decision Point: Weighing Alternatives

a. Write one of the alternatives you are considering: _____
b. In the blanks below list as many negative and positive results as you can that might occur if you followed that alternative. Check whether they are likely or unlikely.
c. If you have many more likely negative results than positive results, you may wish to choose another alternative to pursue.
d. Rank the positive and then negative results in order of their importance to you.

NEGATIVES (Undesirable outcomes)	Likely	Unlikely	POSITIVES (Desirable outcomes)	Likely	Unlikely
_____	_____	_____	_____	_____	_____
_____	_____	_____	_____	_____	_____
_____	_____	_____	_____	_____	_____
_____	_____	_____	_____	_____	_____
_____	_____	_____	_____	_____	_____
_____	_____	_____	_____	_____	_____

e. Compare results:

- Do the positives outweigh the negatives?   Yes _____   No _____

- Overall, do the positives seem more likely and desirable than the negatives? Yes _____   No _____

f. Repeat this procedure for each of your alternatives. Then write a paragraph comparing your results for each alternative. Discuss how these results will affect your final decision.

g. Ten years down the path, which decision would you like to have made? What results might occur only later? Add your insights to the paragraph in f.

h. Spend time choosing your decision; spend some of it alone. Cross the Great Gap!

4. Goals and Strategies

Write down the decision you've chosen to carry out. This becomes your goal. State four or more steps or strategies you will take to accomplish this goal. How soon would you like to accomplish this change and its related strategies?

Decision or goal _____

Is this goal realistic? _____   Does it agree with your values? _____

Steps I will take   *Date to be accomplished*

a._____   _____

b._____   _____

c._____   _____

d._____   _____

e._____   _____

5. Time Management

How will you manage your time in order to reach your goals?

a. State the number of college credits you
   plan to carry in your next term.   _____

b. Allow at least two hours of study for each
   credit or unit (units times 2).   _____

c. State the number of hours you will work
   per week (include family care).   _____

d. Total the number of hours each week you
   have committed so far.   d. ⎡_____⎤

e. Estimate the number of hours per week you devote to

   sleeping   _____

   eating   _____

   commuting   _____

   household chores   _____

   business (bank, dentist, shopping, etc.)   _____

time with family and friends   _____

exercise   _____

recreation/leisure   _____

miscellaneous/unexpected   _____

Add the total   e. ☐

f. Add the totals in boxes d and e to see how many hours per week you spend in all activities—the big total!   TOTAL (d + e). ☐

g. Remember, there are only 168 hours in a week. Do you have too much scheduled? _____ Too little? _____ Just enough? _____

6. Your Weekly Schedule

Fill in a reasonable schedule for yourself. Try to follow it for one week, then revise it.

WEEKLY SCHEDULE

Time	Monday	Tuesday	Wednesday	Thursday	Friday	Saturday	Sunday
6:00							
7:00							
8:00							
9:00							
10:00							
11:00							
12:00							
1:00							
2:00							
3:00							
4:00							
5:00							
6:00							
7:00							
8:00							

Time	Monday	Tuesday	Wednesday	Thursday	Friday	Saturday	Sunday
9:00							
10:00							
11:00							
12:00							
1:00							
2:00							
3:00							
4:00							
5:00							

7. Back to School

If going to college is on your list of possibilities, check (✓) the answers that explain why. If college isn't for you, check any other training alternatives that appeal to you.

Why college?

_____ Not sure, but wish to explore and find out about it

_____ Personal enrichment

_____ Hope to improve basic or other specific skills

_____ Would like to obtain a high school General Equivalency Development (GED) diploma.

_____ Wish to earn a career program certificate

_____ Plan to earn a two-year degree at a community college

_____ Want to earn a BA or BS degree from a four-year college or university

_____ Want to do graduate work

_____ My mother/father/boss/spouse made me come to college!

Other training alternatives?

_____ Apprenticeship programs with unions in various crafts

_____ Adult education in local school district

_____ Proprietary schools (private schools that teach a special job skill)

_____ On-the-job training programs or management training programs

_____ Course work by TV, job experience, weekend college, and other
options for the busy person

8. School Subjects

a. Check (✓) the columns that describe your feelings about school subjects.

	Like	Dislike	Did well	Did not do well	Avoided
Reading	_____	_____	_____	_____	_____
Writing	_____	_____	_____	_____	_____
Speech/drama	_____	_____	_____	_____	_____
Math	_____	_____	_____	_____	_____
Science	_____	_____	_____	_____	_____
Social studies	_____	_____	_____	_____	_____
Arts/crafts	_____	_____	_____	_____	_____
Music	_____	_____	_____	_____	_____
Industrial/technical	_____	_____	_____	_____	_____
Business	_____	_____	_____	_____	_____
Health	_____	_____	_____	_____	_____
Agriculture	_____	_____	_____	_____	_____
Physical education	_____	_____	_____	_____	_____
_____	_____	_____	_____	_____	_____
_____	_____	_____	_____	_____	_____
_____	_____	_____	_____	_____	_____

b. Circle the subjects you'd like to study further.

c. Now look at your "worst" subjects. Are there any you'd like to try again? Not try again?

Try again_____   Not try again_____

9. Some College Majors Arranged by Personality Type and Job Group

Check (✓) majors of interest to you.

R REALISTIC

Mechanical
___ Aero Maintenance/ Operations
___ Air Conditioning/ Refrigeration Technology
___ Air Traffic Control
___ Anaplastology
___ Automotive Technology
___ Biomedical Technology
___ Construction Technology
___ Electronics Technology
___ Engineering/Technology
___ Food Service Technology
___ Hazardous Materials
___ Industrial Administration
___ Laser/Microwave/Digital Technology
___ Machine/Tool Technology
___ Quality Control
___ Radiologic Technology
___ Robotics/Computer-Assisted Manufacturing (CAM)
___ Semiconductor Management
___ Solar Technology
___ Telecommunications
___ Transportation
___ Watch Repair
___ Welding Technology

Industrial: No majors

Nature
___ Agriculture
___ Animal Health Technology
___ Nursery Management
___ Park Management Technology
___ Wildlife Management Technology

Protective
___ Administration of Justice/Private Security
___ Fire Science
___ Safety Engineering

R *(continued)*

Physical Performing
___ Physical Education/ Kinesiology

I INVESTIGATIVE

Scientific
___ Biological science
___ Agriculture
___ Animal/Avian
___ Bacteriology
___ Biology
___ Botany
___ Conservation
___ Enology
___ Entomology/Pest Science
___ Environmental Science
___ Food Science
___ Forest Science
___ Genetics
___ Kinesiology
___ Marine Biology
___ Microbiology
___ Nutrition
___ Soil/Water/Wood Science
___ Toxicology
___ Zoology
___ Cybernetics
___ Engineering
___ Aeronautical/ Aerospace
___ Agricultural
___ Bioengineering
___ Civil
___ Computer Science
___ Electrical/Electronic
___ Environmental/Earth Resources
___ Material Science
___ Naval Architecture
___ Nuclear
___ Robotics
___ Science
___ Systems

I *(continued)*
___ Transportation
___ Linguistics
___ Mathematics/Statistics/ Applied
___ Medical
___ Dentistry
___ Medical Technology
___ Medicine/Surgery
___ Optometry
___ Pharmacy/Pharmacy Technology
___ Veterinary Medicine
___ Physical Sciences
___ Chemistry
___ Geology/Earth Science
___ Meteorology/ Atmosphere
___ Oceanography
___ Physics/Astronomy
___ Social Sciences
___ Anthropology
___ Consumer Economics/ Science
___ Ethnic Studies
___ Geography
___ History
___ Peace and Conflict Studies
___ Psychology
___ Sociology
___ Urban/Rural Studies
___ Women's Studies

A ARTISTIC

Applied Arts
___ Architecture
___ Commercial Art
___ Computer-Assisted Design (CAD)
___ Fashion Design
___ Film/Photography
___ Graphics
___ Interior Design
___ Industrial Design
___ Journalism

A *(continued)*
___ Landscape Design/ Ornamental Horticulture
___ Media Specialty
___ Printing/Lithography/ Desk-Top Publishing
___ Radio/TV
___ Technical Drafting/ Modelbuilding/Illustrating
___ Technical Illustrating/ Writing

Fine Arts
___ Art/Art History
___ Dance/Drama
___ English
___ Foreign Language
___ Humanities
___ Literature
___ Music
___ Philosophy
___ Speech

S SOCIAL

Human Services
___ Community Health Worker
___ Counseling
___ Dental Assistant/Hygiene
___ Dietician
___ Health Science
___ Nursing RN, LVN, Assistant
___ Ophthalmic Dispensing
___ Pediatric Assistant
___ Physical/Occupational Therapy/Assistant
___ Primary Care Associate
___ Psychiatric Technology
___ Psychology–Clinical
___ Public Health
___ Radiology/EKG/ Phlebotomy
___ Respiratory Therapy
___ Social Service
___ Speech Pathology and Audiology

Accommodating
___ Cosmetology

S *(continued)*	S/E *(continued)*	E *(continued)*	C *(continued)*
___ Food Service	___ Labor Studies	___ International Trade	___ Insurance
___ Gerontology	___ Law	___ Law	___ Paralegal
___ Leisure/Travel	___ Library Science	___ Marketing/Sales	___ Secretarial
S/E SOCIAL/ENTERPRISING	___ Management/Supervision	___ Political Science	___ Administrative
Leading/Influencing	___ Manpower Administration	___ Purchasing	___ Clerical
___ Advertising	___ Office Administration	___ Real Estate	___ Legal
___ Business Administration	___ Public Relations	___ Speech/Communications	___ Medical
___ Convalescent Hospital	___ Recreation	**C CONVENTIONAL**	Assistant/Records
Administration	___ Volunteer Administration	*Business Detail*	___ Unit Clerk
___ Education	**E ENTERPRISING**	___ Accounting	___ Word Processing
___ Financial Services	*Persuading/Selling*	___ Banking/Finance	
___ Health Care Management	___ Fashion/Retail	___ Court Reporting	
___ Insurance	Merchandising	___ Data Processing	

10. *Blocks and Barriers: Finding the Keystone*

To find out what is holding you back, ask yourself whether you are dealing with barriers within yourself. Place a check (✓) before any that apply:

Blocks within you

- Locked into your stereotypes
- Too complacent to change the status quo
- Lacking confidence/awash in fear
- Weak skills
- Negative attitudes
- Caught in health or emotional problems
- Bogged down in transitions like divorce, death of spouse, immigration adjustment
- Longing for improved personal relationships
- Afraid to make a commitment
- In the habit of procrastinating
- Over-researching—losing yourself in the library
- Experiencing conflicts about values
- Too many "shoulds"

Barriers outside you

- A really poor job market/economy
- Societal expectations that you accept
- Imperative roles such as parenting
- Physical realities such as illness

What steps can you take to overcome these blocks and barriers?

_____

_____

_____

11. Positive Affirmations

Everyone is a mixture of faults, foibles, and failings along with skills, successes, and strengths. Check (✓) the statements that match your thought patterns. Select one *positive* statement and say it many times a day over a week's time. Know that attitudes and feelings can be changed.

Negatives	Positives
_____ I don't think I'll ever figure out what I want to do.	_____ I can take steps to figure out what to do.
_____ I'm not interested in anything.	_____ I'm interested in many things.
_____ Nothing is much fun.	_____ I enjoy many of my activities.
_____ I'm dumb.	_____ I can learn.
_____ If my first choice doesn't work out, I'm stuck.	_____ I can plan alternatives.
_____ I'm tired of trying because nothing works.	_____ I have the energy to make things happen.
_____ I'm afraid.	_____ I can be courageous.
_____ I never have fun.	_____ I can create a good time.

_____ I can make a good decision!

Group Discussion Questions

1. Describe your decision-making style. What factors might cause you to "decide not to decide"?

2. Share your educational plans. Define lifelong learning and the form it can take in your own life.

3. What new approaches can you take to improve your work/educational/life situation?

4. How do values relate to decisions?

5. What values might prompt a manager to step down to a lower job status?

6. Illustrate how a decision you've made recently reflects your most important values. What values might take the place of work in your life?

7. How can a person prepare for unemployment?

8. Share an important decision you would like to make.

9. What is the most important decision you have ever made in your life?

10. Discuss with a group or write your feelings about important decisions you have made and those you would like to make.

9/

Work Affects the Soul

The Final Analysis

FOCUS

- Review the career decision-making process.

- Gather personal information into one place.

- Review and update your goals.

*T*he Final Analysis is a place to summarize the information you have gathered from the self-assessment exercises in this book. It will give you an overview of the important areas of your life that are affected by work. It will help you assess your career search process and determine how effectively this process has helped you choose the career that will lead to growth and self-fulfillment on all levels. It may help you make some final decisions, and it provides a handy future reference.

To complete the Final Analysis, review the self-assessment exercises and summarize the data here. Feel free to add additional information about yourself and the career/life decisions you are considering.

Chapter 1   Needs, Wants, and Values: Spotlighting YOU

1. Review the Life Problems Checklist (p. 30) and Feelings Checkpoints (pp. 30–31). Then list those areas you would like to expand and those you would like to change or eliminate.

I want to develop   *I want to change*

_____   _____

_____   _____

_____   _____

_____   _____

Reprinted with permission from Mal Hancock.

2. Review Needs and Wants a–c (pp. 28–29). Check the balance in your life. Do you have enough? What do you need or want on these four levels?

I have enough of   *I would like*

Physical level

_____   _____

Emotional level

_____   _____

Intellectual level

_____   _____

Altruistic level

_____   _____

Is your life in balance on these four levels?   Yes _____   No _____

If not, how can you improve the balance? _____

_____

_____

_____

3. Review Rating Values, a–g (pp. 31–33) and write six of your most important values here:

a._____   c. _____   e. _____

b. _____   d. _____   f._____

4. Review your autobiographical data. Summarize what you learned about yourself in exercises a–g in Drawing a Self-Portrait (pp. 36–38).

_____

_____

_____

5. Review Candid Camera—3-D (pp. 34–35). List the four activities you enjoy most.

a. _____   c. _____

b. _____   d. _____

6. Describe success for yourself _____

_____

_____

Chapters 2 and 3   Personality and Job Satisfiers

1. Review the Personality Mosaic in Chapter 2. Then list your types and the scores for each type in order from highest to lowest.

First _____   Fourth _____

Second _____   Fifth _____

Third _____   Sixth _____

2. Which level of involvement with Data, People, and Things do you enjoy? See page 66.

Data   High level _____   Modest level _____   Little or none _____

People   High level _____   Modest level _____   Little or none _____

Things   High level _____   Modest level _____   Little or none _____

3. Circle the numbers of the ten key qualities that represent important skill areas for you. On the line before each skill, write M if you prefer a modest level; H for a high level of ability. Then circle the numbers of the key work qualities you prefer. (See pp. 68–69)

Data/People/Things Qualities

_____ 1. Logical intelligence   _____ 6. Facility with multidimensional forms

_____ 2. Intuitive intelligence   _____ 7. Facility in businesslike contact with people

_____ 3. Verbal ability   _____ 8. Ability to influence people

_____ 4. Numerical ability   _____ 9. Finger/hand agility

_____ 5. Exactness with detail   _____ 10. Whole-body agility

Work Qualities

_____ 11. Repetition   _____ 12. Variety

_____ 13. Physical risk   _____ 14. Status

4. From the Personal Responsibility Skills Checklist (pp. 69–70), list your best personal skills and the ones you could improve.

Best skills   *Could improve*

_____   _____

_____   _____

_____   _____

_____   _____

_____   _____

_____   _____

5. List your work-specific skills.

_____

_____

List the work-specific skills you wish to acquire.

_____

_____

6. List three jobs groups by decimal code and title from the Job Group Chart in Chapter 3 in the order of importance to you.

a. Decimal code _____   Title _____

b. Decimal code _____   Title _____

c. Decimal code _____   Title _____

7. Tell how your top job group matches your personality, skills, interests, and work qualities. Use a separate sheet of paper if necessary.

_____

_____

_____

_____

_____

8. List the job title you would like most. _____

9. Do you want a career or "just a job"? Explain your answer.

_____

_____

10. How does your career choice match your values?

_____

_____

_____

Chapter 4   Work: Challenges, Options, and Opportunities

1. Tell which one of the major challenges is most important to you and why.

_____

_____

2. List three options you would like to be involved with to meet your most important challenge and tell what you would like to do.

_____

_____

_____

3. Does your career choice enable you to be involved with any of these options? How?

_____

_____

_____

4. What does the *Occupational Outlook Handbook* (or similar references) say about the employment outlook for the career of your choice?

_____

_____

_____

5. What is the salary range for the career of your choice? _____

Would this career support your lifestyle?   Yes _____   No _____

6. List three alternate careers you would consider. List one positive and one negative feature of each.

Career	Positive feature	Negative feature
a. _____	_____	_____
b. _____	_____	_____
c. _____	_____	_____

Chapters 5 and 6   Workplaces/Workstyles/Timestyles

1. Use findings from your research to describe the ideal workplace. Consider size and complexity, type of environment, emotional rewards, and work routine you would like.

_____

_____

_____

_____

_____

_____

2. Review the Career Ladder (p. 148). How far up the ladder do you want to go? Explain your answer.

_____

_____

_____

3. Review Researching Workplaces (pp. 207–208) and Workplace Checklist (pp. 210–213). Then list the four corporate values that are most important to you (see Workplace Values, p. 173).

a._____

b._____

c. _____

d._____

4. Review the roles you'll play as you enter the diverse workplace of the future. List three of the ones that are most important to you and tell how they will be affected in the workplace.

_____

_____

_____

Tell how you might like to improve one of your roles. _____

_____

Finish the statement, I'd like to be more accepting of people who are

_____

Circle those major role components of your life that are mot important: career, family, marriage, children, ethnicity/religion, leisure, education, friends.

5. Describe your ideal job.

_____

_____

_____

_____

6. Describe your ideal boss.

_____

_____

_____

7. Describe your ideal work day.

_____

_____

_____

8. Describe your ideal balance of work and leisure.

_____

_____

_____

9. If you were to decide to open your own business, what steps would you take first?

a. _____

b. _____

c. _____

10. Workplace first choice:

a. Where would you like to work?

_____

b. How does this workplace present challenges of interest to you?

_____

_____

c. What positive options does it have that would fit your values?

_____

_____

11. What does work mean to you? Describe your personal work ethic.

_____

_____

_____

_____

Chapter 7   The Job Hunt: Tools for Breaking and Entering

To prepare for the job hunt:

1. Name the title of a job you might apply for. _____

2. List five of your characteristics that relate to that job and tell how.

_____

_____

_____

_____

Chapter 8   Decisions, Decisions: What's Your Next Move?

1. What is your next move in the career search?

   _____

   _____

   _____

2. Educational planning sheet

   a. Do you now have the skills and training you need to obtain a job in the
      field of your choice?   Yes _____   No _____

      If you need more preparation, which of the following do you need?

      _____ Apprenticeship   _____ Workshops or seminars

      _____ On-the-job training   _____ Other _____

   b. If you need more education, which of these alternatives are you
      considering?

      _____ A few courses   _____ A BA or BS degree

      _____ A certificate   _____ Graduate school

      _____ An AA or AS degree   _____ Other _____

   c. List an appropriate major (or majors) for your career choice (see
      pp. 292–293).

      _____   _____

   d. What kind of college do you plan to attend?

      _____ Two year   _____ Out of state

      _____ Four year   _____ Public

      _____ Local   _____ Private

      _____ In state

   e. List colleges that offer the major you have chosen. (Use educational
      references in your library or on the Internet or ask for help at a college
      counseling center.)

      _____

      _____

      _____

f. Obtain catalogs from colleges of interest to you. To gather as much information as possible, visit the campuses and talk with people who are familiar with each school. For example, will you need any of these?

_____ Financial aid   _____ Housing

_____ Special entrance tests   _____ A specific grade point average

_____ Other _____

g. Begin course planning here:

Major requirements	*General or graduation requirements*	*Electives*
_____	_____	_____
_____	_____	_____
_____	_____	_____
_____	_____	_____

3. I plan to complete my degree (or training) by (date) _____

I plan to be employed in the job of my choice by (date) _____

4. Review the inventories and your autobiography. Check each item in the Final Analysis. Does it all hang together?   Yes _____   No _____

Hang Loose

MICHELE F. BAKARICH

I'm
just
going
to
hang
loose
,
that's
the
best
way
to
go

© 1978 Reprinted with permission.

Appendix

Sample Résumés and Letters

The sample résumés and letters in this Appendix are those of real job seekers ranging from college student to former homeless parent, from health care manager to houseperson returning to work. Each résumé is unique to one person as your résumé will be unique to you. But you can use these sample résumés in a number of ways. Notice the variety of forms and styles. Select the ones that seem to fit your situation best. Use them as models to create your own unique résumé.

The sample résumés can be used for role-playing also. As you read them, pay attention to the person behind the résumé as an interviewer would. Think of questions you might ask the person represented by each résumé, and use these questions in mock interviews.

The letters that accompany résumés are called "cover letters." In addition to "covering" your résumé, letters may be used to thank people who have interviewed you and to keep in touch with them until you are actually employed. A letter of resignation is also included here.

5096 W. Monroe Street
South Bend, Indiana 46637
May 22, 1999

Mr. William A. Cline
U.S. Department of Forestry
115 E. Birch Bark Lane
Sault Ste. Marie, Michigan 49783

Dear Mr. Cline:

This is to let you know that I am still interested in working with the Forest Service in the Michigan area. I expect to be in touch with you around November regarding the jobs of recreation assistant and resource assistant that you mentioned to me for next year.

By the way, I applied for (and got) the spotted owl project job at Gifford Pinchot National Forest last summer. Thanks for notifying me about it. (It was never listed with Civil Service.)

If you know of any promising late-opening summer jobs in your area this year, I would appreciate it if you would let me know.

Thanks again.

Yours truly,

Daniel P. Magee

(219) 555-1212

Figure A-1   Letter maintaining contact with a prospective employer

KATHLEEN M. NEVILLE
791 Peony Lane
Mountain View, CA 95040
(408) 555-1696

POSITION OBJECTIVE Supervisor/Inventory Control

QUALIFICATIONS IN BRIEF

AS in Restaurant Management
BA candidate in Business Management
Supervisory experience
Good human relations skills
Reliable, responsible, creative worker

EDUCATION

SAN JOSE STATE UNIVERSITY, San Jose, CA	Present
Major: Business Management	
MISSION COMMUNITY COLLEGE	1993
AA Degree in Restaurant Management	

WORK EXPERIENCE

LINDA'S DRIVE-IN, Mountain View, CA   August 1990 to Present
Supervisor/Cook
Inventory, order, prepare, and stock food supplies. Settle employee and customer problems and complaints. Orient/train new employees; evaluate employee performance. Do minor repairs/maintenance. As occasional acting manager, open and close shop, handle cash/cash register.

Baby-sitting and housekeeping throughout junior   Prior to 1990
high and high school.

ACTIVITIES

GIRL SCOUTS   1985–89
Supervised day camp; planned activities, taught games, arts and crafts, sports, camping skills, and first aid. Solved conflicts. Received art award.

MUSIC/DRAMA   1983–93
As Assistant Director supervised costumes, sets, props. Performed in Summer Theater Workshop. Foothill Youth Symphony, Jazz, Symphony, Marching/Pep Bands from elementary school through community college. Overseas tour 1986.

Figure A-2   Chronological résumé of a young person applying for a first full-time job. It is the résumé of the college student whose work skills provided the example of the "Candid Camera—3-D" exercise in Chapter 1. Her brief statement of qualifications emphasizes education and transferable and personal responsibility skills.

KATHLEEN M. NEVILLE
541 Austria Drive, Sunnyvale, CA 95087
(408) 555-9829

POSITION OBJECTIVE Food Service Coordinator

QUALIFICATIONS IN BRIEF

AA in Restaurant Management
BA in Business Management
Computer capability for production and inventory control
Supervisory experience
Good human relations skills
Organized, reliable, responsible, creative worker

EDUCATION

SAN JOSE STATE UNIVERSITY, San Jose, CA BA Degree   Present
Major: Business Management
Minor: Restaurant and Hospitality

MISSION COMMUNITY COLLEGE   1993
AS Degree in Restaurant Management

WORK EXPERIENCE

GARDNER FOODS, San Jose, CA   June 1997 to Present
Administrative Assistant/Supervisor

Provide administrative support to Executive Chef. Supervise kitchen staff in daily operations. Meals on Wheels Food Coordinator for the Santa Clara County program. Control complete database; maintain current operating inventory, initiate all product changes; and purchase supplies from approved vendor catalog. Data entry for all operations areas.

PIZZA TIME THEATERS, Milpitas, CA   June 1993 to May 1997
Order Entry Supervisor/Inventory Control

Supervised complete order entry operations for 260 locations. Buyer for all inventory and supplies. Maintained three million dollar inventory. Researched discrepancies in report files and corrected any errors. Responsible for receiving data entry.

LINDA'S DRIVE IN, Mountain View, CA August 1990 to June 1993
Supervisor/Cook

COMMUNITY ACTIVITIES Community music and theater groups

Figure A-3   Résumé of same individual as on previous page, some years later as she is moving up

541 Austria Drive
Sunnyvale, CA 95087
September 17, 2001

Mr. Archibald Manx
Gato Food Corporation
1000 Back Street
Los Gatos, CA 95030

Dear Sir:

Recently your accountant, Bruce McDougall, said that you are beginning the search for a food service coordinator.

I have worked fourteen years in the food service industry and most recently as administrative assistant/supervisor in food services at Gardner Foods. I feel that I could bring my experience and good skills to the management of your well-known and very fine food service operation.

Enclosed is a copy of my résumé. I will call you next week for an appointment to discuss this with you further.

Sincerely yours,

Kathleen M. Neville

Figure A-4   Cover letter to accompany preceding résumé

AMALIA LENA
1643 W. Davis Drive
Fort Lauderdale, FL 33325
(305) 555-3669

JOB OBJECTIVE Medical Office Manager

QUALIFICATIONS IN BRIEF Five years' experience as medical secretary/receptionist; six years as bank teller, four years as bank manager, preceded by four years of clerical work. Extensive community service activities. Special skills: current computer fluency. Especially good at business contact with people; fluency in Italian; limited fluency in Spanish; excellent memory for names.

WORK EXPERIENCE

CYPRESS MEDICAL CLINIC, Fort Lauderdale, FL   1993–Present
   Medical Secretary/Receptionist   Answer phone, make appointments in a high traffic office; greet patients and show them to examining rooms; interact with three doctors; evaluate patient problems; prepare examining rooms; prepare and update charts.

MANATEE NEON SIGN COMPANY, Manatee, FL   1989–1993
   Bookkeeper, Computer Operator, Clerk

CIVIC FEDERAL SAVINGS, Fort Lauderdale, FL   1979–1989
   Head Teller, Manager   Typed, cashiered, dealt with public at teller window, paid bank bills. Worked with computer. Handled transactions and answered banking questions by phone. As manager, did general supervision of personnel and procedures, including management of vault cash.

DADE COUNTY SANITATION DISTRICT, Miami, FL   1966–1969
   Office Clerk   Filed, typed, handled radio communication with personnel in the field, did general telephone work, paid department bills; occasional payroll management.

MIAMI MEDICAL CLINIC, Miami, FL   1965–1966
   Medical Records Clerk   Checked and delivered medical records to doctors' offices.

EDUCATION
   ST. VINCENT'S HIGH SCHOOL, Ft. Lauderdale, FL
   Concentration in business education courses.
   Subsequent workshops dealing with human relations and crisis counseling.

COMMUNITY SERVICE ACTIVITIES
   Girl Scout/Cub Scout Leader, seven years
   Elementary School Teacher Aide
   Hospitality Chairperson for PTA Group
   Crisis counseling, individually and in small groups

Figure A-5   Chronological résumé showing career path of a woman who returned to work after raising a family

REINALDA GUZMANN
146 Perdido Avenue
Watsonville, CA 95076
(408) 555-1212

POSITION OBJECTIVE Community Outreach Director

EDUCATION

CABRILLO COLLEGE, Aptos, California: AA Degree   June 1999
Sociology Major
Took additional courses in psychology and Latin American History.

EXPERIENCE SUMMARY

PAJARO VALLEY SHELTER SERVICES,   February 1998 to Present
  Watsonville, CA

Facilities Manager
Interviewed prospective families for transitional housing; set up and ran
orientation programs for residents that included budgeting, home
maintenance, and conflict resolution; supervised maintenance of buildings;
collected rental fees. Did community liaison work by contacting various
agencies for client services; worked with churches and other agencies to
meet needs of homeless families.

Office Manager
Answered phone, set up appointments, wrote letters, kept mailing list up
to date, set up newsletter content, did mailouts to over 1,000 supporters.

PERSONAL PARAGRAPH

As a child of migrant farmworkers and a former homeless parent with three
children, I understand the needs of poor families in this area. Working with
community agencies and similar families has given me valuable experience.

**FIGURE A-6 Chronological résumé of a formerly homeless mother with three
children who lived and worked at a shelter and returned to school. Because she
worked at only one place, her résumé looks almost functional.**

JERRY MARTIN-PITTS, M.H.C., R.C.P
3320 Saddleback Way, Tucson, AZ 85733
(602) 555-1213

OBJECTIVE
To develop and manage health care services

QUALIFICATIONS
- Cardiopulmonary Department Manager for nineteen years
- Master's degree in Health Counseling
- Arizona State License, Respiratory Care Practitioner
- Excellent human relations, organizational, teaching, and facilitation skills

EXPERIENCE SUMMARY
Pilar Hospital:
- Coached and developed a staff of 53 people
- Interviewed, hired, oriented, and evaluated staff
- Resolved personnel issues
- Scheduled staff
- Developed and managed multiple budgets
- Planned, designed, and developed department facilities
- Participated in and chaired multiple-service meetings
- Taught and implemented continuous process improvement skills
- Managed equipment and supplies for seven departments
- Developed and implemented policies and procedures
- Handled patient, visitor, physician complaints and relations
- Developed and coordinated employee recognition programs
- Developed, coordinated, and facilitated employee/volunteer mission/values
  retreats; developed mission/values statements
- Developed ethical guidelines for health care decision making
- Prepared department for outside regulatory agency surveys/licensing
- Developed and expanded respiratory services in skilled nursing facilities
- Developed and coordinated patient-focused care models
- Developed Therapist Driven Protocols and Clinical Pathways

Community Experience:
- Thunderbird Medical Clinic: Facilitate Smoking Cessation Program   1997–Present
- American Cancer Society: President of Tucson Board of Directors   1997–1999
- American Lung Association: President-Elect of Board of Directors   1994–1997
  Chairperson of Human Resources
  Committee
- Arizona Society of Respiratory Care: President   1999–2001
- Samaritan Counseling Center: Founding Board of Directors   1995
- Hospice Caring Project of Tucson: Founding Board of Directors   1988
- Pilar Hospital Speakers Bureau Lecturer on Stress Management, Living   1990–1998
  with Chronic Illness, Smoking Cessation, Working with the Dying

EDUCATION
- University of Connecticut   B.A., B.D.   1974
- Arizona State University   Teacher's Certification   1975
- Samaritan Respiratory School   CRTT   1982
- Xavier University   M.H.C.   1994

**Figure A-7   Health care manager in transition because of hospital downsizing
and restructuring**

1085 Blue Meadows
Bowling Green, KY 42101
March 17, 2000

Dr. Gladys C. Penner, Chancellor
University of the Trees
369 Dogwood Blvd.
Bowling Green, KY 42l0l

Dear Dr. Penner:

After considerable thought, it has become clear that a career change is appropriate for me at this time. As of June 1, 2000, I will be resigning from the University of the Trees as Career Center Coordinator and Counselor.

I have enjoyed and greatly profited from my years of teaching and counseling at UOT. Your considerable expertise, openness to innovation, and general professionalism have been a significant factor in my job satisfaction.

Perhaps on occasion I might return to teach a short course or a night class, for I plan to stay in the field of Career Development. I will be expanding my private practice and my consulting in that area.

I wish to express my appreciation to the college community for the many years of support it has given me, for its commitment to excellence, and its dedication to students.

Sincerely yours,

Allison E. Stevenson

Figure A-8   Letter of resignation

NOTES

CHAPTER 1
Needs, Wants, and Values:
Spotlighting YOU

1. Page Smith, *Redeeming the Time: A People's History of the 1920s and the New Deal,* Vol. 8 (New York: McGraw-Hill, 1986), p. 953.
2. "Potpourri," Financial Resource Center, Santa Cruz, California, May 1992.
3. Jim Frederick, "The End of Eureka!" *Working Woman,* February 1997, p. 40.
4. *INC,* February 1995, p. 6.
5. Bill Cane, *Through Crisis to Freedom* (Chicago: Acta Books, 1980), p. 21.
6. Clarissa Pinkola Estés, *Women Who Run with the Wolves* (New York: Ballantine, 1992), p. 221.
7. Victor Frankl, *Man's Search for Meaning* (New York: Washington Square Press, 1963).
8. Page Smith, *Old Age Is Another Country* (Watsonville, CA: Crossing Press, 1995), p. 223.
9. Eileen R. Growald and Allan Luks, "A Reason to Be Nice: It's Healthy," *American Health Magazine,* reprinted in the *San Francisco Chronicle,* March 4, 1988, p. B-4.
10. "For a Better World," *World Monitor,* January 1989, p. 95.
11. World Bank, June 1996, in *Ministry of Money,* August 1996, p. 2.
12. *Ministry of Money,* August 1996, p. 6.
13. David Shi, "Thoreau Rides with Today's Commuters," *Christian Science Monitor,* December 13, 1996, p. 19.
14. See Gary Carnum, "Everybody Talks about Values," *Learning,* December 1972; S. B. Simon, S. W. Howe, and H. Kirschenbaum, *Values Clarification* (New York: Hart, 1972), pp. 30, 113–115.
15. Robert Marquand, "'Globerati' Try to Find 'Common Values,'" *Christian Science Monitor,* September 15, 1997, p. 7.
16. Edward Goss "Patterns of Organizational and Occupational Socialization," *Vocational Guidance Quarterly,* December 1975, p. 140.
17. Stephen Covey, "The Beliefs We Share," *USA Weekend,* July 4–6, 1997, p. 4.
18. Ken Keyes, Jr., *Handbook to Higher Consciousness* (Saint Mary, KY: Cornucopia Institute, 1975), p. 52.
19. Adapted from Abraham Maslow, *Motivation and Personality* (New York: Harper & Row, 1954), p. 91; see also Marilyn M. Bates and Clarence Johnson, *A Manual for Group Leaders* (Denver: Love Publishing, 1972), and Keyes, *Handbook to Higher Consciousness.*
20. Carter Henderson, "The Frugality Phenomenon," in John G. Burke and Marshall C. Eakin, eds., *Technology and Change* (San Francisco: Boyd & Fraser, 1979), p. 233.
21. *Sojourners,* February 1987, p. 13.
22. Kathleen Sullivan, "Naomi Gray's Spirit Is No Surprise—She's a Taurus," *Register-Pajaronian,* April 13, 1996, p. 3.
23. Pat Mathes Cane, "The Call to Be Brothers and Sisters," *Integrities,* Spring 1989, p. 8.
24. Ruth Hunter, "Public Pressure Counts in Fight for Human Rights," *Santa Cruz Sentinel,* March 3, 1996.
25. Michelle Locke, "Labor Secretary Speaks at Berkeley," *Register-Pajaronian,* May 10, 1995, p. 7.
26. Rebecca Smith, "The Power of Persuasion," *San Jose Mercury News,* February 27, 1995, p. 1D.
27. Center for Living Democracy, RR #1 Black Fox Road, Brattleboro, VT 05301.
28. David Suzuki, "Towards a New Ecological Future, the Importance of Grass Roots," *Talking Leaves,* Winter 1992, p. 3.
29. *Catalyst,* Summer, 1991, p. 16.
30. U.S. Department of Health, Education, and Welfare, *Work in America* (Cambridge, MA: MIT Press, 1973), pp. 186–187.
31. Lance Morrow, *Time,* May 11, 1981, p. 94.
32. S. Norman Feingold, "Career Education: A Philosophy," B'Nai B'rith Career and Counseling Service, 1640 Rhode Island Avenue, N.W., Washington, DC, September 1973, p. 11.
33. Virginia Y. Trotter, "Women in Leadership and Decision Making: A Shift in Balance," *Vital Speeches,* April 1, 1975, pp. 373–375.
34. Hans Selye, *Stress without Distress* (Philadelphia: J. B. Lippincott, 1974), p. 96.

35. Fernando Bartolomé and Paul A. Lee Evans, "Must Success Cost So Much?" *Harvard Business Review,* March/April 1980, p. 142.

CHAPTER 2

Personality and Performances: Pieces of the Puzzle

1. John Holland, *Making Vocational Choices: A Theory of Careers* (Englewood Cliffs, NJ: Prentice-Hall, 1973).

2. Rose Marie Dunphy, "Why I Sew," *The Christian Science Monitor,* May 20, 1985, p. 34.

3. Wynne Busby, "Chips Off the Old Block," *Creation Spirituality,* Winter 1994, p. 47.

4. *This Time,* from H.O.M.E., Fall 1988, p. 7.

5. Compiled from the following sources: U.S. Department of Labor, *Dictionary of Occupational Titles,* vol. 2, 1965; *Guide for Occupational Exploration,* New Forum Foundation, distributed by the American Guidance Service, Publications Building, Circle Pines, MN 55014, 1984; *U.S. Army, Career and Educational Guide,* Counselor Edition, 1978.

6. *Regeneration,* September/October 1989, p. 10.

7. Jean Houston, "The Church in Future Society," taped address to the Lutheran Brotherhood Colloquium, University of Texas, Austin, January 1979.

8. See Sydney A. Fine, "Counseling Skills: Target for Tomorrow," *Vocational Guidance Quarterly,* June 1974, and "Nature of Skills: Implications for Education and Training," *Proceedings,* 75th Annual Convention of the American Personnel Association, 1967.

9. Nancy Gibbs, "The EQ Factor," *Time,* October 2, 1995, p. 60.

10. Daniel Goleman, *Emotional Intelligence* (New York: Bantam Books, 1995).

11. Compiled from the following sources: U.S. Department of Labor, *Dictionary of Occupational Titles,* vol. 2, 1965; *Guide for Occupational Exploration,* New Forum Foundation, distributed by the American Guidance Service, Publications Building, Circle Pines, MN 55014, 1984; *U.S. Army, Career and Educational Guide,* Counselor Edition, 1978.

CHAPTER 3

The Career Connection: Finding Your Job Satisfiers

1. U.S. Department of Labor and National Forum Foundation, *Guide for Occupational Exploration,* 1979 and 1984 (Washington, DC: U.S. Department of Labor).

2. Compiled from the following sources: U.S. Department of Labor, *Dictionary of Occupational Titles,* vol. 2, 1965; U.S. Department of Labor and National Forum Foundation, *Guide for Occupational Exploration,* 1979 and 1984; U.S. Army, *Career and Education Guide,* Counselor Edition, 1978; U.S. Department of Labor, *Handbook for Analyzing Jobs,* 1972 (Washington, DC: U.S. Department of Labor).

3. U.S. Department of Labor, *Dictionary of Occupational Titles,* 1978.

4. *The Enhanced Guide for Occupational Exploration,* 1991 (formerly by U.S. Department of Labor, 1979), JIST Works, Inc., 720 N. Park Avenue, Indianapolis, IN 46202; (317) 264-3720.

5. *The Enhanced Guide for Occupational Exploration.*

6. *The Enhanced Guide for Occupational Exploration.*

CHAPTER 4

Work: Challenges, Options, and Opportunities

1. John Peers lecture at Mission College, November 11, 1982.

2. Thomas Merton, *Raids on the Unspeakable* (New York: New Directions, 1996), p. 70.

3. Jeremy Rifkin, "The Clocks That Make Us Run," *East West Journal,* September 1987, p. 44.

4. "The Invisible Farmer," *Christian Science Monitor,* October 20, 1993, p. 18.

5. *Statistical Abstracts of the United States* (Washington, DC: U.S. Bureau of the Census, 1990), pp. 395, 387.

6. "The Invisible Farmer," *Christian Science Monitor,* p. 18.

7. Jeremy Rifkin, *The End of Work* (New York: G.P. Putnam's Sons, 1995), p. 110.

8. James Burke, *Connections,* a PBS Series.

9. Jonathan Rowe, "Just Words, but They Linger," *Christian Science Monitor,* May 17, 1989, p. 12.

10. Stephen J. Kline, "What Is Technology?" *Reporter,* January 1986, p. 1.

11. Priscilla Enriquez, "An Un-American Tragedy," *Food First Action Alert,* Summer 1992, p. 4.

12. Arthur S. Miller, "The Right to a Job," *San Jose Mercury News,* July 13, 1986, p. P-1.

13. Thomas J. Peters, "Competition and Change," *Santa Clara Magazine,* Summer 1989, p. 10.

14. Sarah van Gelder, "A New Civilization," *In Context,* Winter 1995–96, p. 6.

15. George Gendron, "Small Is Beautiful," *INC Special Report 1995,* p. 39.

16. Lester R. Brown, Christopher Flavin, and Sandra Postel, "A Planet in Jeopardy," *Futurist,* May/June 1992, p. 10.

17. Thomas Berry, *The Dream of the Earth* (San Francisco: Sierra Club Books, 1988), p. 73.

18. Manus van Brakel and Maria Buitenkamp, "Our Fair Share," *In Context,* No. 36, 1993, p. 38.

19. Letter, Acción International, Fall 1998.

20. Michael Renner, "Chiapas: An Uprising Born of Despair," *World Watch,* January/February 1997, p. 12.

21. Renner, "Chiapas," p. 12.

22. *Statistical Abstracts of the U.S.* (Washington, DC: U.S. Census Bureau, 1996), pp. 465, 476.

23. "Raising the Minimum Wage," *1998 Wage Gap Organizing Kit* (Boston, MA: United for a Fair Economy/Responsible Wealth), p. 21.

24. Maria Foscarinis, "Helping the Homeless," *Christian Science Monitor,* July 25, 1997, p. 18.

25. "Malnutrition Kills Six to Seven Million Children Annually," *Register-Pajaronian,* December 16, 1997, p. 22.

26. John J. Sweeney, "Labor Unions Are Ready to Face the Challenges," *Register-Pajaronian,* April 17, 1998, p. 4.

27. John Cassidy, "Who Killed the Middle Class?" *New Yorker,* October 16, 1995, p. 113; "Time for a Living Wage around the World," *Global Exchanges,* Fall 1998, p. 5.

28. "Historical Income Tables–Households," U.S. Census Bureau, http.www.census.gov/hhes/www/income. html, September 1997.

29. Charles Frago, "Global Shakedown," *Streetwise,* June 9–June 22, 1998, p. 4.

30. "Looking for Hope," *Ministry of Money,* April 1998, p. 3.

31. Cassidy, "Who Killed the Middle Class?" p. 113.

32. Sharron Cordaro, "Readers' Forum," *In Context,* Winter 1995–96, p. 5.

33. Holly Sklar and Chuck Collins, "Forbes 400 World Series," *Nation,* October 20, 1997, n.p.

34. Gary Gunderson, "Keeping Faith for Children," *World Ark,* Fall 1996, p. 12.

35. "U.S. Consumption: Equal to That of 13 Billion Poor," *World Watch* May/June 1998, p. 6.

36. Curtis Runyan, "Ecological Footprint: Taming the Consumer Culture," *World Watch,* July/August 1997, p. 35.

37. David Clark Scott, "Retailers Move Early to Foil Yule Grinch," *Christian Science Monitor,* November 18, 1985, p. 31.

38. David C. Korten, *When Corporations Rule the World* (West Hartford, CT: Kumarian Press, Inc., 1995), p. 221.

39. "Earth Notes, Price of Ads," *Creation Spirituality,* July/August 1992, p. 6.

40. "So Many Lists, So Little Time," *USA Weekend,* March 15–17, 1996, p. 4.

41. "The Page That Counts," *YES! A Journal of Positive Futures,* Spring 1997, p. 11.

42. "The Page That Counts," *YES! A Journal of Positive Futures,* Winter 1997/1998, p. 11.

43. Lance Morrow, "The Weakness That Starts at Home," *Time,* June 4, 1979, p. 81.

44. Korten, *When Corporations Rule the World.*

45. Helena Norberg-Hodge, Director, International Society for Ecology and Culture, "Lessons from Traditional Cultures," *Futurist,* May/June 1992, p. 60.

46. Laura Van Tuyl, "Her Design Is to Save the Earth," *Christian Science Monitor,* January 28, 1991, p. 14.

47. *Comic News,* Resource Center for Nonviolence, January 1994, p. 8.

48. Marshall Ingwerson, "Tales of Golf-Ball Gulping 'Gator and Reptile's Return to Florida," *Christian Science Monitor,* July 2, 1986, p. 3; Rushworth M. Kidder, "Agenda for the 21st Century," *Christian Science Monitor,* September 23, 1986, p. 1; see also p. 37.

49. Brad Knickerbocker, "Conversations with Outstanding Americans," *Christian Science Monitor,* August 15, 1997, p. 11.

50. Source unknown.

51. Howard Youth, "Flying into Trouble," *World Watch,* January/February 1994, p. 10.

52. Robert Gilman, "Ecological Limit," *In Context,* Fall 1993, p. 12; Molly O'Meara, "The Risks of Disrupting Climate," *World Watch,* November/December 1997, p. 10.

53. Thomas Gartside, "Planting 1,000 Trees," *Christian Science Monitor,* March 6, 1990, p. 18.

54. Peer Weber, "Neighbors under the Gun," *World Watch,* July/August 1991, p. 35.

55. Christopher Flavin, "Climate Change and Storm Damage, the Insurance Costs Keep Rising," *World Watch,* January/February 1997, p. 10.

56. "One-fifth of Americans Said to Be Drinking Dangerous, Dirty Tap Water," *Register-Pajaronian,* June 1, 1995, p. 2.

57. Sandra Postel, *Last Oasis, Facing Water Scarcity* (New York: W.W. Norton, 1997); www.worldwatch.org.

58. Scott, "Retailers Move Early," p. 31.

59. Runyan, "Ecological Footprint," p. 35.

60. Gilman, "Ecological Limit," p. 12.

61. Runyan, "Ecological Footprint," p. 35.

62. Gilman, "Ecological Limit," p. 12.

63. Colin Woodard, "Lessons from 'the Year the Earth Caught Fire,'" *Christian Science Monitor,* February 4, 1998, p. 1.

64. "Matters of Scale," *World Watch,* January/February, 1994, p. 39.

65. "Matters of Scale," *World Watch,* January/February, 1994, p. 39.

66. Colin Woodard, "Troubles Bubble under the Sea," *Christian Science Monitor,* September 10, 1997, p. 1.

67. Matthew Fox, "A Call for a Spiritual Renaissance," *Creation,* January/February 1989, p. 10.

68. Weber, "Neighbors under the Gun," p. 35.

69. Lester R. Brown, "Can We Raise Grain Yields Fast Enough?" *World Watch,* July/August 1997, p. 8.

70. "Vital Signs," *World Watch,* May/June 1990, p. 6.

71. Arthur Getz, "Community Supported Agriculture," *Earth Save,* Spring/Summer 1992, p. 8.

72. "Spotlight, the Loaves and the Fishes: 1980s Style," *Regeneration,* March/April 1989, p. 5.

73. Alan B. Durning, "Trends: U.S. Poultry Consumption Overtakes Beef," *World Watch,* January/February 1988, p. 11.

74. Karen Free, "Poverty Housing Sets Families Adrift," *Habitat World,* February/March

1998, p. 2; http//www. fedstats.gov/index20.html.

75. "Quinientos Milliones de Personas Viven Sin Hogar en Las Ciudades Que No Paran de Crecer," *Perspectiva,* January 1996, p. 8.

76. Lester R. Brown, "Facing Food Scarcity," *World Watch,* November/December 1995, p. 10.

77. Barbara Marx Hubbard, "Critical Path to an All-Win World," *Futurist,* June 1981, p. 31.

78. Francois Dusquesne, "The Making of a Sacred Planet," *One Earth,* 2, p. 6.

79. Sandra Postel, *Last Oasis* (New York: W.W. Norton, 1992), p. 23.

80. "New Entries," *Boycott Quarterly,* Spring 1994, p. 38.

81. Sharron Cordaro, "Readers' Forum," *In Context,* Winter 1995–96, p. 5.

82. "Almanac," *Organic Gardening,* April 1985, p. 126.

83. Robert Rodale, *Regeneration of Health and the Human Spirit* (Emmaus, PA: Rodale Press, 1986).

84. "Mitraniketan," *Community Service Newsletter,* March/April 1988, p. 3.

85. Howard Youth, "Iguana Farms, Antelope Ranches," *World Watch,* January/February, 1991, p. 36.

86. Jo Roberts, "Rubber Tapper Chico Mendes Murdered," *Catholic Worker,* March/April 1989, p. 1.

87. "New Ground," *Organic Gardening,* July/August 1989, p. 12.

88. Alan Weisman, "¡Gaviotas! Oasis of the Imagination," *YES! A Journal of Positive Futures,* Summer 1998, p. 11.

89. Kathryn True, "Healing Technologies," *In Context,* Fall 1995, p. 24; The Green Center, 237 Hatchville Road, Falmouth, MA 02536.

90. Thomas Gartside, "Planting 1,000 Trees," *Christian Science Monitor,* March 6, 1990, p. 18.

91. "'Global Releaf' Project," *Greenhouse Gasette,* Spring 1989, p. 11.

92. Susan Meeker-Lowry, *Catalyst,* May/June 1987, p. 2.

93. Brad Knickerbocker, "Draft Horses Pull Their Weight for Endangered Fish," *Christian Science Monitor,* September 9, 1997, p. 13.

94. Alexandra Marks, "Seal of Approval," *Christian Science Monitor,* June 24, 1997, p. 10.

95. Joanna Poncavage, "Walnut Acres: The Farm That Gandhi Grew," *Organic Gardening,* February 1991, p. 58.

96. Eliot Coleman, "Living Soil," *Organic Gardening,* October 1989, p. 67.

97. "Who Gardens? Most Are Women," *Register-Pajaronian,* March 29, 1996, p. 25.

98. Cathryn J. Prince, "All Built Up, Places to Grow," *Christian Science Monitor,* September 17, 1997, p. 1.

99. John Kuhn, "Biointensive Gold Mining," *Ecology Action Newsletter,* February 1997, p. 1.

100. Christina Waters, "Natural Phenomenon," *Metro Santa Cruz,* April 4–10, 1996, p. 11.

101. Christina Waters, "Seeding the Future," *Metro Santa Cruz,* September 5–11, 1996, p. 5.

102. Elizabeth Schilling, "Natural Products Find Market Niche," *Register-Pajaronian,* January 14, 1991, p. 11.

103. Chela Zabin, "Watsonville-Based Business Had Its Start in the Kitchen," *Register-Pajaronian,* October 25, 1994, p. 1.

104. Lester R. Brown, "Facing Food Scarcity," *World Watch,* November/December 1995, p. 10.

105. "In This Issue," *World Watch,* March/ April 1990, p. 3.

106. "Americans Spending Billions on Offbeat Medical Treatments," *Register-Pajaronian,* June 27, 1993, p. 1.

107. "Almanac," *Organic Gardening,* April 1985, p. 126.

108. Former Stanford University Assistant Dean Michael Closson, founder of the Center for Economic Conversion in Mountain View, California, works with industry, business, and institutions in conversion projects.

109. George Hoffman, "Converting Swords into Environmental Plowshares: Laudable Transitions from Weaponry into Environmentally Benign Technology," *Environmental Council,* Summer 1993, p. 9.

110. Christopher Flavin, "Last Tango in Buenos Aires," *World Watch,* November/December 1998, p. 10.

111. Christopher Flavin and Nicholas Lenssen, "Here Comes the Sun," *World Watch,* September/October 1991, p. 10.

112. Christopher Flavin and Molly O'Meara, "Solar Power Markets Boom," *World Watch,* September/October 1998, p. 23.

113. Craig Savoye, "An All-Solar Home in the North Country? It Can Be Done," *Christian Science Monitor,* April 14, 1983, p. 14; "Superinsulation Means Super Savings in Canada's Cold," *Christian Science Monitor,* July 14, 1983, p. 14.

114. Terri Franklin, "Building Houses Made of Straw," *Habitat World,* June 1995, p. 12.

115. Peter Tonge, "Fuel-Stingy Z Stove: Could It Be the Answer for Fuel-Poor Third World?" *Christian Science Monitor,* January 6, 1984, p. 25.

116. Christopher Flavin, "Power Shock: The Next Energy Revolution," *World Watch,* January/February 1996, p. 10.

117. Darren Waggoner, "Wind Energy Picks Up Speed in the Midwest," *Doing Democracy,* Spring, 1997, p. 9.

118. Seth Dunn, "The Electric Car Arrives—Again," *World Watch,* March/April 1997, p. 19.

119. John Dillin, "Emerging Plans to Cut U.S. Oil Imports," *Christian Science Monitor,* February 7, 1991, p. 1; also Christopher Flavin, "Conquering U.S. Oil Dependence," *World Watch,* January/February 1991, p. 28.

120. Marcia D. Lowe, "Bicycle Production Rises Again," *World Watch,* September/October 1994, p. 38.

121. Flavin, "Conquering U.S. Oil Dependence," p. 28.

122. Christopher Flavin and Seth Dunn, "Kyoto: The Days of Reckoning," *World Watch,* November/December 1997, p. 21.

123. "Eco-Actions," *CO-OP America Quarterly,* Winter 1992, p. 8.

124. Knickerbocker, "Draft Horses Pull Their Weight," p. 13.

125. "It's Called the Automobile and Here's How It Works!" *Environmental Council of Santa Cruz County Newsletter,* January 1997, insert.

126. Amory B. and L. Hunter Lovins, "Carbon Reductions Can Make You Money," *Christian Science Monitor,* December 22, 1997, p. 16; Bill Cane, "Study Guide for Group Leaders," *Circles of Hope* (New York: Orbis Books, 1992), p. 6, Rocky Mountain Institute, 1739 Snowmass Creek Road, Snowmass, CO 81654.

127. Colin Norman, "The Staggering Challenge of Global Unemployment," *Futurist,* August 1978, p. 224.

128. Robert Gilman, interview with Bob Berkebile, "Restorative Design," *In Context,* 35, 1993, p. 9.

129. David W. Orr, "Breaking Ground," *YES! A Journal of Positive Futures,* Winter 1998/1999.

130. Michael N. Corbett, *A Better Place to Live, New Designs for Tomorrow's Communities* (Emmaus, PA: Rodale Press, 1981).

131. Sarah van Gelder, "Cities of Exuberance," *In Context,* 35, 1993, p. 46.

132. Stuart Cowan, "A Design Revolution," *Yes! A Journal of Positive Futures,* Summer 1998, p. 27.

133. Cowan, "A Design Revolution," p. 27.

134. Howell Hurst, "Focus," *INC,* February 1991, p. 15.

135. Frank Swoboda, "Labor Secretary Challenges National 'Competitiveness' Issue," *Register-Pajaronian,* September 24, 1994, p. 22.

136. Cindy Mitlo, "A Matter of Principles," *CO-OP American Quarterly,* Spring 1996, p. 18.

137. *National Green Pages 1998,* CO-OP America, 1612 K Street NW, #600, Washington, DC 20006.

138. Muhammad Yunus, "A Lesson in the Price of Bamboo," *World Ark,* Summer 1997, p. 28.

139. Acción International Conference, Chicago, June 11–13, 1998.

140. "Green Business," *CO-OP America Quarterly,* Winter 1994, p. 25.

141. Michael E. Porter, "The Rise of the Urban Entrepreneur," *INC Special Report: The State of Small Business 1995,* p. 89.

142. Marj Halperin, "Women Helping Women Worldwide," *Building Economic Alternatives,* Spring 1987, p. 19.

143. Trickle Up Program, Inc., 54 Riverside Drive PHE, New York, NY 10024-6509

144. Greg Ramm, "Community Investment Is Coming of Age," *Building Economic Alternatives,* Spring 1987, p. 9; *Custody & Finance World,* May 1997.

145. Rifkin, *The End of Work,* p. 241.

146. Hazel Henderson, "Will the Real Economy Please Stand Up," *Building Economic Alternatives,* Summer 1986, p. 3.

147. "New Loans," *ICE Update,* April 1998, p. 3.

148. Chuck Matthei, "Why Do We Have a Housing Shortage?" *Catholic Worker,* October/November 1987, p. 1.

149. *Adobe Magazine,* Autumn 1998 Issue, Cover.

150. Beth Burrows, "Ethics and Other Irrational Considerations," *Boycott Quarterly,* Spring 1994, p. 20.

151. Quotes from Christopher Cerf and Victor Navask, *The Experts Speak* (New York: Pantheon Books, 1984).

152. TRW advertisement, 1985.

153. *Regeneration Newsletter,* September/October 1988, p. 8.

154. *Catholic Women's NETWORK,* March/April 1998, p. 13.

155. "The Page That Counts," *YES! The Journal of Positive Futures,* Spring 1997, p. 11.

156. "Responsible Investing," *CO-OP American Quarterly,* Spring 1998, p. 13.

157. May 1998 phone bill.

158. Oscar Arias, "Global Demilitarization," *Christian Science Monitor,* November 3, 1997, p. 15.

159. John Robbins, "Growing Impact," *Earth Save,* Winter 1991, p. 2.

160. Kirsten A. Conover, "Public Groundswell Sways Organic Guidelines," *Christian Science Monitor,* May 14, 1998, p. 14.

161. Brad Knickerbocker, "Earth Day Has Helped Turn America 'Green,'" *Christian Science Monitor,* April 22, 1998, p. 3.

162. "World's 'Vital Signs' Getting Better," *Register-Pajaronian,* October 19, 1992, p. 1.

163. Ed Ayres, "Environmental Intelligence," *World Watch,* July/August 1994, p. 6.

164. Responsible Wealth, c/o United for a Fair Economy, 37 Temple Place, Fifth Floor, Boston, MA 02111, *Update,* February 1998.

165. "Facts Out of Context," *In Context,* Winter 1995–96, p. 13.

166. *Tightwad Gazette,* RR1, Box 3570, Leeds, ME 04263.

167. Iain Guest, "Debt—the Next Cause Célèbre," *Christian Science Monitor,* May 27, 1998, p. 20.

168. Ann Japenga, "Why Med Schools Teach Meditation," *USA Weekend,* February 21–23, 1997, p. 8.

169. Frances Moore Lappé and Joseph Collins, *Food First: Beyond the Myth of Scarcity* (New York: Ballantine Books, 1979), pp. 50–52; *Time,* November 15, 1976, quoted in Lappé and Collins, *Food First.*

170. "Odds and Ends," *Ecology Action Newsletter,* October 1992, p. 4.

171. "Odds and Ends," p. 4.

172. "Odds and Ends," p. 4.

173. "Odds and Ends," p. 4.

174. John Young, "The New Materialism," *World Watch,* September/October 1994, p. 37.

175. Michael Renner, "Monitoring Arms Trade," *World Watch,* May/June 1994, p. 21.

176. Campaign against Arms Trade, 5 Caledonian Road, London NI 9DX.

177. Flavin and Dunn, "Kyoto: The Days of Reckoning," p. 21.

178. "Indicators," *YES! A Journal of Positive Futures,* Winter 1997, p. 7.

179. Colin Norman, "The Staggering Challenge of Global Unemployment," *Futurist,* August 1978, p. 224.

180. "Looking Ahead to 1997: Post-Election Considerations," *Maryknoll Newsnotes,* November/December 1996, p. 1.

181. "Special Report," *Oxfam America News,* Winter 1983, p. 3.

182. "Citings," *World Watch,* May/June 1993, p. 8.

183. Korten, *When Corporations Rule the World,* reviewed by Toni Nelson, in *World Watch,* January/February 1996, p. 37.

184. Job market statistics synthesized from a variety of sources: "Ninth Annual Listing: Twenty-five Hottest Careers," *Working Woman,* July 1994, p. 37; Knight-Ridder Survey, "Growth Occupations," *San Jose Mercury News,* September 4, 1994, p. D-1.

185. David R. Francis, "Jobs and Jobs Galore: Who Are the Workers?" *Christian Science Monitor,* April 9, 1997, p. 8.

186. David R. Francis, "Sizing Up the Yuppies and the Dinks Gives Population Insights," *Christian Science Monitor,* April 11, 1988, p. 14.

187. Bureau of Labor Statistics: Occupational Outlook Handbook, http://www.fedstats.gov/index20.html.

188. U.S. Department of Labor, Bureau of Labor Statistics, *Occupational Outlook Quarterly,* Spring 1994, pp. 10–45, 47.

189. Bureau of Labor Statistics: *Occupational Outlook Handbook* Fastest-Growing Occupations: http://www.fedstats.gov/ index20.html.

190. George Silvestri, "Employment Projections," Bureau of Labor Statistics: http://stats.bls.gov/ecopro.table7.htm, December 29, 1997.

191. Hunter Lovins and Michael Kinsley, "Ingredients for Success," *Idea Bulletin,* Summer 1987, p. 3.

192. Jean Houston, "The Church in Future Society," address to the Lutheran Brotherhood Colloquium, University of Texas, Austin, January 1979. See also Jean Houston, *The Possible Human* (Los Angeles: J.P. Tarcher, 1982).

193. John O'Donohue, *Anam Cara* (New York: HarperCollins, 1997), p. 148.

194. O'Donohue, *Anam Cara,* p. 148.

195. Virginia Y. Trotter, "Women in Leadership and Decision Making: A Shift in Balance," *Vital Speeches,* April 1, 1975, pp. 373–375.

196. Adapted from Leonard Steinberg, Long Beach State University, Long Beach, California.

CHAPTER 5
Workplaces/Workstyles: Companies That Work

1. Adele Scheele, "Moving Over Instead of Up," *Working Woman,* November 1993, p. 75.

2. Robert Vahl, Small Business Assistance Service, Clymer, NY, quoted in *In Business,* January/February 1986, p. 15.

3. Erving Goffman, *Asylums* (New York: Doubleday, 1961).

4. Barbara Garson, "Women's Work," *Working Papers,* Fall 1973, p. 5.

5. *Nations' Restaurant News,* December 1984.

6. "MIT's Engineering Students Seek Better Ways to Coat M&Ms," *Register-Pajaronian,* January 2, 1991, p. 20.

7. Robert Levering and Milton Moskowitz, "The Workplace 100," *USA Weekend,* January 22–24, 1993, p. 4.

8. Christy Heady, "Time Is Now for Women to Take Control and Start Investing," *Christian Science Monitor,* June 16, 1997, p. 8.

9. "20 Facts on Women Workers," *Facts on Working Women* (Washington, DC: U.S. Department of Labor, Women's Bureau, September 1996), p. 3.

10. David R. Francis, "Downsizing: A Fad That Spins Wheels," *Christian Science Monitor,* June 11, 1997, p. 9.

11. James Kouzes and Barry Posner, "Credibility Makes a Difference," *Santa Clara Magazine,* Fall 1994, p. 12.

12. Michael Hopkins and Jeffrey L. Seglin, "Americans at Work," *INC Special Issue,* May 20, 1997, p. 77.

13. James C. Collins, "Building Companies to Last," *INC Special Issue: The State of Small Business,* 1995, p. 83.

14. Dale Kurschner, "The 100 Best Corporate Citizens," *Business Ethics,* May/June 1996, p. 24.

15. U.S. Trust gets such information from a variety of sources—companies' annual reports, Securities and Exchange Commission reports, findings of the Investor Responsibility Research Center, the National Labor Relations Board, the Council on Economic Priorities, and the Interfaith Center on Corporate Responsibility.

16. Dawn-Marie Driscoll and W. Michael Hoffman, "It May Be Legal, but Is It Ethical?" *Christian Science Monitor,* December 8, 1997, p. 15.

17. Ron Scherer, "Eye on Firms That Use 'Cheap Labor' Abroad," *Christian Science Monitor,* November 14, 1997, p. 3.

18. Jeffrey W. Helms, "Green Investing," *Gardenia,* Winter 1994, p. 6; Anne Zorc, "Checking Up on Corporate Claims," *CO-OP America Quarterly,* Fall 1991, p. 16.

19. Jill Andresky Fraser, "Changing of the Card," *INC 500 97,* p. 84.

20. Loretta Graziano, "I'm Optimal, You're Optimal—an Economist's Way of Knowledge," *Propaganda Review,* Winter 1988, p. 36.

21. "Eco-Actions," *CO-OP America Quarterly,* Summer 1997, p. 7. Graduation Pledge Alliance, MC Box 152, Manchester College, North Manchester, IN 46962 or NJWollman @Manchester.edu for online brochure or questions.

22. "Worth Repeating," *Money Matters from Working Assets,* Fall 1994, p. 4.

23. Robert Levering and Milton Moskowitz, "The Workplace 100," *USA Weekend,* January 22–24, 1993, p. 4.

24. Kouzes and Posner, "Credibility Makes a Difference," p. 12.

25. William Bridges, "A Nation of Owners," *INC Special Report: The State of Small Business,* 1995, p. 89.

26. "Doubting Sweden's Way," *Time,* March 10, 1975, p. 42.

27. Sabrina Brown, "The Diversity Advantage," *Santa Clara Magazine,* Spring 1994, p. 22.

28. Elie Wiesel, "The Foreigner in Each of Us," *Christian Science Monitor,* August 7, 1991, p. 23.

29. "Bar Association Honors Lawyers Who Fought for Women's Equality," *Register-Pajaronian,* August 7, 1995, p. 8.

30. "Statistically Speaking: Issues Women Face," *Habitat World,* April/May 1998, p. 14.

31. "Facts Out of Context," from the United Nations Development Report, *In Context,* Winter 1995–96, p. 13; Toni Nelson, "Women's Work Undervalued by $11 Trillion," *World Watch,* November/December 1995, p. 7.

32. "Facts Out of Context," p. 13; Nelson, "Women's Work Undervalued by $11 Trillion," p. 7.

33. "Facts Out of Context," p. 13; Nelson, "Women's Work Undervalued by $11 Trillion," p. 7.

34. "Statistically Speaking: Issues Women Face," p. 14.

35. "Statistically Speaking: Issues Women Face," p. 14.

36. "Statistically Speaking: Issues Women Face," p. 14.

37. Cassandra Burrell, "Census: Half of U.S. Poor Are Children," *Register-Pajaronian,* August 19, 1996, p. 1.

38. "20 Facts on Women Workers," *Facts on Working Women* (Washington, DC: U.S. Department of Labor, Women's Bureau, September 1996), p. 2; Editorial: "Equal Pay for Equal Work," *Christian Science Monitor,* September 18, 1997, p. 20.

39. "Women and Work Factsheet," *Women at Work* (Washington DC: Wider Opportunities for Women, 1997).

40. "American Women: A Profile," *Bureau of the Census Statistical Brief* (Washington, DC: Bureau of the Census, July 1995).

41. Donna K. H. Walters, "Gender Pay Gap Narrows Because Men Lose Ground," *Register-Pajaronian,* September 14, 1992, p. 10.

42. "Women and Work Factsheet."

43. "Women and Work Factsheet."

44. "Women and Work Factsheet."

45. "Women Appear in Few Front-Page Stories," *Register-Pajaronian,* April 16, 1996, p. 14.

46. Shelley Donald Coolidge, "At Home: Career Change for 90s," *Christian Science Monitor,* December 8, 1997, p. B1.

47. Harris Collingwood, "The Mommy Tax," *Working Woman,* February 1997, p. 35.

48. Nelson, "Women's Work Undervalued by $11 Trillion," p. 7.

49. Peggy McIntosh, "Unpacking the Invisible Knapsack," *Creation Spirituality,* January/February 1992, p. 33.

50. Lisa Genasci, "Women's Work, More Take on Non-traditional Jobs," *Register-Pajaronian,* March 11, 1995, p. 11.

51. *Women and Nontraditional Work,* National Commission on Working Women of Wider Opportunities for Women (1325 G St. N.W. Lower Level, Washington, DC 20005), November 1989, p. 1

52. Shelley Donald Coolidge, "Climbing Career Ladder Tips Balance at Home," *Christian Science Monitor,* July 15, 1997, p. 1.

53. Mark Lloyd, "Affirmative Action: Solution or Problem?" *Christian Science Monitor,* January 18, 1991, p. 19; "Final Hearings Held on the Glass Ceiling," *Register-Pajaronian,* September 27, 1994, p. 14.

54. Mitch Finley, "My Three Sons," *Santa Clara Magazine,* Fall 1990, p. 47.

55. James A. Levine and Todd L. Pittinsky, "Working Fathers," *INC,* July 1997, p. 83.

56. "Millions of Youngsters Live in 'Blended' Families, Census Bureau Analysis Shows," *Register-Pajaronian,* August 30, 1994, p. 15.

57. Harry F. Rosenthal, "Study Shows Divorces, Out-of-Wedlock Births Declining," *Register-Pajaronian,* March 6, 1996, p. 13; "Study Shows Americans Slower to Get Married," *Register-Pajaronian,* March 13, 1996, p. 18.

58. Shira J. Boss, "Let's Honor Fathers—Single Fathers, Too," *Christian Science Monitor,* June 13, 1997, p. 19.

59. "Fewer Households Are Made Up of Married Couples," *Christian Science Monitor,* July 2, 1997, p. 2.

60. James L. Tyson, "Mother's Day an Increasingly Longer Day: Work vs. Family," *Christian Science Monitor,* May 9, 1997, p. 1.

61. "Obstacles Remain for Women and Working Mothers, U.N. Says," *Register-Pajaronian,* February 16, 1998, p. 9.

62. Anne-Marie Foisy-Grusonik, "The Superwoman Fallacy," *Santa Clara Magazine,* Winter 1992, p. 44; cf. Pamela Kruger, "All Twentysomething Women Want Is to Change the Way America Works," *Working Woman,* May 1994, p. 61.

63. Nancy K. Austin, "What Balance," *INC,* April 1997, p. 37.

64. "Family-Leave Law Goes into Effect," *Register-Pajaronian,* August 3, 1993, p. 3.

65. Scott Baldauf, "More Stay-at-Home Dads Drop Baby Bottles for Briefcases," *Christian Science Monitor,* March 26, 1997, p. 1.

66. Randolph E. Schmid, "Minding the Kids," *Register-Pajaronian,* October 8, 1997, p. 9.

67. Lillian Hellman, *An Unfinished Woman: A Memoir* (Boston: Atlantic Monthly Press, 1969).

68. Zalman Schachter-Shalomi and Ronald S. Miller, *From Age-ing to Sage-ing* (New York: Warner Books, 1995).

69. Ann Crittenden, "Temporary Solutions," *Working Woman,* February 1994, p. 35.

70. Political letter, 1988.

71. "Snapshot of America: Older, More Interracial," *Christian Science Monitor,* March 27, 1997, p. 14.

72. William H. Carlile, "All Anglo No More, a Latin Phoenix Rises," *Christian Science Monitor,* August 6, 1997, p. 1.

73. Lucia Mouat, "Despite Minority Gains, Gap between Races Still Looms Large," *Christian Science Monitor,* November 21, 1990, p. 8.

74. Gregory Rodriguez, "Multiracial Americans Deserve Better Than 'Other,'" *Christian Science Monitor,* October 14, 1997, p. 19.

75. "Reaching New Heights," *Vista,* September 1996, p. 23.

76. Carmen Teresa Roiz, "!En Pleno Crecimiento! Las Empresas De Los Latinos," *Vista/Register-Pajaronian,* October 1, 1996, p. 8.

77. Isabelle de Pommereau, "Why Black Financial Progress Is Running into Speed Bumps," *Christian Science Monitor,* February 4, 1998, p. 5.

78. Terence Wright, "Liberation, My Nation, Migration," *Diaspora,* Fall, 1980, p. 1.

79. Adair Lara, "If You're So Smart, Why Are You So Stupid?" *San Francisco Chronicle,* August 4, 1994, p. E 10.

80. Susanna Heckman, "ADA Burden Not All on Business," *Register-Pajaronian,* March 14, 1992, p. 11.

81. Shelley Donald Coolidge, "Finding Love, 1990s Style: Cupid Strikes at the Office," *Christian Science Monitor,* February 13, 1997, p. 1.

82. Hans Selye, 1936, 1950, cited in David Barlow and Mark Durand, *Abnormal Psychology*

(Pacific Grove, CA: Brooks/Cole, 1995), p. 335.

83. "Pieces," *Good Money,* November/December 1984, p. 7.

84. Shelley Donald Coolidge, "Vacations Feel the Pinch, as Workers Feel Pressure of Changing Workplace," *Christian Science Monitor,* June 3, 1997, p. 1.

85. David Holmstrom, "Leisure Time in the '90s: TV Soaks Up the Hours," *Christian Science Monitor,* June 3, 1997, p. 13.

86. "Fit Employees Keep Health Costs Down on the Job," *Register-Pajaronian,* September 20, 1995, p. 19.

87. John Kenneth Galbraith, "The Economics of an American Housewife," *Atlantic Monthly,* August 1973, pp. 78–83.

88. Marilyn Gardner, "Striking for Home Time, not Dollars," *Christian Science Monitor,* February 4, 1998, p. 1.

89. Bernard Lefkowitz, *BREAKTIME: Living without Work in a Nine to Five World* (New York: Penguin Books, 1979).

CHAPTER 6
Timestyles/Workstyles: Alternatives That Work

1. Elyse M. Friedman, Ed., "Almanac, a Statistical and Informational Snapshot of the Business World Today," *INC Special Issue,* May 20, 1997, p. 120.

2. Marilyn Gardner, "Wanted: Employees to Work 30-Hour Weeks," *Christian Science Monitor,* March 30, 1997, p. 10.

3. Charlotte-Anne Lucas, "Bechtel Employees Like Short Week," *Register-Pajaronian,* January 3, 1991, p. 16.

4. Marilyn Gardner, "Wanted: Employees to Work 30-Hour Weeks, p. 10.

5. Christine Nifong, "How Part-Timers Fare in U.S. Economy," *Christian Science Monitor,* August 14, 1997, p. 4.

6. Paula Ancona, "Temporary Workers in Demand," *Register-Pajaronian,* October 8, 1994, p. 24.

7. *Manpower Inc. Fact Sheet,* March 1998.

8. Stephen Barr, "Government Issues Rules on Temporary Employees," *Register-Pajaronian,* September 21, 1994, p. 14.

9. Shelley Donald Coolidge, "Tele-work Still a Slow Commute," *Christian Science Monitor,* October 14, 1997, p. 1.

10. *Women and Office Automation: Issues for the Decade Ahead* (Washington, DC: U.S. Department of Labor, Women's Bureau, 1985), p. 24.

11. *Futurist,* February 1984, p. 82.

12. *Franchise Fact Sheet,* International Franchise Association, 1350 New York Avenue, N.W., Suite 900, Washington, DC 20005 (202) 628-8000, Spring 1994; Echo Montgomery Garrett, "The 21st-Century Franchise," *INC,* January 1995, p. 79; Echo Montgomery Garrett, "Looking for a Unique Work Environment?" *INC,* April 1997, Ad Pages.

13. Ylonda Gault, "Rising-Star Franchises," *Working Woman,* November 1993, p. 85.

14. Vivian Hutchinson, *Good Work, an Introduction to New Zealand's Worker Co-operatives,* Taranaki CELT, P.O. Box 4101, New Plymouth East, New Zealand.

15. "Global Cooperation," *CO-OP American Quarterly,* Summer 1994, p. 22.

16. Susan Meeker-Lowry, *Economics As If the Earth Really Mattered* (Philadelphia: New Society, 1988), p. 113.

17. Associated Press, "UAL Workers Sport 'Owner' Buttons," *Register-Pajaronian,* July 13, 1994, p. 16.

18. Tom Richman, "The Hottest Entrepreneur in America," *INC,* February 1987, p. 50.

19. Editor's Notebook, "The State of Small Business 1997," *INC Special Issue,* May 20, 1997, p. 11. See also Chapter 5, this volume.

20. "Women at Work," *Women and Work Factsheet,* 1997, p. 4

21. "Women at Work," p. 4

22. "Women at Work," p. 4.

23. Christy Heady, "Time Is Now for Women to Take Control and Start Investing," *Christian Science Monitor,* June 16, 1997, p. 8.

24. "An Outlook of Change," *Small Business* (from the U.S. Small Business Administration) Spring 1995, p. 3.

25. Carmen Teresa Roiz, "Cumbre Mundial: 'El Poder Económico de la Mujer,'" *Vista,* April 1997, p. 29.

26. Jerry Useem, "Start-up Chasers Track New-Bis Story," *INC,* April 97, p. 22.

27. "Small Businesses Cast a Big Shadow at White House Conference," *Small Business Success,* April 1996, p. 2.

28. Michele Wucker, "Keep On Trekking," *Working Woman,* December/January 1998, p. 32.

29. Jim Frederick, "The End of Eureka!" *Working Woman,* February 1997, p. 38.

30. Tom Ehrenfeld, "The Demise of Mom and Pop?" *INC,* January 1995, p. 46.

31. Luke Elliott, "$1,500 and a Kitchen Table," *Back Home,* Winter 1990–91, p. 20.

32. Jeremy Joan Hewes, *Worksteads* (Garden City, NY: Doubleday, 1981), pp. 7, 5; see also Bernard Lefkowitz, *BREAKTIME: Living without Work in a Nine-to-Five World* (New York: Penguin Books, 1979).

33. Richard Vega, "Fat Cats on Campus," *USA Weekend,* March 26–28, 1993, p. 8.

34. "CEO's Notebook," *INC,* July 1997, p. 105.

35. Brochure, The Drucker Foundation, 666 Fifth Avenue, 10th Floor, New York, NY 10103.

36. Author visit and tour, September 30, 1994.

37. Heather MacLeod, "Crossover," *INC Special Issue,* May 20, 1997, p. 100.

38. Friedman, "Almanac, a Statistical and Informational Snapshot of the Business World Today," pp. 108, 117.

39. John Case, "The Wonderland Economy," *INC Special Issue 1995: The State of Small Business,* p. 14.

40. David Friedman, "Job Detection," *INC Special Report 1995: The State of Small Business,* p. 33.

41. John Cassidy, "The Comeback," *New Yorker,* February 23, 1998, p. 122.

42. "Hotline Plugs Honest Mechanics," *Register-Pajaronian,* April 28, 1993, p. 5.

43. "Ethnic Marketing, Turning Obstacles into Opportunities," *Small Business,* Spring 1995, p. 42.

44. Marilyn Ferguson, *Aquarian Conspiracy: Personal and Social Transformation in the 1980s* (Los Angeles: J.P. Tarcher, 1982).

45. Richard Pitcairn and Susan Hubble Pitcairn, *Dr. Pitcairn's Complete Guide to Natural Health for Dogs and Cats* (Emmaus, PA: Rodale Press, 1995).

46. Bill Cane, *Through Crisis to Freedom* (Chicago: Acta Books, 1980), p. 8.

47. Tom Shanks and Peter Facione "The Case of the Cyber City Network," *Santa Clara Magazine,* Winter 1996, p. 25.

48. David Brewster, "Civil Society, Democracy and the Yearning for Community," *YES! A Journal of Positive Futures,* Fall 1996, p. 17.

49. Suzanne Morse, "Reweaving the Fabric of Democracy," *YES! A Journal of Positive Futures,* Fall 1996, p. 33; Arlene Hestherington and Lou Piotrowski, "Democracy in the Woods," *YES! A Journal of Positive Futures,* Fall 1996, p. 41.

50. Robert Marquand, "Wendell Berry, Plowman-poet," *Christian Science Monitor,* October 10, 1986, p. 1.

51. *Occupational Outlook Quarterly,* Spring 1983, p. 11.

52. Shelley Donald Coolidge, "Mentors Give a Tug along Career Path," *Christian Science Monitor,* July 22, 1997, p. 8.

CHAPTER 7
The Job Hunt:
Tools for Breaking and Entering

1. James L. Tyson, "As Lawsuits Rise, Companies Use Detectives to Cull Job Applicants," *Christian Science Monitor,* February 12, 1997, p. 1.

2. Martha Stoodley, "Choosing the Right Tool," *National Business Employment Weekly,* January 14, 1990, p. 9.

3. Jeremy Rifkin, *The End of Work* (New York: Jeremy Tarcher, 1995), p. 149.

4. Hanna Rubin, "One Little Résumé and How It Grew," *Working Woman,* April 1987, p. 100.

5. James L. Tyson, "Bosses: Even If You Can Say Something Nice, Don't," *Christian Science Monitor,* February 21, 1997, p. 9.

6. "Franchise Inc.," *INC,* June 1997, Advertising Section.

7. *Personnel Administrator,* May 1981, pp. 71–78.

8. Toni St. James, Interview Workshop, California Employment Development Department, 1977.

9. Lorie Parch, "Testing . . . 1, 2, 3," *Working Woman,* October 1997, p. 74.

10. Toni St. James, Interview Workshop, California Employment Development Department, 1977.

11. George S. Odiorne, "Bait and Switch, Corporate-Style," *Working Woman,* May 1987, p. 50.

CHAPTER 8
Decisions, Decisions:
What's Your Next Move?

1. Ashleigh Brilliant, *I Have Abandoned My Search for Truth, and Am Now Looking for*

a Good Fantasy (Santa Barbara, CA: Wood-bridge Press Publishing Company, 1985), p. 128.

2. David Keirsey and Marilyn Bates, *Please Understand Me, Character and Temperament Types* (Del Mar, CA: Prometheus Nemesis Books, 1978), p. 22.

3. Key Keyes, Jr., "Oneness Space," Living Love Recording (St. Mary's, KY: Cornucopia Center; Ken Keyes College, The Vision Foundation, 790 Commercial Avenue, Coos Bay, OR 97420).

4. Betts Richter and Alice Jacobsen, *Make It So!* (Sonoma, CA: Be All Books, 1979).

5. Olive Ann Burns, *Cold Sassy Tree* (New York: Dell Publishing, 1984), p. 379.

6. Bill Schackner, "College Students' Attitude: Give Us Latitude," *Register-Pajaronian,* August 21, 1997, p. 8.

7. "Worker Training: Competing in the New International Economy," *OTA (Office of Technology Assessment) Report Brief,* September 1990.

8 Editorial, "Candidates Avoid the Hard Choices," *Register-Pajaronian,* September 8, 1994, p. 24.

9. "20 Facts on Women Workers," *Facts on Working Women* (Washington, DC: U.S. Department of Labor, Women's Bureau, September 1996), p. 3.

10. Scott Baldauf, "Nations Catching Up to U.S. in Productivity and Education," *Christian Science Monitor,* April 25, 1997, p. 4.

11. John Cassidy, "Who Killed the Middle Class," *New Yorker,* October 15, 1995, p. 113.

12. David R. Francis, "Business Leaders Say Dropout Problem Calls for Action," *Christian Science Monitor,* March 8, 1991, p. 8.

13. *CBS Evening News,* September 25, 1994.

14. Jonathan P. Decker, "Howard University Becomes 'Hot Pick,'" *Christian Science Monitor,* June 2, 1997, p. 12.

15. "Graduation Rate Rises for Blacks," *Register-Pajaronian,* September 5, 1996, p. 7.

16. Chris Eftychiou, "At 82, She's a Student, Reporter, Senior Citizen," *Register-Pajaronian,* April 30, 1997, p. 11.

17. Suzi Parker, "In Ever-Changing Workplace, Two-Year Colleges Fill Niche," *Christian Science Monitor,* October 27, 1998, p. 3.

18. Susan Ager, "After Exiting the Executive Suite," *San Jose Mercury News,* October 25, 1981, p. 6E.

19. Brilliant, *I Have Abandoned My Search for Truth,* p. 118.

20. Walter Chandoha, *Book of Kittens and Cats* (New York: Bramhall House, 1973), p. 8.

21. Lyle Crist, "Twain's River Holds Depths for Exploring," *Christian Science Monitor,* May 16, 1989, p. 17.

22. Alan Lakein, *How to Get Control of Your Time and Your Life* (New York: N.A.L. Dutton, 1989).

23. Peter F. Drucker, "My Life As a Knowledge Worker," *INC,* February 1997, p. 76.

24. See Connie Stapleton and Phyllis Richman, *Barter: How to Get Almost Anything without Money* (New York: Scribner's, 1982).

25. John Cassidy, "All Worked Up," *New Yorker,* April 22, 1996, p. 51.

26. Feature, *Catholic Women's Network,* September/October 1994, p. 10.

27. *Lotus,* Fall 1991, back cover.

28. H. B. Gelatt, *Creative Decision Making* (Los Altos, CA: Crisp Publications, 1991), p. 11.

29. Robert Klose, "A Son Begins to Widen His Orbit," *Christian Science Monitor,* October 10, 1997, p. 16.

30. Joseph Campbell, *The Power of Myth* (New York: Doubleday, 1988), p. 91.

31. Ted Berkman, "Wanting It All," *Christian Science Monitor,* January 27, 1983, p. 21.

INDEX